Israel Divided

ISRAEL DIVIDED
Ideological Politics in the Jewish State

Rael Jean Isaac

The Johns Hopkins University Press
Baltimore and London

Copyright © 1976 by The Johns Hopkins University Press

Manufactured in the United States of America

The Johns Hopkins University Press, Baltimore, Maryland 21218
The Johns Hopkins University Press Ltd., London

Library of Congress Catalog Card Number 75–36944
ISBN 0-8018-1737-4

Library of Congress Cataloging in Publication data
will be found on the last printed page of this book.

To the memory of my beloved aunt
Rebecca Friedman Isaacs

Contents

LIST OF MAPS

Acknowledgments

I would like to thank all of the members of the Land of Israel Movement and the peace movement, as well as others whom I interviewed, and those with whom I corresponded for their cooperation. I am especially grateful for the help of Samuel Katz, a member of the Land of Israel Movement, who has been an unfailing and patient source of information and suggestions for several years, and who, beginning as an informant, has become a friend.

As any woman seeking to perform more traditional roles simultaneously will appreciate, an entire household becomes involved, in one way or another, in an effort of this sort. My son Gideon did much of the typing of initial drafts and served as preliminary copy editor, through refusing to carry on if I did not call a halt to my habit of constructing interminable sentences. My son Gamaliel acted at crucial junctures as babysitter, cook, gardener, and interested reader. Without the absolute confidence I was able to put in my housekeeper, Isabel Marazite, who gave love and concern as well as physical care to four children, I should never have been able to give this work the concentration required to bring it to completion.

Part of the material for this book came from my doctoral dissertation in sociology at the City University of New York written under the guidance of Gideon Sjoberg, whose suggestions and criticisms I found invaluable.

Above all, this book owes a debt to my husband, Erich Isaac. He encouraged me, he prodded me, he rescued me from dead ends, he pointed out new approaches, he criticized, he suggested sources, he drew the maps. Without him this book would not have been written.

Israel Divided

1
Introduction

B y 1930 it was clear that the social reform movement in the United States, which found its national political embodiment in the Progressive party platform of 1912, had failed. It was clear to the reformers, and many of the participating national committees themselves had died. When in the mid-1930s, in response to the Depression, the great majority of the demands of the movement and many of the specific programs it advocated were enacted into law, no one thought of the reform movement of an earlier decade. It had failed, and only recently has historical scholarship reminded us of the reform movement's existence and its belated impact, for it created the ideology which made possible the speedy enactment of its programs under conditions of emergency.[1]

For movements to arise which provide the ideological frameworks that decision makers ultimately adopt, and to disappear, their contribution forgotten, is presumably not infrequent. While the tendency of historians to overlook small movements that never achieved—or perhaps even sought—power is understandable, it might be expected that political scientists and sociologists, paying close attention to the decision-making process, should be in a better position to identify the importance of the ideological movement. Yet the inclination of social scientists to dismiss the two opposing ideological movements within Israel that form the basis of this study is already apparent, although these movements, we shall argue, are essential for an understanding not merely of Israeli policy in the last seven years but of the development of Israel's political structure in the years ahead. While it is possible only to speculate concerning the reasons for this neglect, they may lie with the methods of study adopted by social scientists. Decision making has been approached through studying decision makers or through focusing upon actual decisions and attempting to trace the way in which they were made. The decision makers in turn have been identified by some students through examination of the official leadership of institutional structures and by others through the so-called reputational method, which relies upon the perceptions of knowledgeable people in a community as to who the most influential persons are. In this method of study many are presumed to be behind the scenes and thus not identifiable merely through examination of institutional structures.[2] Not surprisingly, the two methods yield different perspectives on the process of decision making; but however decision makers are identified—and even if the focus is on the major decisions themselves—the importance of individuals who neither occupy central positions in institutional structures nor are perceived by others to influence or control those in such positions is bound to be overlooked. In this case, it is instructive that the individuals who compose the leadership of the movements under study were not identified in a broadly ranging survey of Israel's political elite.[3]

But there is perhaps another reason why the ideological movements under study here have received little attention. As we shall see, they do not provide wholly new ideas but, rather, present traditional ideas which had largely been lost, at least within the dominant circles of the labor parties that have ruled Israel since the establishment of statehood. While there are within the ideologies certain elements that are without traditional foundation, on the whole the movements systematize traditional concepts of the nature of the Zionist task, declare them applicable to current circumstances, and provide a program for their implementation.

The political movements under study here arose following the Six-Day War of June 1967; they are already in process of reduction in significance, in some cases of disappearance, through becoming part of established (minority) political entities. They will be splinter extremist movements that failed, small and marginal groupings, no more than footnotes in especially ambitious texts. Nonetheless both of these movements, by clarifying the essential ideological alternatives before the state, will have had profound impact upon Israel's political structure. There is, moreover, a curious twist in the fate of these movements. At a time of potential triumph of one ideology as a result of internal dynamics, external constraints have been introduced to implement the ideology of the *losing* movement. The study of these movements becomes particularly interesting because the slow process of adoption by decision makers, first of the program of action of one movement, and presumably necessarily eventually of the ideological assumptions underlying that alternative, has been abruptly interrupted. The consequent disorientation has threatened to produce profound alterations in the functioning of the Israeli political system. Instead of a new consensus based on once-dismissed values, there now looms a confrontation of two opposed ideologies, each adopted by major elements within the political system.

The Yom Kippur War of October 1973 brought radical change to the Middle East not so much by altering the balance of military power—Israel's army still proved superior to that of combined Arab antagonists—as by bringing to the fore again the great power constraints that had been in abeyance for the six years after the Six-Day War. In terms of Israeli experience, it was those six years, when there was relative freedom to formulate policy—even if, as we shall see, the freedom was not in fact taken—that were the exception. Years before the Six-Day War, historian Ben Halpern argued that Israel had been so peculiarly subject to external constraints that it had scarcely known the luxury of formulating foreign policies at all: "Neither Zionist principles nor other ideological factors, neither long-range geopolitical calculations nor a clever grasp of short-range tactical opportunities were truly decisive. The external pressures on Israel were so severe, and the country was forced into so tight a corner, that the basic principles of its foreign policy became hardly an exercise of sovereignty at all, but rather an acceptance of necessities to which there was no alternative."[4]

As the Soviet Union and the United States join together to attempt to impose a settlement, Israel experiences once again the familiar bond of constraint. Actually, the situation has grown worse since Halpern wrote. Originally finding common cause at least temporarily with France and moral support on the African, Asian, and South American continents, Israel has now become almost wholly isolated; the United States serves as her sole buffer against the overwhelming hostility of the United Nations, which is potentially easy to mobilize in actions against her. And it is the ideology of one of the indigenous Israeli movements to be discussed here that the United States seeks to impose; significantly, one function of the movement in the eyes of its leadership was precisely to provide the ideological basis that would permit acceptance by the Israeli public of what was seen as an inevitable imposed settlement.

The movements that developed in the immediate aftermath of the Six-Day War and determined the character of the debate on foreign policy issues until the Yom Kippur War were the Land of Israel Movement, known in Israel as the *Tenuah Lemaan Eretz Yisrael Hashlema*, which more precisely translated would be the "Movement for a Whole Land of Israel"; and the peace movement, an assemblage of small ideological groups which, unlike the Land of Israel Movement, never overcame ideological divergences to form a single unified body. The first, as its name suggests, had as its avowed aim ensuring that all the territories taken in the Six-Day War remained part of Israel. The peace movement's persistent theme was that the government of Israel must seek to obtain what might initially be less than full peace through the return of almost all territory taken in the war, although there was disagreement regarding the appropriate body or bodies to which the land should be returned.

The 1973 war had a sharp impact upon both movements. Logically, it might have been expected to vindicate the analysis of the Land of Israel Movement, which the government already was moving slowly, reluctantly—but steadily—to implement. But the ambiguous outcome meant that the war confirmed the views of both movements concerning the rightness of their original positions. The Land of Israel Movement was convinced that only the buffer space provided by the territories had averted catastrophic losses to the civilian population, while the peace movement argued that if its proposals had been followed, a settlement with the Arabs would have been reached and the Arab attack would never have taken place. In any event the war, by bringing external constraints to bear upon an internally divided public, served to reverse the pattern of prewar developments and to bring closer to reality the programs of the peace movement.

From the standpoint of social movements, these movements provide interesting case studies of the way in which small fringe ideological groupings composed almost wholly of intellectuals can contribute to undermining a governmental consensus. The concepts of winning and losing in relation to these movements become complex and difficult to apply; the movement whose ideas were winning in the domestic political arena stands to lose through external intervention. In another sense both movements have won; from representing extremist positions held by relatively small groups, they became, within a few years, competing ideologies debated by the leaders of the ruling party among themselves. Indeed, by the time the Yom Kippur War was over it was clear that these ideological movements had offered, not merely possible alternative ideologies, but the only feasible alternatives. Yet in spite of this ideological triumph, in another sense both movements are losers; they are examples of a type of movement generally ignored precisely because, if successful in that its programs are implemented, the implementation is not brought about by the movements themselves. In this case, the fact that their contribution was to give contemporary relevance to traditional beliefs would make it even more probable that the role of these movements would be forgotten.

The appearance of both the Land of Israel Movement and the peace movement, if nothing in human events is inevitable, was at least predictable. Sociologists, perhaps belaboring the obvious, point out that social movements arise under conditions of strain, under the stimulus of a precipitating event, and in the absence of perceived available alternative means of expression.[5] The basic condition of strain was, of course, the underlying Arab-Israeli conflict. It was brought to the extreme tension of a precipitating event by the Six-Day War and, equally important perhaps, by the waiting during the weeks preceding that war.

Memory of the atmosphere surrounding events fades, as it rapidly comes to appear as if the outcome could not have been other than it was. The Six-Day War was such an overwhelming victory for Israel that in retrospect the outcome appears foreordained and the contest a wholly unequal one. Those outside Israel, especially Jews who identified with the fate of the Jewish state, may remember the tension during the period of United Nations debates after Nasser closed the Tiran straits to Israeli shipping, dismissed the U.N. force from Egyptian territory, and began a build-up of forces in the Sinai desert. Israel appealed to the world body and, when that failed, to the Western countries, especially the United States, to lift the blockade; but although the United States made some efforts to find European support for a fleet that would challenge the blockade and put pressure on Israel to take no action in the interim, nothing came of these efforts. Israel was isolated, ringed around with enemies that had formed a united front to destroy her and proclaimed their intention daily. Violent street mobs in Cairo were visible on television screens, shouting their determination to drive the Jews finally into the sea. After the six days in June many of those abroad who had been most deeply worried about the ability of the Jewish state to survive an Arab onslaught began to see their own fears as absurd in the light of events, and assumed that the Israelis had possessed a clear notion of their own strength and, though others had doubted them, at least had not been obsessed with self-doubts.

Overconfident as the Israelis appear to have been prior to the war of 1973—to the point that the political and military leadership did not even credit intelligence reports of the buildup of forces as meaning imminent Arab attack—prior to the Six-Day War of 1967, the Israeli public and the Israel government harbored the deepest self-doubts. The weeks preceding the war were terrifying ones, particularly as the waiting brought daily testimony to the probability of concerted Arab attacks. A unified command was set up for the states ringing Israel (with the exception of Lebanon); the isolation of the state in the international arena became clear as the powers that in theory were guaranteeing Israel's security openly backed away from the obligation; and so did the indecision of Israel's own leaders, who not only merely waited as Arab forces were massed in the formerly empty Sinai but also stumbled in speeches and were obviously casting about for direction. The government prepared mass graves in city parks and elsewhere visible to the general public for the anticipated many thousands of civilian casualties. Military leaders warned that each day's delay meant thousands of additional casualties. Druggists reported that some concentration camp survivors were begging for poisons so that if Israel fell they would not fall once again into an enemy's hands.

A number of those who would become prominent in the Land of

Israel Movement had been worried about Israeli security for many years. They had formed part of the circle around the political party Rafi, which Ben-Gurion formed when he broke away from the ruling Mapai party, and to which Moshe Dayan belonged. Their primary concern was the security of the state at a period in the early 1960s when the leaders of Mapai (the Labor party) spoke hopefully of international detente in a "Spirit of Tashkent" and of a supposed de facto emerging peace with the Arab states. The Israeli army had begun to seem primarily an adult educational center teaching semi-literate North Africans to read; it was widely praised abroad for its feats in this area—splendid public relations, no doubt, but those around Rafi wondered if any emphasis remained on how to fight. Israel's atomic reactor at Dimona—and its presumed eventual production of atomic weaponry—came under attack from within the Labor party during the years prior to the Six-Day War. Fearful of the state of Israel's military preparedness, alienated from Israel's political establishment though some of them had originally formed part of it, these men found the weeks before the war verifying all their worst fears. Then the war came and Israel was saved. One member of the Land of Israel Movement described the war's impact in these words: "When the Six-Day War broke out, it was an incredible experience. I have been in this country for forty years, and many of us have been here a long time, but there was never such a deep, sharp experience."[6] Part of the initial dynamic for the Land of Israel Movement on the psychological level was simply the resolve never to be in a position to be so frightened again.

The peace movement in Israel was slower to develop because in the period immediately following the war it appeared that the government had adopted the policy the peace movement was shortly to advocate. The announced position was that all the territories—except eastern Jerusalem—were negotiable for peace treaties with the Arab states. Moshe Dayan, shortly before the 1973 war to move closest of the Labor Alignment leaders to the ideological position that the territories must remain part of Israel, in 1967 said that he waited "for a phone call from Hussein." One component group of the peace movement did come into existence almost immediately after the war. Ironically, in view of the influence its program was to assume both outside of and within Israel, this group died not long after its birth for lack of supporters. Uri Avnery, of Israel's Haolam Hazeh party,[7] had advocated since the Sinai War of 1956 that Israel establish a federation with "Palestine." The idea was scarcely practical at the time it was first advocated, since Palestine (Jordan) had no desire to enter such a federation, nor did Avnery have any idea how to create interest in the proposal on the part of the Arabs. But the Six-Day War suddenly made the idea capable of realization, for Israel now controlled the West Bank and could presumably create a Palestinian state in federation with itself. In June 1967, Avnery wrote an open letter to Levi Eshkol, then Prime Minister, demanding that Eshkol immediately offer to create a Palestinian state and conduct a plebescite to this end among the population of the West Bank. A number of intellectuals joined with Avnery in creating the Movement for a Federation of Israel-Falastin.[8] (See Appendix 3.) The other component groups of the peace movement emerged later, when it became apparent that the phone calls from Arab leaders would not come, and that the government's policy of direct negotiations leading to withdrawal from some territories in exchange for peace meant prolonged inaction, since the Arabs were not prepared to negotiate directly and Israel would not offer concessions without direct negotiation. Various programs were offered by the different groups that emerged, most of which were to join the umbrella Movement for Peace and Security; but all had in common the insistence that the Israeli government could take more active initiatives to secure agreement with the Arab states. For those who joined the peace movement, then, the war provided a unique opportunity to achieve the long-dreamed-of goal of peace through demonstration of Israeli generosity—a demonstration, it was believed, that would ease the fears of the vanquished Arab states concerning Israeli intentions.

In the case of these movements, existing institutional channels for expression of their perspective were not wholly lacking; however, such channels, for a variety of reasons, were perceived as unavailable by those who joined. As far as the Land of Israel Movement was concerned, Herut, the dominant element in the Gahal bloc, Israel's largest opposition coalition, had never fully accepted the boundaries established by the 1949 armistice. Even after the War of Independence Herut maintained its traditional motto "Israel on both sides of the Jordan." In other words, the Herut party continued to claim after statehood, as its leaders had claimed prior to statehood, that Israel should have the boundaries of the British Palestine Mandate as originally proposed; those boundaries were in turn based largely on historic boundaries of ancient Israel, including not merely the provinces of Judea and Samaria taken in the war but present-day Jordan as well. Up until the election of 1965 Herut had as one of its electoral planks, "The right of the Jewish people to the Land of Israel in its historical completeness is an eternal and inalienable right." To be sure, Herut had never suggested going to war to achieve these boundaries, but had rather insisted upon the importance of sustaining the claim so that in the event a new war was forced upon Israel in which these territories were conquered the claim to legitimacy of Israeli rule over them would have been maintained. But in 1965 Herut joined with the Liberal party to form the Gahal bloc, and in deference to the new partner there was no reference to the historic boundaries of the Land of Israel but rather the pledge of a "constant striving for peace with the Arab peoples."[9] Despite the erosion of Gahal's enunciated position over time, if the war had convinced a variety of influential members of Israeli society that Israel's boundaries should be expanded to include the territory taken in the six days of June, those individuals might have been expected to rush to join Gahal.

But there were a number of reasons why this alternative was perceived as unavailable. To begin with the less important ones, even if one ignored the muting of its public demands upon joining with the Liberals, Herut's ideology was not precisely the ideology the members of the Land of Israel Movement embraced. Herut had repeatedly emphasized that its claim included the entire state of Jordan but no other territory, in principle making it possible to achieve peace treaties on the basis of the 1949 boundaries with all other Arab states. Herut's traditional ideology, therefore, required it to assert Israeli sovereignty not only over the West Bank, which Jordan had itself conquered in 1948, but also over Transjordan, which Israel did not conquer in 1967. The ideology, however, did not necessarily bind Herut to assert Israeli sovereignty over the Golan and above all over Sinai, which had been conquered. The Land of Israel Movement's leaders were insistent upon claiming all territory Israel presently controlled, but to some of them it was equally important that Israel not claim more than it already possessed. The manifesto of the Movement said: "The whole of Eretz Yisrael is now in the hands of the Jewish people," and some of its leaders saw Israel's potential historic claim to the other side of the Jordan as well as to other territories which were in different historical periods part of the Jewish land as bargaining counters: in return for Arab acceptance of the status quo, Israel would formally relinquish claims of right to any further territory.[10]

In addition, Gahal was at least temporarily muzzled after the war, for, while the uncertainty and fear were at their height prior to the Six-Day War, Israel's Labor party had acquiesced to demands for creation of a "Government of National Unity" including smaller rival labor parties and the chief opposition Gahal bloc, several of whose leaders became ministers in the Israeli cabinet. Gahal had thus become part of the government; and as long as Gahal remained within, the party was in no position to take public positions at variance with the government. Moreover, it quickly became apparent that Gahal's leaders were not adapting their ideology to events, for in the typical pat-

tern of "leaks" from Israeli cabinet deliberations, it became known
that Gahal's leader, Menachem Begin, was prepared to return Sinai to
Egypt immediately after the war, and that he had gone along with a
cabinet proposal to send messages to the United States relating this
readiness.[11] Eventually Gahal was to become more interested in retaining Sinai, although after 1973 it reverted to its view that Sinai was
negotiable. In any case, the Land of Israel Movement's leaders retained the conviction that they had discovered the importance of Sinai.

But the most important reason why Gahal was perceived as unavailable must be found in Israel's tradition of bitter ideological politics.
While in the post-independence period that tradition lost force, the
bitterness lingered, especially between individuals who had participated actively in the parties which were ideologically farthest apart.[12]
The major lines along which Israeli politics have fractured are economics, religion, and questions of national definition, the latter two
often becoming intertwined. Parties embodying various socialist doctrines have battled with one another, and all these have engaged what
was perceived as the capitalist enemy; at the same time, parties of
varying economic policy have fought over the question of what Israel's
self-definition in respect to the boundaries of the land should be and,
in the pre-state period, over the question of the nature of the sovereignty that should be exercised. As Alan Arian has pointed out, in the
pre-state period, the very impotence of the various Zionist parties encouraged ideological confrontations: "Issues of ideological purity and
party infighting were paramount, for such issues were actual to the
leaders and results could be influenced by their efforts; matters of policy and execution, on the other hand, were less relevant, since the
locus of power lay elsewhere. The 'government in exile' mentality
which they developed and the patterns of behavior which they learned
over the long pre-State years were not entirely dissipated even in the
face of the mammoth problems which the first years of statehood
introduced."[13]

Israel's system of proportional representation has preserved the mul-
ti-character party system characteristic of the pre-state Zionist Movement and the pre-state representative institutions of the Jewish community in Palestine, and this too has encouraged ideological self-
definition and made possible the preservation of ideological purity, at
least for those willing to pay the price of remaining outside government coalitions. Any group that could mobilize the support of 1 percent of the voting population was assured of representation in Israel's
Knesset.

There were countervailing forces to the potential disruption of ideological politics. In the pre-state period there was the consensus on im-

plementation of Zionist ideology and, in the latter part of that period, on the achievement of independence. After independence there was the ongoing Arab threat, but also there were the advantages to be gained from participating in government coalitions which the ruling Mapai party perennially had to form, since it consistently lacked a clear majority. Mapai sought to build ruling coalitions, not according to the size principle suggested as theoretically optimal by William Riker (51 percent), but by including as many parties as possible. "Israeli coalitions are large, compromise-oriented bodies which strive to generate consensus in policy-making. They reflect a wide spectrum of public opinion and are consciously created with that purpose in mind. They do not behave as smaller coalitions in other countries often behave, and are not used merely as vehicles through which a few parties can cooperate to control the rest of the Parliament."[14] The religious parties, staple features of Mapai's coalition cabinets, behaved like special-interest parties, concerned primarily with preserving religious control over matters of personal status, a share of public funds for education, etc. At the elite level, then, there had grown an increasingly marked climate of consensus,[15] with the parties becoming ideologically dogmatic only at election time.[16] Finally, in 1969, the long dream of the various labor factions to achieve unity was realized, although even then Mapam, one of the labor parties, merely "aligned" itself with the United Labor party in the so-called Labor Alignment. (Moreover, the strain between former factions within the United Labor party itself remained considerable.)

The ideological debate, in which ideological "style" increasingly replaced substantive ideological politics, was primarily concerned with internal politics and not national issues.[17] On questions of foreign policy and defense after 1949 there was less and less dissent. Soviet hostility helped in this trend, for it made the Israeli non-communist left, once strongly anti-Western, participate in the foreign policy consensus that orientation to the West was necessary for Israel's survival.

Nonetheless, until 1967 Herut (by 1967 part of Gahal), along with the Communists, had remained outside the pale of permissible governing partners. By many in the labor parties it was viewed, not merely as an opposing party, but as an embodiment of evil. This was not primarily because Herut represented what was considered within the Israeli framework a right-wing economic position (It combined a welfare state approach with greater emphasis than the labor parties on free enterprise), since Mapai had formed coalitions with parties representing middle class interests without difficulty. Furthermore, the traditional economic labels looked increasingly absurd when Herut actually drew its preponderant voting strength from the poorest of the

Israeli proletariat, notably those from the North African countries, while the strength of the socialist labor parties came from middle- and upper-middle-class districts. The difficulty stemmed rather from the fact that Herut was the political outgrowth of the underground Irgun Zvai Leumi of the pre-state period and was led by Menachem Begin, once leader of the Irgun. In the pre-state period the most left-wing of the labor parties had repeatedly branded the Irgun, together with the Revisionist party of which it was an offshoot, as fascist. The term, of course, had especially strong connotations in a community composed to such a large degree of the refugees from and survivors of Nazism.

In addition, deriving from that period was a virtual blood feud between the leaders of Herut and the labor parties; when Begin had been leader of the Irgun, the leaders of Israel's labor parties had been dominant figures in the Jewish Agency, which had turned over Irgun members to the British. Even after the war with the Arabs had been joined, on the orders of the labor leadership, the elite Palmach troops (The Palmach itself was a specifically labor-oriented force) had destroyed an Irgun ship, the Altalena, on which Begin himself stood, as it tried to unload arms obtained from France to be used in the war against the Arabs.[18] The reason for this action was the labor leadership's fear that the Irgun would be unduly strengthened by these arms and might pose a subsequent political threat.

By 1967 even Gahal's Herut leadership had moved far toward accepting both the economic and the foreign policy framework established by the succession of labor governments and this, under conditions of national emergency, made it possible to incorporate Gahal into the government. Nonetheless, events at the top of the political pyramid had moved much more rapidly than the rank and file of party members recognized, and the ideological rhetoric that continued to characterize Israeli politics was partly responsible for the lag in perception. Thus for individuals who had not merely sympathized with one or another of the labor parties, but had played significant parts within them, it was impossible overnight to join Gahal.

In public perception, then, the chief drama of the Land of Israel Movement—and historically one of its major achievements—was in drawing together individuals who had long and serious accounts with each other from labor, religious, and nationalist parties into a single framework, albeit a non-party one. This was the first time that Israelis from such diverse ideological backgrounds had been able to unite in any kind of framework to advocate common political goals. Efraim Ben-Haim, at one time Israel's ambassador to the Central African Republic, and from a labor background, noted: "There has been no precedent for a movement like this where people from the extreme left and right sit with each other. . . . I can tell you that never in my life would I have sat and talked with people like Samuel Katz or Israel Eldad or Eri Jabotinsky or Uri Zvi Greenberg. They were beyond the pale. I'm from a kibbutz of the Achdut Haavoda and I never met people like that. I knew them by name only. The mere fact that we can speak one language is fantastic."[19]

Of the figures to which Ben-Haim referred, Israel Eldad had been a member of the high command of the yet more extreme underground organization, Lechi, or Fighters for the Freedom of Israel, known abroad more widely as the Stern gang. Eri Jabotinsky was the son of Vladimir Jabotinsky, ideological father of the Revisionist party of which Herut is a descendant. Uri Zvi Greenberg, one of Israel's major poets, was the author of a series of long, intensely nationalist poems which had inspired the underground movement; in the 1930s he had written, for example:

> And there will be a day when from the River of Egypt to the Euphrates
> And from the sea to beyond Moab my young warriors will ascend
> And they will call my enemies and haters to the last battle
> And blood will decide who is the only ruler here.[20]

The reaction to these and similar lines by labor groups who believed at that period that the only just wars were class wars can be imagined.

Ideological differences were translated into personal ones. Bitterly attacked by the kibbutz movement of the Achdut Haavoda (known as the Hameuchad), Greenberg replied by deriding their settlements in his poetry and by a famous never-to-be-forgiven quotation from King David, "Let there be no more dew on the hills of Gilboa." (The parent kibbutz of the movement stood at the foot of the mountains of Gilboa.) Samuel Katz, who was to become a leader of the Land of Israel Movement, had once been a member of the high command of the Irgun (although he was no longer associated with Gahal) and, as author of a book on the Irgun, had been invited not long before the Six-Day War to the high school of a left-wing kibbutz to present the Irgun's version of the Altalena incident. Invited to present the opposing point of view in debate with him had been Benny Marshak, who in the period of the Altalena incident had been a political officer of the Palmach. Marshak had refused to enter into a direct debate on the grounds that he would not enter the same room as Katz.[21] A few months later they were to work together in the executive of the Land of Israel Movement. That these men, and others among whom differences had been no less intense (sections of the labor movement had been bitterly anti-religious and members of the groupings were now to work together with ultra-orthodox leaders), should join together in one movement seemed scarcely less remarkable both to those involved and to the Israeli public, patient witness to the long struggles, than an agreement between the leaders of Israel and the Arab states would have been.

For many, the Land of Israel Movement provided a transitional forum which enabled individuals for whom direct transfer of allegiance to Gahal would have proved intolerable, gradually to become socialized into acceptance of a perspective in which Gahal became an available alternative. The first decisive step was taken in 1970 when Gahal resigned from the Government of National Unity and it was proposed that Gahal join with the Land of Israel Movement to create a "Committee Against Retreat." A few labor members of the Movement then dropped out rather than join in such an alliance, and they created a committee within the labor party to work toward the same goals. By 1973 the majority of labor members of the Land of Israel Movement were prepared to go further than this: prior to the elections these members formed a "Labor Movement for a Whole Land of Israel" which then joined the new opposition Likud bloc, dominated by Gahal but composed also of other small nationalist parties. Gahal's ideology had in turn come closer to that of the Land of Israel Movement, although the two still were not identical; on the question of the future of Sinai, Gahal remained willing to compromise.

The peace movement, unlike the Land of Israel Movement, never achieved unity. Instead, the peace movement foundered on traditional ideological differences over matters of internal politics as well as on ideologically formulated issues in respect to foreign policy, for example: Had the 1967 war been a just war? What constituted a moral solution to the conflicting claims of Arabs and Jews to Palestine?

While existing institutional frameworks might also have provided avenues of expression for members of the peace movement, again for a variety of reasons these were perceived as unavailable. The majority of those who became members of the peace movement had been part of the Mapam party, the most left-wing of the Zionist labor parties, but Mapam could no longer serve as an avenue of expression because it had become part of the ruling Labor Alignment (Maarach) and so was committed to government policy. There were three other small political parties in existence at the time of the Six-Day War with which those who joined the various groupings of the peace movement might in theory have affiliated themselves. These were Israel's two Communist parties, Maki and Rakah (product of a split in the leadership in 1965), and Uri Avnery's Haolam Hazeh party. However, of the Communist parties Rakah had become the Arab nationalist party, hewing closely to the Soviet line, and Maki had moved in respect to foreign policy to a position difficult to distinguish from that of the government. Furthermore, both these parties were communist, and most of those who joined the peace movement were not in sympathy with communist ideology. As for Haolam Hazeh, many of those who joined the peace movement considered both the party and the magazine frivolous. Moreover, most of those who joined the peace movement were to the left of center on economic issues and suspected Avnery of being right-wing in this area. In 1969 some sections of the peace movement joined together to run a "peace list" in the national elections, but they failed to obtain a single seat.

In 1973, in reaction to the formation of the right-wing Likud, those in the peace movement and in the peace-oriented political parties (except for the Soviet-oriented Communist party) sought to set up a left-wing alignment, but continuing dissension on a variety of issues made this impossible. The two existing parties, standing for a more radical program to achieve peace, maintained their separate existences; each absorbed segments of the peace movement, and both gave themselves new names, Meri and Moked respectively, to indicate their changed make-up. By the time of the outbreak of the 1973 war, then, both the Land of Israel Movement and the peace movement were clearly moving toward institutionalization within party frameworks, even though the Land of Israel Movement continued its formal independent existence and sections of the peace movement did not join either the Meri or the Moked party.

Both movements began, as so many social movements do, as optimistic crusades. The leaders of the Land of Israel Movement had no conception of any opposition; they felt, rather, that they would be initiators of a mass movement which would make it easier for the government *to pursue a policy it wished to pursue.* One of the Movement's members observed: "At the beginning Rachel Yanait [wife of Israel's former President, Yitzhak Ben-Zvi] said that we're helping the government, we're not in opposition. At the beginning there was such elation, it was assumed the government must want to do this too. Slowly it turned out it was not so simple."[22] Paradoxically, as the Movement's ideas gained strength within Israel, the Movement itself lost strength. In the beginning the Movement had sharp impact, not only because of its success in drawing together figures from a variety of political backgrounds, dramatic enough in itself, but also because its initial sponsors included men of the highest literary talent. There could scarcely be surprise that Uri Zvi Greenberg should become part of such a movement, but S. Y. Agnon, Israel's first Nobel Prize winner in literature, also joined, as did Nathan Alterman, often referred to as Israel's national poet, and Judah Burla and Haim Hazaz, both distinguished novelists. Again it must be understood that in Israel poets and writers have a much more important position than they do in present-day Western society, for they traditionally have defined the national experience. While Western writers and poets have moved to assert the privacy of the artist's world (and many of Israel's newer generation of writers, in rebellion against their own past tradition, are now moving toward a similar assertion), Israel's writers had seen their function quite explicitly as shaping national consciousness. Former military leaders who joined included Dan Tolkowsky, a former Air Force commander, Ya'akov Dori, the first chief of staff of the Israel Defense Forces, and Avraham Yaffe, the commander of the force that broke through to Sharm el Sheikh in the Sinai campaign. At the outset, then, the Land of Israel Movement had the dynamic of great self-confidence, distinguished members from a great variety of backgrounds, and novelty. The last wore off. Self-confidence was eroded, for although confidence in rightness was untouched, confidence in the ability to convince decision makers was quickly shaken. Membership did not grow significantly; some of the most famous members, in fact—including Dori, Agnon, Alterman, Hazaz, Chaim Yachil, and Eliezer Livneh—died within a few years. And, most important, the developing opposition to the Movement, from both the counter-movement and the government, served to brand it as extremist and fanatic.

In the case of the peace movement as well, there was optimism at the outset concerning a great public response; disillusionment followed at the actual response of public and government. Gad Yatsiv, an instructor in sociology at the Hebrew University who headed the unsuccessful "peace list" in 1969, wrote in 1970 that the Movement for Peace and Security, which had hoped to win the heart of the government and serve as a counterweight to the annexationists "spawning in rivers of intoxication of the senses," had been pushed by the government into an opposition position, and that now even many of those who agreed with the peace movement's attitudes were fearful of public association with them.[23]

Yet the increasing marginality of the movements as such does not mean that their impact became minimal. The key function of an ideological movement is to provide alternative sets of justifications and courses of action for decision makers, who may be brought to adopt the alternative thus defined under pressure of constraints which limit their power to continue in the course they have defined as desirable. Constraints, in social movement literature, are generally treated as internal to social systems; the best known method of studying social movements is the natural history approach, which emphasizes the internal dynamic of movements even if they are seen as arising in some cases as a response to disequilibrium produced by outside forces. Social movements are conceived of as moving serially through stages, barring abortion through successful exercise of institutional power. The fate of the Land of Israel Movement and the peace movement as ideological movements depends upon the interplay of internal pressures, great power constraints, and Arab pressures—the last of which are being exercised, of course, upon both Israel and the oil-hungry world.

The impact of these movements has already been profound. For one thing, they have virtually introduced movements of public opinion into a society which, partly because of its electoral structure and the special character of its parties, has had little room for such movements. The system of proportional representation has meant that party representatives have been more dependent on party approval than responsive to the will of any more general public. Moreover, Israeli parties are unusual in that the more important of them provide or assist with housing, jobs, recreational facilities, and general ideological education; thus, they fulfill many of the functions performed in other societies by voluntary associations.

More important, these movements have contributed to a reawakening of ideological energy in Israel. Both movements emphasized the importance of ideology as the basis for action to a leadership that had become increasingly impatient with all ideologies and prided itself on pragmatic orientation to the real world, seen without the distorting spectacles of ideological preconceptions. Both movements argued that ideology was essential, indeed the only realistic basis for action, although the insistence emerged more emphatically from the Land of Israel Movement, which advocates an ideology that brings Israel into conflict with the stated wishes of virtually the entire world. What the Land of Israel Movement emphasized was that the absence of ideology invited pressure, for in the absence of a principled basis for action Israel became more open to the pressures of those outside the state who were at liberty to define any course of action as momentarily expedient. In the aftermath of the 1973 war there was a growing sense of the weakness resulting from lack of clear ideological direction within the Labor party.

Not only have these movements given renewed emphasis to ideology; they have also treated the national issue, secondary in concern to many Zionist parties even through much of the pre-state period, as the single overriding issue. This conception of the political task as overwhelmingly one of national self-definition has become increasingly convincing to Israeli decision makers with the result that Israeli political parties, almost all of which have had their "hawks" and "doves" on foreign policy issues, show sharp internal tensions. While such tensions are perhaps most apparent in the National Religious party, riven between its pragmatic (dovish) and ideological (hawkish) wings, tensions also exist in the United Labor party and in each of its component wings, including Achdut Haavoda, Rafi, and Mapai. The same is true of the Likud, where the tensions are not merely between Herut and the Liberal party, which as essentially a party of middle-class economic interests could be expected to retain its reservations about Herut's nationalist preoccupations, but within Herut itself and the other splinter parties that joined to form the Likud. Given the heightened sense of the national-foreign policy issue as overriding, once crucial decisions have to be made, there is the potential for a general political realignment which will affect most parties. The Land of Israel Movement was the first group to break down traditional cleavages to achieve unity on issues of national destiny and the meaning of the Jewish state in the present period. The Likud, with its component of Land of Israel Movement members from a labor background, represents a break with old patterns on the party level; soon the old forms may give way to quite new configurations.

In addition, the movements—even before the Yom Kippur War— increasingly provided the competing ideologies of the decision makers themselves, debated within the cabinet. While from the conclusion of the Six-Day War there were within the Labor party those whose points of view were essentially sympathetic to either the Land of Israel Movement or the peace movement (This was to be expected since these movements articulated ideologies based on traditional Zionist conceptions), these feelings could receive no systematic formulation within the Labor party, with its pragmatic and even anti-ideological bias, its need for day-to-day adjustment among a variety of conflicting conceptions and interests, and its formal commitment to a program of exchanging territories (extent undefined) for "true" peace. Articulation of alternatives based on definitions of the central values of Zionism necessarily had to come from outside the Labor party, and those who more and more lost sympathy with the government's announced program of action were forced to depend upon systematic formulations of ideas coming from the movements.

The existence of *both* movements was extremely important. We shall see that the government gradually moved toward implementation of the programs of the Land of Israel Movement in the years between 1967 and 1973. That the government did not move farther and more decisively in this direction was in good part due to the opposition which was focused in the peace movement. The peace movement was consistently able to mobilize support against those actions taken by the government which were advocated by the Land of Israel Movement. While the peace movement was not necessarily successful in specific efforts to block action, the knowledge that strong opposition existed—within a small minority that was nonetheless capable of mobilizing broader support among the public on specific issues—gave strength to elements within the government who themselves opposed the action and gave pause to those who might have wanted to move faster. This braking force exerted by the peace movement was crucial because it meant that after the 1973 war, which produced a reversal of government policy, there were fewer *faits accomplis* in the territories than would otherwise have been the case; further, the pattern of existing settlements had a decisive impact on post-1973 government policy.

Much of the potential ideological strength of both the Land of Israel Movement and the peace movement derived from the fact that they embodied traditional interpretations of the basic values of Zionism, kept alive in institutional form by the parties we have indicated were not perceived as available. It is possible to view both the Land of Israel Movement and the peace movement as embodying deviant traditional perspectives within Zionism. This would presumably be Ben Halpern's view, for he has pointed out that the dominant strain in Zionism viewed sovereignty as a means, a means to solve the problem of the Jews, whether this problem was defined chiefly as one of culture or one of physical survival, but that there also was a strand in Zionist thought which believed that the problem of the Jews could never be solved without prior achievement of sovereignty over the entire Land of Israel.[24] Yet Halpern overstates the divergence: the difference he describes between the dominant and the minority strain was tactical, ultimately only a question of priority. Normative Zionism never denied the claim of the Jews to title over an undivided Land of Israel; it merely put the claim aside as of less importance under a particular set of historical circumstances than achievement of sovereignty over *some* of the land in order to create a Jewish state under what were, in hard fact, conditions of severe external constraint. But when, against Israel's plan or will, sovereignty was achieved over the whole Land of Israel, dilemmas were posed for a Zionist government as the problem became that of renouncing sovereignty over the core areas of the ancient land, when it is upon the ancient right that the claims to sovereignty of a Jewish state ultimately stand. Thus, from an ideological point of view, the chief strength of the Land of Israel Movement is that it represents in fact normative Zionism. The peace movement, on the other hand, derives from a deviant but traditional strain that saw the basic task of Zionism as reaching agreement with the Arabs; ironically, as we shall see, the post-1967 bearers of this tradition proposed for that end tactics which were diametrically opposed to those which had been offered in the past. Sociologist Samuel Eisenstadt has noted that alternative definitions of basic values may remain latent, constituting important foci for change under propitious conditions.[25] The Six-Day War, and the events preceding it, were important primarily for providing such conditions by "unfreezing" the situation which had obtained since the cease-fire of 1949 and was only temporarily changed by the Sinai War of 1956.

2
Normative Zionism: The Bond to the Land

We have noted that the major force of the Land of Israel Movement's ideology is that it represents normative traditional Zionism. The territorial debates which rent the Zionist organization in the 1930s did not stem from disagreement concerning what the boundaries of a Jewish state should be; rather, they came out of disagreements over the advisability of accepting British proposals for truncating the territory of the Jewish National Home established by the League of Nations Palestine Mandate to Britain in the hope that such acceptance would mean Jewish sovereignty somewhere and would thus provide the possibility of rescue for the millions of increasingly desperate Jews trapped in Nazi-threatened Europe. The alternative, to the majority in the Zionist movement that accepted British proposals for reducing the territory of the Jewish National Home, appeared to be no home at all. But until British pressure developed for reducing the size of the territory open to Jewish settlement, there was no disagreement within the Zionist movement concerning the Jewish people's rightful claim to the territory of historic Israel. More than that, there was agreement that a future Jewish state should claim a territory greater than that over which the Jews, for most of the ancient period, had sovereignty. The future state, it was agreed, should profit from the strategic problems that had faced its ancient predecessor, and should incorporate the territories from which the chief invasions had come.

The Zionist title, of course, rested upon more than history. Although most Zionists were not religious (Religious Jews for the most part originally opposed Zionism), and although Herzl's motivation was to give Jews security through making them a nation like other nations with a geographical territory, the Zionist claim was inescapably a religious as well as a historical one. It rested upon the divine promise to Abraham in Genesis 15:18, "Unto thy seed have I given this land, from the river of Egypt unto the great river, the river Euphrates." Martin Buber in *Israel and Palestine: The History of an Idea* has sought to explain the unique tie between the Jewish people and the Land of Israel. In the religious conceptions of Judaism, the essential mystery involves the need of the people for the land, and of the land for the people, which together are called upon to cooperate in the task of contributing to the perfection of the world as the Kingdom of God.

Only in association with the Land of Israel can the people of Israel become what according to the Bible they are meant to be: a blessing. Buber asserts that, with however little or much right in each case the nations can accuse each other of being robbers, such a charge against Israel is unjust, for Israel acted under authority: "So long as it sincerely carried out the command it was in the right and is in the right in so far as it still carries it out. Its unique relationship to its land must be seen in this light. Only in the realm of perfect faith is it the land of this people. But perfect faith does not mean faith in one's own right or one's own Lebensraum or anything of that kind, but faith in the commander and the command, in the giver of the commission and in his commission."[1] Ultimately, Buber notes, in the Jewish perspective, the world can be redeemed only by the redemption of Israel, and Israel can be redeemed only by reunion with its land. It was the religious nature of the claim to the land that made it impossible for the Zionist organization to accept Herzl's proposal—when all effeorts to obtain Palestine proved hopeless in the face of the Turkish Sultan's opposition—for establishing a Jewish National Home in Uganda when the British government suggested such a possibility. Historic ties might have been overcome by the combination of need and opportunity; the religious tie could not be abrogated.[2]

But although the tie to the Land of Israel was clear, as was the sense of Jewish ownership by divine mandate that time could not alter, what the boundaries of the land were constituted a separate problem, a problem that of course only assumed importance once the possibility of a Jewish National Home[3] under British sponsorship became a real one. For one thing, there were several divine promises in the Bible which varied as to boundaries. And then there were the borders of actual historical settlement, and they varied over time. Never did the borders of any of the promises seem to have conformed to the areas of Jewish settlement at any period. Should the Zionist Organization claim territory on the basis of historic settlement? If so, on the basis of settlement at which period in ancient Israel's history?

The original promise to Abraham, "from the river of Egypt unto the great river, the river Euphrates" was clear in the sense that the river of Egypt is the Nile—generally taken to be the former eastern Pelusian branch—but vague in that rivers flow for long distances and that where the boundary was to touch these rivers was not specified. But there is also the promise of Numbers 34:2 (repeated with some changes in Ezekiel 47:15–20). These borders are detailed, almost like a surveyor's description, but include places that can no longer be identified. While scholars cannot agree on what the various border specifications refer to, with rare exceptions they concur that the promise of

Numbers represents a sharply circumscribed border in comparison to that of the promise to Abraham.[4] (See Map I.) For a long time the discrepancy between the promised borders of Genesis and of Numbers was explained by treating the borders of Numbers as an ex post facto promise—as the borders of historic settlement. In this view, once the conquest was completed, the promise was reinterpreted to conform to the actual borders held by the tribes of Israel. The most obvious difficulty with this interpretation is the clear discrepancy between the promise of Numbers and the actual conquest of Joshua. The distinguished Biblical historian Yehezkel Kaufmann has argued that the borders of Numbers represent an ancient strategic plan of conquest, drawn up before the invasion of the tribes, that was never completely fulfilled.[5] There is yet another type of promise. From Psalms 72:8–11 comes prophecy of a future king:

May he have dominion also from sea to sea,
And from the River unto the ends of the earth.

The "ends of the earth" may well have had a specific geographic meaning. Reconstructions of early Greek world maps show that the Greeks conceived the ends of the earth to be in the area of southern Arabia and Somalia, where the "world ocean" was supposed to surround the world's lands.[6] The prophetic messianic kingdom may well have been conceived of as covering the lands between the great known bodies of water in the Israelite world view: the Nile, the Mediterranean, the Euphrates, the Persian Gulf, and the Red Sea.

As an alternative to the promised borders there were the historical borders, concerning which there was less dispute, but which varied sharply over time. In Kaufmann's view, the territory of the Jewish ethnic settlement was established in the period of the Judges and included the land from Dan to Beersheba and from the western desert to the Mediterranean.[7] The area of settlement thus included Israel in the borders of 1949, the Golan, the occupied land west of the Jordan, eastern Jordan (including most of the present-day Hashemite Kingdom of Jordan), and present-day Lebanon up to ancient Sidon (including the southern course of the Litani River). Neither the southernmost part of the Negev nor the Sinai Peninsula was part of the ethnic settlement. (See Map II.)

Thereafter the people of Israel were subject to endless vicissitudes. By the time Saul became King, considerable territory had been lost; David's conquest restored the old boundaries, except for the territory of five Philistine cities on the coastal plain, and extended the boundaries sharply to the south and in the north as far as the Euphrates. With the division of the kingdom after Solomon's death into the kingdoms of Judah and Israel, there were periodic losses and recovery of

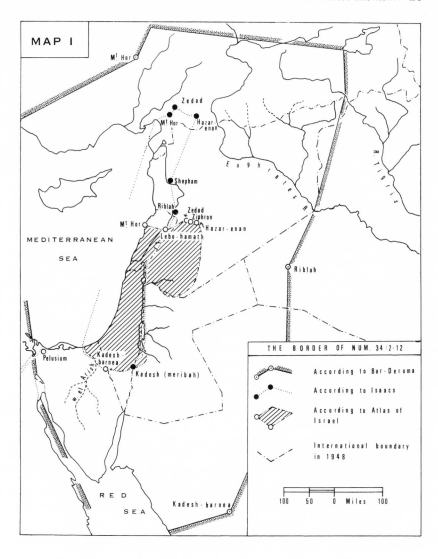

MAP I

M! Hor

Zedad
M! Hor   Hazar-
         enan

Euphrates R.

R. Tigris

Shepham

Riblah   Zedad
         Ziphron
M! Hor   Hazar-enan
         Lebo-hamath

MEDITERRANEAN

SEA

Riblah

Pelusium

Kadesh-
barnea

Kadesh (meribah)

THE   BORDER   OF   NUM. 34:2-12

According to Bar-Deroma

According to Isaacs

According to Atlas of
Israel

International boundary
in 1948

100   50   0   Miles   100

RED

SEA

Kadesh-barnea

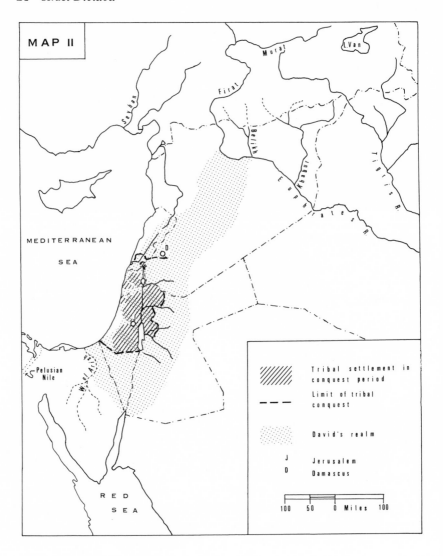

territory by the separate kingdoms. Eventually the kingdom of Israel was eliminated by the Assyrians; and the kingdom of Judah, whose mountainous terrain offered a longer refuge, was left with a core area from north of Jerusalem through the mountains of Hebron and south through the Beersheba Valley and the Negev to Wadi El Arish. (See Map III.) With the return from the exile after the destruction of Judah by Babylonia, there was similar fluctuation in boundaries. Beginning in a small area around Jerusalem, Jewish settlement expanded until eventually the Hasmoneans included in their empire most of the area of ancient Jewish settlement. With the Hasmoneans the last independent Jewish kingdom ended. The Second Temple was destroyed in the first unsuccessful revolt against Rome in 70 A.D. The last stand in the desperate second war against the Romans in 135 A.D. occurred at Betar, the present Battir, southwest of Jerusalem. (The village has been under Israeli control since the Six-Day War, and a group of Israelis who pitched tents there in a symbolic effort to assert Jewish rights to resettle the area were removed by the Israeli military authorities in 1970.)[8]

Thus, while over a thousand years of Hebrew sovereignty in the Land of Israel boundaries expanded and contracted, the core area where Hebrew sovereignty was first asserted, maintained for the longest period, and reestablished after exile, was what is now Jerusalem and the Israeli-occupied West Bank. Jewish sacred literature reflects this historical circumstance. The rabbinic literature defines the boundaries of the Holy Land in terms of what might be called orders of sacredness. The area of greatest holiness was seen to reside in the province of Judea, for this was the area of Jerusalem, where the *shechinah* ("divine spirit") dwelt. Beyond this, it is interesting that the concept of the promised land loomed larger in the eyes of some rabbis than a history of dense Jewish settlement in defining the area where Biblical laws (including tithe and sabbatical laws) concerning Eretz Yisrael applied. Thus Transjordan, although settled by the Hebrews in part even before Joshua's conquest, was viewed as partaking in sacred obligations to a lesser degree than even an area like the Lebanon, or Syria up to the Euphrates, for these were part of the promise of Numbers.[9]

Much has been written concerning Zionism as a secular movement arising in response to the general development of nationalism in nineteenth century Europe, an emphasis that has gained credibility through the assimilated background of the founders and early leaders of the Zionist movement and the active opposition of much of religious Jewry to the movement. But to look upon Zionism as yet another movement of national liberation—which can then be paralleled to the

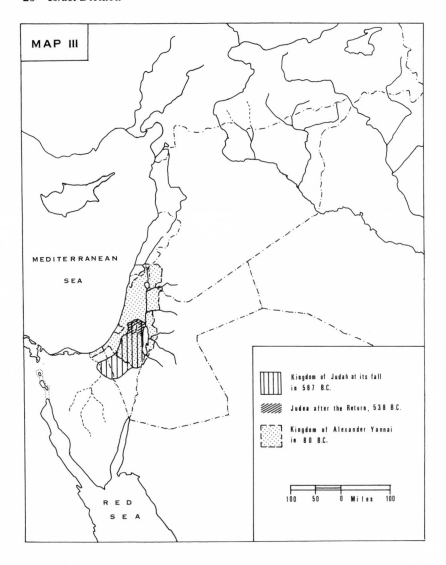

MAP III

MEDITERRANEAN

SEA

RED
SEA

Kingdom of Judah at its fall
in 587 B.C.

Judea after the Return, 538 B.C.

Kingdom of Alexander Yannai
in 80 B.C.

100   50   0   Miles   100

Arab nationalist movement which developed only slightly later—is to ignore the foundation of modern Jewish nationalism in religious tradition.[10] In the close to two thousand years of the Jews' loss of sovereignty over the Land of Israel, the tie to the land never ceased to be part of that tradition; and the most cursory examination of the Jewish prayer book shows the overwhelming majority of prayers affirming the tie linking the Jewish God, the Jewish people, and the Holy Land. The strength of the tie is rather dramatically evidenced by some of the rabbinic homilies of midrashic literature, in which the rabbis asserted that dwelling in the Land of Israel outweighs all the commandments of the Torah. Another homily says that anyone who resides in the Land of Israel remains without sin.[11]

Retaining faith in their ultimate return to the Land of Israel, the Jews, under conditions of dispersion and persecution, increasingly tied that faith to the coming of a messianic leader. A series of false messiahs arose to raise and then shatter Jewish hopes. The most widely accepted figure was Shabbetai Tzevi, who stirred the Jewish world of the seventeenth century. Whole communities disposed of their homes and possessions in anticipation of their imminent and miraculous transportation to the Land of Israel. With his conversion to Islam, hopes for a messiah were dealt a blow from which they did not recover. And with this disappointment, religious Jews—for all that their emotional tie to the Land of Israel was strongest—paradoxically became the least willing to initiate or accept proposals to transfer the Jews as a people to the Land of Israel. For the individual to live in the Holy Land remained a high value, and poverty-stricken Jewish communities in Europe supported individuals in the holy cities of Jerusalem, Hebron, Tiberias, and Safed in a life of prayer and study. But there was profound suspicion among an important section of orthodox Jewry when the Zionist movement arose, both in reaction against the messianic implications of the return to the Land of Israel and against the secular, even atheistic, guise in which that return was overtly planned. Nonetheless, one can as readily see the Zionist movement as a last, finally successful, effort of the Jewish people to return to Zion as see it as yet another movement of national liberation characterizing the nineteenth century. Presumably, the sudden growth of national liberation movements provided the context in which this traditional religio-historical aspiration of union of people and land could find sufficient understanding and sympathy in European society for the ancient claim to be recognized and supported.

The need for the re-creation of the claim to specific boundaries, following the Balfour Declaration calling for establishment of a Jewish National Home "in Palestine," presented obvious dilemmas. Should the boundaries be drawn in reference to the promise? If so, which promise? And how did one determine precisely what geographic boundaries either "promise" promised? There were those who argued in terms of using the promise as the basis for the boundaries of a modern Jewish state. Samuel Isaacs, for example, wrote *The True Boundaries of the Holy Land* to show the magnitude of Israel's inherited territory, based on the promise in Numbers, the boundaries of which Isaacs attempted to establish on the modern map.[12] Isaacs' map went north along the Mediterranean as far as southern Turkey, embraced eastern Syria and of course all of Lebanon, and in the south went to Wadi El Arish in northern Sinai. (See Map I.)

Zionist leaders, however, dismissed the borders of the promise as unrealistic. The promise to Abraham spoke of borders from the Euphrates to the Nile; but Egypt was on the Nile and Syria on the Euphrates. The promise of Numbers was hopelessly obscure, for it involved locations that could not be verified. In any case, only for a very brief time in history—if ever—might Israel have been said to have expanded to the borders of either promise, however interpreted.

In 1917 three important Zionist publications paid attention to the problem of boundary definition: *Zionism and the Jewish Future; Palestine,* the organ of the British Palestine Committee; and *Eretz Yisrael,* a study of the geography and history of modern Palestine by Yitzhak Ben-Zvi, who was to become Israel's second President, and David Ben-Gurion, her first Prime Minister. There was consensus that the Zionist claim was to be based on historical settlement and that the boundaries of the past should serve, not as a precise model, but rather as an object lesson.[13] It was argued that the secular failure of the ancient Jewish state had stemmed largely from its unfavorable military position, which was a result of unsatisfactory boundaries. Zionist leaders then sought to supplement the basic "Dan to Beersheba" boundaries with regions that would give the country the basis both for sound modern economic development and for adequate military defense.[14]

The proposed Zionist map, as finally drawn, included all the land between the Mediterranean Sea and the Jordan River, from the Litani River in the north to the Sinai desert in the south, as well as Transjordan, eastward to the edge of the desert, northward to Mount Hermon, and southward to the Gulf of Eilat (Aqaba). (See Map I.) The northern frontier was drawn with a view toward providing the Jewish homeland with the water resources that would enable small and barren Palestine to provide the economic base to absorb the millions of Jews from Europe and Russia which the Zionists hoped it would attract in order to solve "the problem of the Jews." Included within the Zionist northern frontier were the Litani River, the headwaters of the

Jordan, the snows of Hermon, the Yarmuk and its tributaries, and the Jabbok. Military considerations required that Palestine should include the desert areas of the south and east from which nomad invaders had come, as well as the Baka'a valley in the north, the gate of entry between the slopes of Lebanon and Mount Hermon. Military considerations also dictated the inclusion of the Hauran and of the Yarmuk valley from which invaders had penetrated into the Esdraelon lowlands and cut the ancient Jewish state in two by separating Galilee from Judea. Since the Zionist hope of making the country a commercial entrepôt required control of ports to both the west and the east, not only must the ports of the Mediterranean coast be part of the country, but so must Aqaba, with its outlet to the Red Sea.[15]

In the end, the Zionist map was to be sharply cut. Indeed, Frischwasser-Ra'anan in *The Frontiers of a Nation,* a study of the way in which the boundaries of the Mandate came to be drawn, argues that it was the mutilation of the frontiers proposed by the Zionist Organization which subsequently made it impossible to find a solution to the Palestine question when Zionist and Arab nationalism came into conflict. The borders of the national home were already so small that no partition was feasible, and partition proposals prior to World War II— when a Jewish state could still have saved a substantial part of European Jewry—foundered on the recognition of their unworkability by commissions sent to investigate practical schemes.[16] The northern frontier, for which the Zionist leaders fought most stubbornly since it was to provide the water which could be channeled to make the deserts bloom and to create the power for industrial development, was to prove their greatest disappointment. Unknown to the Zionists, England had entered into the Sykes-Picot agreement with France in 1916. This treaty divided the Middle East into French and English spheres of influence and placed the area of the Zionist map into seven different political entities. The French sphere of influence was to extend to just north of Haifa, and all of Galilee was thus to be excluded from the Jewish national home. Ultimately that border was modified. In the Zionist view, the determining factor in drawing the final border was the Zionist decision to defend the cut-off Jewish colonies in the north in the face of Arab attack, but it must be remembered that even before the defense of Tel Hai there had been agreement between Clemenceau and Lloyd George on September 15, 1919, that "the territories occupied by British troops will then be Palestine, defined in accordance with its ancient boundaries of Dan to Beersheba."[17] The persuasive argument with the French was English insistence upon the historical claim as represented by the Biblical phrase "from Dan to Beersheba" rather than Zionist needs, even though Lloyd George, pressed by

Clemenceau to point out Dan on the map, was unable to do so.[18]

Although the discovery by the Zionists of the terms of the Sykes-Picot treaty created early anxiety concerning the ultimate shape of the northern boundary, the Zionists hoped that in the east their plans would meet with greater success, since England was the only negotiating partner involved. The eastern boundary originally planned for the Mandate by Britain took in considerably more territory than the Zionist map, which stopped west of the Hejaz railway. Britain sought to secure her line of overland communications with the Persian Gulf and included a large section of the desert of southern Syria to enable the Mandate territory to join directly with British-controlled Iraq.[19] But in 1921, following the expulsion of Emir Faysal from Syria by the French, there was a breakdown of order in Transjordan which made the British consider dealing with Transjordan separately from Palestine. The decision was taken when Faysal's brother Abdullah marched from the Hejaz through Transjordan to attack the French in Syria. Fearful of repercussions in the form of a possible French invasion of Transjordan, the British decided to offer Transjordan to Abdullah if he would abstain from the effort to conquer Syria. More than two-thirds of the proposed territory of the Mandate was thus removed from the area of Palestine.

The southern border of the Mandate, from the Gulf of Aqaba to the Mediterranean, had been determined by the Aqaba incident of 1906, in which an English ultimatum in effect forced the Turkish Sultan to abandon his claim to any part of Sinai. Formally this was merely an administrative change, since Egypt, to which Sinai then became attached, was also nominally a part of the Ottoman Empire at the time; but in fact Egypt was under English control, and the reason for the English ultimatum was to secure a broad foreland to protect the Suez Canal.[20]

In Frischwasser-Ra'anan's view, the boundaries of the Mandate were not reasonable ones and bore greater physical resemblance to the map of the Crusader kingdom than to any Jewish state of the past. The Zionists had sought to learn lessons from ancient frontiers, but the result was inferior from the strategic point of view. The frontiers of the Mandate as finally drawn clearly were intended not so much to shape the physical outline of a new national unit as to delimit spheres of influence in the Middle East of the British and French Empires.[21]

What is worth emphasizing—through all the debates and plans, all the disappointments and attempts to avert them—is the fundamental agreement that existed within the Zionist movement on the question of boundaries. Even Vladimir Jabotinsky, later to become the opposition leader within the Zionist movement, made no objections when

Transjordan was detached by Britain in the Churchill White Paper. Chaim Weizmann, then President of the Zionist Executive, reports that he feared the reaction of Jabotinsky, then a member of the Executive. The Executive had been informed by the British government that confirmation of the Mandate was conditional upon the Executive's acceptance of the policy as interpreted by the White Paper. But Jabotinsky merely said that the White Paper would still afford a framework for building a Jewish majority and eventually a Jewish state.[22] Aaron S. Klieman has pointed out that the major reason for the passivity of the Zionist Organization in the face of the addition of Article 25 to the Mandate in 1921, which provided for local administration of Transjordan and entitled England "to postpone or withhold application of provisions of the Mandate relating to Zionism in relation to that territory, was probably that Zionist leaders did not understand its meaning. An editorial in *Palestine* of April 30, 1921, five days after Zionist leaders had been informed by the Colonial Office of the change in the Mandate, said: "The appointment of Abdullah east of the Jordan does not necessarily imply separation from the rest of Palestine, and in any arrangement that may be made the essential oneness of Palestine should be recognized."[23] By December, the Zionists had begun to wake up to the fact that Article 25 had broader implications and that Transjordan was to be treated, not as an administratively distinct province of Palestine, but rather as an entirely separate entity. Weizmann no less than Jabotinsky expressed severe disappointment.[24] Nonetheless, as late as 1930 Zionist leaders were including Transjordan in their settlement plans.[25]

Bitter debate within the Zionist movement developed; but again, it it must be emphasized, the disagreements between the Zionist mainstream led by Weizmann and the Revisionist party led by Jabotinsky were over tactics and not over fundamental principles. As the British moved to sabotage the Jewish National Home they had undertaken to establish, disagreement arose over how to deal with the problem. Weizmann, in Jabotinsky's view, followed a policy of appeasement of the British and did not push with sufficient energy to achieve mass transfer of the Jews of Europe to Palestine. From Weizmann's perspective, there was no alternative to following a policy of "moral persuasion" of the British. As for the mass transfer of Jews to Palestine, Russia had been the prime hoped-for source of Jewish immigrants, and with the Bolshevik revolution this reservoir dried up. While some Jews continued to make their way to Palestine from the Soviet Union, it became progressively more difficult as the Soviet government's hostility to Zionism hardened; in 1927 the exodus of Soviet Jews essentially came to a halt.[26] As for other European countries, where Jews were comfortably established they were reluctant to leave, and where they lived in conditions of great poverty, massive entry into Palestine would bring a threat to the orderly building up of a new society. Weizmann was sympathetic to the labor movement within Palestine, with its emphasis upon agriculture, socialism, and the creation of an ideal society. In Jabotinsky's view, Weizmann muted political goals in order to emphasize practical work in Palestine, when ultimately the only practicality lay in political action. The broad disagreement over the method to achieve generally agreed-upon Zionist goals in turn affected the question of boundaries, and the disputes over boundary issues grew sharper over time.

Once Jabotinsky had resigned from the Zionist Executive the fate of Transjordan, now that the implications of Article 25 were fully apparent, became a major issue for him and his Revisionist party within the Zionist Organization. In 1934, the Revisionists submitted a petition to the League of Nations asking that the Mandate be interpreted as meaning a Jewish state on both sides of the Jordan; the League refused. When Jabotinsky eventually broke away from the Zionist Organization to found the New Zionist Organization in 1935, the declaration signed by each member said: "My aim is a Jewish state on both sides of the Jordan, and social justice without class war within Palestine Jewry."[27] This aim continued to characterize both the Revisionists and the underground Irgun Zvai Leumi that was an offshoot from them and continued, as noted earlier, to constitute a formal part of the ideological platform of Herut until 1965. It is interesting that the basic Revisionist criticism of the Mandate boundaries concerned the exclusion of Transjordan, rather than the drawing of the northern frontier which had eliminated the water sources essential to the rapid expansion of the economic absorption capacity of the country for large numbers of immigrants. This was because the Revisionist argument emphasized the historic right of the Jews to the land. Thus, while a northern border in the neighborhood of Dan could be justified, the East Bank of the Jordan had clearly been part of ancient Israel and for many centuries had continued, although periodically torn from Jewish sovereignty, to be settled by Jews.

The tactical dispute became still sharper in the 1930s as the situation deteriorated, the position of the Jews in Europe became intolerable, and the British imposed ever sharper restrictions upon Jewish immigration into Palestine. In 1920 Max Nordau, a former president of the Zionist Organization, proposed that a million Jews be transferred to Palestine in one year so as to create a Jewish majority in the country. Considered an insane fantasy by Weizmann, the policy of immediate mass population transfer was advocated by the Revisionists after the

rise of Hitler. In the meantime the British set up a succession of commissions to investigate the Arab-led disorders in Palestine, and these
commissions recommended restrictions on the National Home policy
as a way of satisfying the majority population. In 1937 the Peel
Commission, on the heels of the Arab revolt of 1936, announced that
the Mandate was unworkable and recommended partition of western
Palestine into a Jewish and an Arab state. The partition proposal was
based upon the existing distribution of populations, not taking into
account possibilities of immigration, although by this time Jewish pressure to enter Palestine was intense. It suggested that the Jewish state
receive all of Galilee, the Haifa district, the Sharon Plain, and Tel Aviv
and its vicinity. (See Map IV.) None of the areas of vital historic association was included: neither the great cities of Jewish history, Jerusalem and Hebron, nor any part of the province of Judea. From the
strategic point of view, there was little hope of defense. Jabotinsky,
who was no longer within the Zionist Organization, was relieved on
hearing the details of the plan: it was so absurd, he said, there was
no danger of the Zionist Congress falling into the trap.[28]

Jabotinsky was wrong; the Zionist Congress voted, after sharp internal debate, to "discuss" the proposal with the British. But what must
be emphasized is that there was no disagreement that *all* of Palestine
belonged by right to the Jews. What was debated was the tactical wisdom of reaching out for the prospect of a quarter of a loaf in the hope
that sovereignty, no matter how small the area over which it might be
exercised, could permit the rescue of some portion of European Jewry.
But even those who argued that acceptance was a tactical necessity
felt called upon to reassert the legitimacy of the entire claim. *The New
Judea* reported excerpts from Weizmann's speech:

The choice lies between a Jewish minority in the whole of Palestine or a
compact Jewish State in a part. . . . He made a sharp distinction between
the present realities and the Messianic hope, which was part of them, a hope
embedded in their traditions and sanctified by the martyrdom of thousands
of years, a hope which their nation cannot forget without ceasing to be a
nation. A time shall come when there shall be neither enemies or frontiers,
when war shall be no more, and men shall be secure in the dignity of man.
Then Eretz Yisrael will be ours. He told the Commission: God has promised
Eretz Yisrael to the Jews. This was their Charter. But they were men of their
own time, with limited horizons, heavily laden with responsibility toward
the generations to come.[29]

While Weizmann was prepared to put aside the realization of Israel's
claim to some messianic end of days, Ben-Gurion was not prepared to
wait so long. "The Jewish State now offered," he said, "was only a stage
in realization of Zionism."[30] While agreeing with Weizmann that the

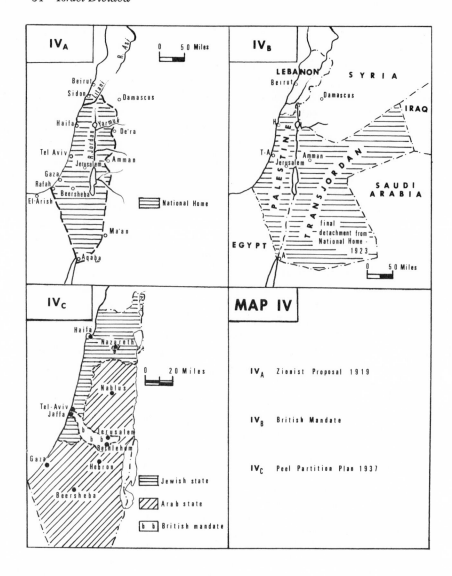

IV_A   Zionist Proposal 1919

IV_B   British Mandate

IV_C   Peel Partition Plan 1937

proposal be pursued, he asserted that the Jews must not cease to insist upon their right to the whole of Palestine. This proposed Jewish state was not to be the end, but only the beginning.

But although Jabotinsky's followers were no longer within the Zionist Organization (except for a rump group which called itself the Jewish State party), there was a large dissenting minority within the Zionist Organization which felt that even treating the Peel proposals as a basis for discussion would mean Zionist repudiation of the legitimacy of its claim, and that—whatever the short-term benefit—this could not be done. The religious parties were particularly adamant on this issue. Rabbi Meir Berlin (later Bar-Ilan), the Mizrachi spokesman, asserted that even if a partition plan had been offered providing full scope for economic and cultural development, Palestine in its entirety must still have been their uncompromising demand. "It was their religious duty to pray for the restoration of the whole of the Holy Land and to do so would, if the partition scheme was adopted, be in contradiction to their political obligations which would entail peace with their Arab neighbors. Palestine was not a reply to the demand for a land of refuge; it was theirs by virtue of their historic connection and divine promise, and they must have the land once more. They could not accept a Jewish state that would not include Jerusalem and Hebron. . . . They believed in the redemption of the whole of the land not merely of part of Eretz Yisrael."[31] Even a reform rabbi, America's Stephen Wise, argued: "We are only trustees for an everlasting people and dare not act as proposed. . . . We should not give our signature to the document that reduces the Jewish State to a twentieth of what we originally expected."[32]

Within the General Zionist party, the position was led by Menachem Ussishkin. "The Jews would never relinquish their right to any part of Palestine. . . . He was not in favour of withdrawing from the greater part of Palestine and leaving it to the remote future to recover possession of it. Would they teach their children in the schools of Tel Aviv that they had an Irredenta? Would the Arab people believe that the Jews would be content with the small area now offered? A living people had no right to repudiate a large part of its heritage."[33] Golda Meyerson (later Meir) also opposed partition from within the Labor party; she argued in favor of a transfer of the Arab population of Palestine to the vast territories over which there was Arab political control.[34]

In the end Britain abandoned the idea of partition because the Arabs opposed it, still hoping to receive all of Palestine if they held out for it. With the 1939 White Paper, the Arabs almost fully obtained their way, as England sought to counter pro-Axis sentiment in surrounding

Arab states. Palestine was not constituted as an Arab state, but Jewish immigration was frozen to an allotment of 15,000 persons a year.

During World War II the Zionist movement once again, despite earlier acceptance of the idea of partition, affirmed its claim to the entire land. In 1943 the New York Biltmore Conference, attended by all American Zionist organizations, a variety of non-Zionist organizations, and representatives of the various Zionist groups within Palestine, called for the establishment of a Jewish state in all of Western Palestine. On the face of it the program seemed unlikely of achievement. Britain, which had been unwilling to allow even modest Jewish immigration, could scarcely be expected to undertake the role assigned to her by the Zionists—maintaining order while the Jewish Agency took over the task of bringing in huge numbers of immigrants until the Jewish majority was established and the British could simply leave. But the Zionist Organization felt that, after the war, the constellation of forces would have changed and the time might finally be ripe for achieving, within the framework of a new international order, the traditional Zionist aim.

The fact that the Zionist Organization had moved toward affirming the goal of Jabotinsky's Revisionist party (even if there was no mention of the other side of the Jordan) did not prevent continued tactical disagreement that was almost to erupt into civil war within the Yishuv, as the Jewish community of Palestine was called. Internal disagreements arose over the proper tactics to be taken to obtain Jewish sovereignty, and specifically over the issue of terrorism. In 1931, a section of the Haganah (the underground defense force under the control of the Jewish Agency) broke away, giving itself the title "The Irgun Zvai Leumi in Eretz Yisrael." In 1937, during the Arab riots, a reunification with the Haganah was effected. The result was a new split as those opposing the move, which meant acceptance of the Haganah policy of *havlagah* (purely defensive operations), formed a group which gave itself almost the identical name, "The Irgun Zvai Leumi." There was yet another split in 1939 within the Irgun; this time, the majority decided to support Britain so long as the war continued, while the minority, under the leadership of Abraham Stern, decided to embark immediately upon a policy of active opposition to British rule. This group became the Lechi, or Fighters for the Freedom of Israel. In 1944, with the outcome of the war against Germany clear, the Irgun joined in the battle against the British. Both underground organizations were bitterly attacked by the Zionist Organization and by the Jewish Agency, the chief organization representing the Yishuv, although the Haganah, pushed by British policy to an active opposition, cooperated with the others for nine months in 1945 and 1946. Predictably, the Irgun and Lechi were more radical in their territorial claims, the Irgun claiming Israel on both sides of the Jordan, and Lechi, the more ideological of the two organizations, claiming the boundaries of Genesis 15:18—from the Euphrates to the Nile.[35]

Britain, finding Palestine ungovernable as a result of the activities of the underground organizations, and tiring of the moral odium attached to her policies of turning back refugees, turned over the Palestine problem to the United Nations. After that organization had voted for a partition plan, the various parties within the Zionist movement, with few exceptions, reacted with enthusiastic acceptance—despite the fact that the terms of the partition were not an overwhelming improvement over the Peel proposal. On objective grounds there appeared little reason for the euphoria that seized the Yishuv: the historic area of Jewish settlement was not included; the proposed territory of the state consisted of three separate segments linked by narrow corridors scarcely capable of defense (see Map V); Arab opposition was unabated; British cooperation was non-existent. But, with the prospect for sovereignty suddenly real, all such considerations were at least temporarily overlooked. Even the religious Mizrachi party gave up its opposition. Its attitude was summed up by the national president of the American branch: "It is with deep anguish . . . that we must now accept partition of Eretz Yisrael, but we have no alternative at this crucial stage of Jewish history."[36] Even the Revisionists did not react sharply against the U.N. plan, although in this case it was because they did not believe the partition would ever be implemented. In a typical essay in the Revisionist *Jewish Herald,* a writer pointed out that Jewry had been granted, not partition, but only the right to fight for partition, and that they would be fighting for something better than that. Thus little could be gained by fighting the partition proposal on an abstract basis.[37] Steadfast opposition came from the underground organizations and two left-wing parties: one was the Achdut Haavoda, which held out for an "undivided" Land of Israel under Jewish sovereign rule (temporarily under U.N. trusteeship); the other was the Hashomer Hazair, which was a forerunner of the peace movement within the Zionist movement. The Hashomer Hazair also insisted upon maintaining the indivisibility of the land—but under bi-national, Arab and Jewish, political rule.[38]

Within the Zionist movement, the Hashomer Hazair after 1936 constituted the major grouping which offered persistent criticism of the leadership for failing to give adequate attention to the problem of the Arabs. In different terms, Martin Buber argued that, with every encounter of people and land, the divine task was set afresh for the people of Israel, and that if this task were not mastered, all other

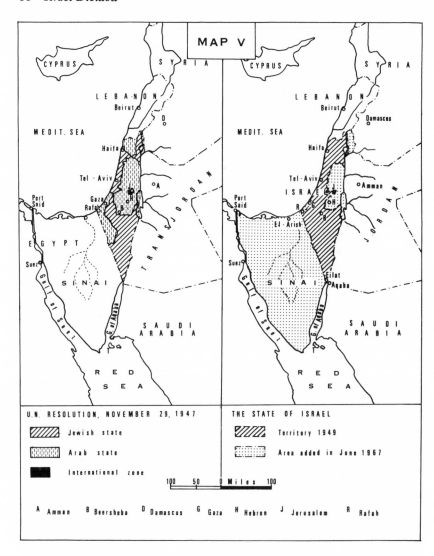

MAP V

CYPRUS · SYRIA · LEBANON · Beirut · MEDIT. SEA · Haifa · Tel-Aviv · Port Said · Gaza · Rafah · EGYPT · Suez · SINAI · Gulf of Suez · Gulf of Akaba · SAUDI ARABIA · RED SEA · TRANS-JORDAN

CYPRUS · SYRIA · LEBANON · Beirut · Damascus · MEDIT. SEA · Haifa · Tel-Aviv · ISRAEL · Amman · Port Said · El-Arish · Suez · SINAI · Eilat · Aqaba · Gulf of Suez · Gulf of Akaba · SAUDI ARABIA · RED SEA · JORDAN

U.N. RESOLUTION, NOVEMBER 29, 1947
- ▨ Jewish state
- ▨ Arab state
- ■ International zone

THE STATE OF ISRAEL
- ▨ Territory 1949
- ▨ Area added in June 1967

100   50   0 Miles   100

A Amman   B Beersheba   D Damascus   G Gaza   H Hebron   J Jerusalem   R Rafah achievements fell in ruin. At this period in history, according to Buber the task was to coexist with another people in the same country, a people foreign in tradition, social structure, and outlook.[39]

The bearers of this divergent interpretation of the function of Zionism differed on the extent of the concessions they were prepared to make to win Arab acceptance of the Jewish enterprise in Palestine. The Hashomer Hazair refused to consider limiting Jewish immigration into Palestine, and sought instead to calm Arab fears of an eventual Jewish majority by creating a political structure which would ensure equal Arab representation regardless of the existence of a Jewish majority. Hashomer Hazair's proposals in this regard resembled those put forward by a number of the leaders of the Zionist Organization, including Weizmann and Haim Arlosoroff, in the early 1930s after the Yishuv came under pressure of British proposals to create representative institutions in Palestine, which in that period would have meant giving the Arabs, with their overwhelming numerical advantage, a decisive voice. But Hashomer Hazair maintained this proposal long after the others had abandoned it.[40] There were groups prepared to go further. In 1925 the *Brit Shalom* ("Covenant of peace") society was founded, and a central feature of its program was that the Zionist Organization should proclaim "an open and clear surrender of the idea of erecting a Jewish state."[41] Always too small to constitute a party within the Zionist movement, Brit Shalom was quiescent during the middle 1930s, but it reorganized under the name *Kedmah Misraha* ("In the direction of the Orient") after the 1936 Arab uprisings in Palestine. In August 1939 the League for Arab-Jewish Rapprochement, consisting of many of the same people but augmented by recent German immigrant intellectuals, was formed "to unite all those who recognize the imperative need to solve the problem of Palestine on the basis of economic progress and the free development of Jews and Arabs along national, cultural, and social lines."[42] After initial hesitation the Hashomer Hazair joined the League in the summer of 1942, once the League had agreed to include statements in its constitution affirming the right of Jewish immigration, the connection between the Jews and Palestine, and its opposition to Jewish minority status in Palestine.[43]

In September 1942 still another association was formed, the Ihud, which joined the League and like it sought Jewish-Arab cooperation in a bi-national Palestine. Among the Ihud's chief members were Martin Buber; Judah Magnes, President of the Hebrew University and long associated with Brit Shalom; and Ernest Simon, professor of education at the Hebrew University. These men were imbued with the standards of western humanistic liberalism; members of the group, with few exceptions, came from Western Europe and the United States. The Ihud, like its intellectual predecessors, argued that the

Zionist political leadership had worked in the framework of traditional colonialism. Instead, the Ihud's intellectuals argued, Zionist policy should have been oriented to an awakening Middle East.[44] The Ihud also attacked the Biltmore program as fictitious and without hope of realization.

Partition was also opposed on the ground that it would mean intensification of chauvinism on both sides. The Jews might win over the Arabs in a war, but, wrote Judah Magnes, "That is the day, I think, when we shall be sowing the seed of an eternal hatred of such dimensions that Jews will not be able to live in that part of the world for centuries to come."[45] The Ihud went further than the Hashomer Hazair. In its testimony before the Anglo-American Commission of Inquiry in Jerusalem in 1946, the Ihud suggested limiting Jewish immigration, provided 100,000 Jewish survivors of the European camps were admitted right away. As a long-term policy, the Ihud urged that Jews have the possibility of becoming fifty percent of the population, with approximately 30,000 Jews to be permitted entry each year after the first 100,000 had been admitted.[46]

It must be noted that common to all groups emphasizing agreement with the Arabs as the fundamental task of Zionism was the belief that the land of Israel should not be divided, but rather that *within* shared borders Jews and Arabs should work out a common destiny. Indeed the language used by the Hashomer Hazair often echoed that of religious Zionists, despite the fact that the Hashomer Hazair was militantly anti-religious. For example, in arguing against partition proposals at a Zionist Congress in 1947, Jacob Riftin asked how the Jews could possibly give up Jerusalem and the Dead Sea, the very heart of Palestine.[47] After the Six-Day War, the peace movement sought as wholly Jewish a population as possible in boundaries which would give permanent legitimacy to the land's partition. The shift was a reasonable one in the context of continuous assumptions: Jews and Arabs both had legitimate national claims to Palestine that must be satisfied. Traditionally, those emphasizing peace with the Arabs as the major target had argued that both should be satisfied together within one land; more recently, they have argued that each should be satisfied separately in contiguous space.[48] The shift was significant; given its traditional assumptions, the peace movement could have argued (and one small segment did) for a restoration of the bi-national principle.

The factional arguments within the Zionist Movement became academic as the U.N. passed the partition proposal, the Arab states attacked the new state, and new boundaries were established on a de facto basis on July 20, 1949, after a series of abortive truces. Thereafter, from a practical point of view, there was virtually complete acceptance by the citizens of the new state of the resulting boundaries. These, of course, represented a significant gain of territory for the Jewish state as compared to the U.N. drawn boundaries. Western Galilee, all of the south and the Negev, the area to the Gulf of Eilat (Aqaba), Jaffa (previously intended as an Arab enclave), and western Jerusalem became part of the state of Israel. (See Map V.) The large Arab population which had threatened to swamp a Jewish state under a democratic regime fled to the neighboring Arab countries, leaving a manageable ten percent minority within the state. The tension for achievement of Jewish sovereignty over the entire land assigned under the Mandate evaporated with the winning of sovereignty over a part. Initially, two parties—Herut, the political outgrowth of the Irgun, and the Fighters for the Freedom of Israel—formally continued to list as part of their platforms the restoration of Israel in its historic borders on both sides of the River Jordan. The latter lost its single Knesset member after the first election, leaving only Herut formally asserting the goal for a while longer; but even Herut viewed it as a goal to be achieved some day, somehow, by peaceful means.

Herut's abandonment of all but lip service to the goal prompted the formation of a small ideological grouping without Parliamentary representation, revolving around Israel Eldad, a former Lechi commander. The critique that was to become characteristic of the Land of Israel Movement after the Six-Day War can be found in its publication *Sulam* ("The Ladder") in the years after 1949. In *Sulam's* view, all the political parties treated the state of Israel as a completed political creature whereas it was properly seen as but a means to the sovereignty of Israel in the territory of the promise—defined in *Sulam* as from the Euphrates to the Nile, the Amanus Mountains to the Red Sea, and the Mediterranean to the desert. (See Map VI, VII.) This was the territory into which the entire Jewish people would be ingathered, for just as a state in only a partial territory of the promised land was repudiated, so was an ingathering of only a part of the Jewish people. The ideological group around Eldad was without influence, except in so far as *Sulam* was regarded as a nuisance by the government since it provided ideological ammunition for the Arab states. It was the map distributed by Eldad showing Israel in the borders of the promise that the Arab states claimed hung in the Knesset and constituted the true goal of the government of Israel. But even Eldad had difficulty, as he admitted in *Sulam*, in maintaining the desired radical perspective. It was hard to avoid criticizing this or that aspect of the state, rather than the state's basic view of itself, and by the time of the Six-Day War *Sulam* had ceased publication.

In practice, then, the irredentism that had worried men like Ussish-

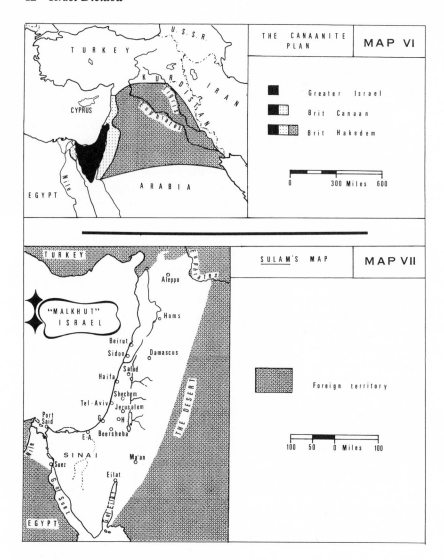

kin as a possible result of partition never developed. There were individuals who mourned the loss of the ancient holy sites, but of the irredentism that argued for action to restore the lost areas of the Land of Israel to make Israel "complete" or "united" there was none. The satisfaction with the existing situation characterized those who had once advocated renouncing Jewish sovereignty as well as those who had once insisted that the entire land must be Jewish. From Mapam (the party created by the Hashomer Hazair in conjunction with the Achdut Haavoda) came suggestions that Israel take the initiative in compensating the refugees and/or in offering to take some of them back in token of her good will. Mapam also objected to the continuance of the security laws that prevented free movement of Israel's own Arab population, and the laws were given up. But there was no more mention of a bi-national state as an overall solution to the continuing problem of securing Israel's place in the Middle East.

Nonetheless it is noteworthy that no ideological commitment was made to the boundaries of 1949, however willing Israel was in practice to live within them. Israel has remained a state without boundaries, the armistice lines lacking not only Arab or international recognition but internal Israeli recognition as well. Both internal and external constraints impeded Israel's recognition of the armistice lines as borders. Internally, there was fear of rupturing the delicate consensus through which the state functioned.[49] Some of those who had once advocated bi-national political arrangements now spoke of establishing "corridors" through Israeli territory to allow direct linkage between the Arab countries whose access to each other was blocked by Israel's presence. More numerous, of course, were those who refused to give formal sanction to the relinquishment of the historic boundaries of Israel. Definition of borders would also have been an embarrassment in Israel's international relationships, for the armistice lines were explicitly defined as subject to change through negotiation for final peace treaties. Formal definition of boundaries by Israel would have been interpreted as a declaration that Israel was unprepared to negotiate.

The Sinai War of 1956 produced territorial change, but only for a very brief period, as the United States put pressure upon Israel to return the land to Egypt.[50] And while Ben-Gurion spoke momentarily of restoring a "Third Kingdom,"[51] the relinquishment of the land caused no serious internal problems in Israel, for even Herut had never defined Sinai as part of the Land of Israel. In a way, the Six-Day War revealed how fully the partition of the land had been accepted by Israel's citizens. In the immediate aftermath of the war there was a massive movement by Israelis to visit the newly acquired lands on the Golan and the West Bank. Some have seen in this the self-assertion of a people who felt they were coming home again to their own land.[52] On the other hand, although Israelis visited, picnicked, and shopped, they returned home to their side of the "green line" (as the old border was called in honor of the color in which the line had been drawn on Israeli maps). As will be seen, the only group for whom the bond to the land retained sufficient force for settlement activity to be taken in direct defiance of government authority was the religious settlement movement, and even here the action was taken by individuals within the movement and not by the movement itself. As far as the overwhelming majority of Israelis were concerned, only the bond to Jerusalem retained overwhelming force. Eastern Jerusalem was the only area to be formally incorporated into the state (Bethlehem petitioned to be included, but the petition was rejected), and the incorporation was accomplished immediately following the Six-Day War.

It is in this sense, then, that it is possible to speak of the Land of Israel Movement articulating a traditional ideology that had been "lost," lost as a group of ideas seen as a basis for action.[53] In the absence of a salient traditional ideology demanding incorporation of the territories into Israel, the government was able to emerge from the Six-Day War with a policy, officially unchanged at the time of the Yom Kippur War six years later, of "territories for peace," a policy that won broad public acceptance. But the expectation that this policy would provide a quick solution for the Arab -Israel conflict evaporated as Dayan failed to receive the awaited phone call from Hussein and the Arab states formulated a policy of continued non-recognition of Israel and unwillingness to enter into negotiations with her. Nonetheless, Israel accepted Security Council Resolution 242,[54] partly in response to international pressure but partly because this resolution in fact reflected Israeli government policy in calling for withdrawal in exchange for "respect and acknowledgment of" the state of Israel. Of course Israel interpreted the resolution differently from the Arab states, for how much territory Israel should give up was not specified in the resolution, and Israel has assumed that withdrawal should be only partial. But when it became increasingly apparent that the policy was not a workable one, since the Arabs clearly were not prepared to accept such territories as the Israeli government might have been willing to relinquish for a peace that would be defined as such by Israel, the government became open to pressure from those with divergent conceptions. It was open to external pressures, but these were weaker than Israel had ever known; so the government became more open to internal pressures from those advocating an alternative policy, whether that policy was one of keeping the territories or of returning them to Arab rule.

3
The Land of Israel Movement

If from one point of view the origin of the Land of Israel Movement was in the strain precipitated by the Six-Day War (The Movement even has a myth of origin which describes its source of inspiration as the words of a dying soldier who urged that the land he was giving his life for not be given up),[1] more fundamentally the Land of Israel Movement represented the revival of a traditional ideology never renounced by some groups within Israel, that had now found both new relevance and unaccustomed bearers as a result of the 1967 war. Adherence to the Land of Israel Movement cannot be explained by that favorite variable of sociologists: class background. The Movement did not represent the class interests of any population segment, nor can it be seen as an "expressive" movement of a class that, passed over and alienated from the existing order, seeks "symbolic goals."[2] The Movement while including retired generals and businessmen, was basically composed of intellectuals, most of them of middle age, born abroad but strongly oriented *inward*. Thus, in terms of Robert Merton's dichotomy between "cosmopolitans" and "locals," if we consider cosmopolitans in this context to be those who are oriented and receptive toward world opinion and foreign cultures, Movement members were emphatically locals. In a subsequent chapter we shall see the contrast the Movement offered in this respect to the rival peace movement.

Because the Movement carried forward traditional ideologies and attracted traditional bearers of those ideologies, it is paradoxical that those with the strongest tradition of allegiance to the ideology the Movement adopted had the least authority in determining the course the Movement would take. The Movement's absorption of individuals from a variety of backgrounds constituted one of its major contributions to the history and development of Israeli politics; but the "converts," although not the largest number of members, were the least expendable, for without them the Movement lost its raison d'être. And the converts were members of the various segments of the labor parties, since it was these parties, dominating the state since its establishment, which had become most deeply committed to acceptance of the partition of Palestine. Other members could continue within or attach themselves to existing frameworks hospitable to the ideology; only for members from the labor parties was the Land of Israel Movement essential as an avenue of expression, and thus only for them did it really need to exist. As a result, the converts ultimately won a determining voice on issues of strategy, the basic initial formulation of ideology, and the boundaries of permissible membership within the Movement. On the other hand, the Movement served as an agent of socialization for labor members, for it brought the majority of members eventually to the point at which they did not really need the Movement and could fit within frameworks previously perceived as closed, that is, the nationalist parties that had traditionally served as bearers of the ideology of the entire land.

The way in which the Movement was created reflects the centrality of converts. The nucleus consisted of a few men from the labor parties who then attracted little groups, "ideological circles" as they are called in Israel, which had formed after the war among groups with traditional allegiance to the idea of an undivided Israel. The key initial figures were Moshe Shamir, a well-known Israeli writer from the Mapam party (on the extreme left wing); Zvi Shiloah, a consistent follower of David Ben-Gurion, first within Mapai and then within the splinter Rafi party; and Nathan Alterman, the Israeli poet, also associated first with Mapai and then with Rafi. And since converts were to be so crucial to the Movement, it becomes interesting to examine the process of conversion of these three key figures. The examination is the easier in this instance because Shamir and Shiloah each wrote a book about his own journey to the Movement. The case of these men —as well as of all those (with a single exception)[3] interviewed by the author—bears out the analysis of Hans Toch, who observes that the convert is a disillusioned person, and that disillusionment is a slow, surreptitious type of change, which represents the cumulative record of the costs of adaptation.[4] In the words of Menachem Dorman, a member of the Movement who also came from a labor background: "The founders of the Movement were those who despaired of all the political parties. Despair of party life existed long before the Six-Day War. . . . In fact the despair of parties and ideologies prepared the way for this national movement of capitalists and socialists, religious and secularists. There were other factors. The years before the war made a tabula rasa, clearing everything away. They were years of unparalleled erosion and we came cleansed to this movement; despairing, disappointed, and cleansed. The war itself was a catalyst, producing us as a movement, but it had been preparing long before."[5]

In the case of Shamir, disillusionment flowed from an increasing awareness of disparity between the definition of the situation provided by the Hashomer Hazair, and the reality—both the reality of the

Hashomer Hazair's practice, and that of the structural imperatives of Israeli existence. Shamir found that, in the kibbutz where he lived prior to 1948, members talked of brotherhood with the Arabs but had no contact with the Arab villages surrounding them. The ideology of the Hashomer Hazair called for class war, but the problem facing the Jews of Palestine was the hostility of the British and Arabs. Despite his reservations, Shamir found it possible to live with the Movement's formulations until the Soviet Union, with which the Hashomer Hazair identified, took an actively anti-Israel political stance. In Shamir's perception, it then became an ideological impossibility to fuse the class war with the survival of the Jewish people.

What Shamir perceived as a positive element in the ideology of the Hashomer Hazair was its stress upon the indivisibility and wholeness of the land. As noted in the previous chapter, in the wedding of Hashomer Hazair Zionism with internationalism, this notion of the land had been translated in the pre-state period into a rejection of partition and an advocacy of bi-nationalism. In Shamir's perception, the movement kept the consciousness of the Land of Israel as "one, whole, natural fatherland" destined in its entirety for the redemption of the Jewish people. It was this perception which enabled Shamir to view his conversion as a natural progression, one in which he could retain what was usable in terms of the Israeli experience and discard the contradictory unusable elements in the Hashomer Hazair ideology.[6]

For Shiloah, who became the central figure administering the Movement after the departure of Moshe Shamir for London (where he served as director of immigration for the Jewish Agency for several years), the disillusioning experience was with a leader rather than with an ideology. Shiloah, whose own ideas had crystallized early, gradually discovered that David Ben-Gurion, whom he had followed for a generation in the belief that he shared his own vision of Israel's role in the area, did not share it at all. The Six-Day War, after which Ben-Gurion stated publicly that he advocated returning all the territories except Jerusalem in exchange for peace, became the final precipitating experience in Shiloah's developing perception of the disparity between his own view of Ben-Gurion and the reality of Ben-Gurion's view. Shiloah called this a blow unparalleled in his life.[7]

For Alterman, the third member of the initiating group, a growing security-mindedness had prepared the way for his response to the Six-Day War. For Alterman as for a number of other members once prominent in Mapai, the chief party within the Labor Alignment, the Lavon affair became a turning point in his alienation from the "establishment." This labyrinthine affair of the 1950s, originally concerned with assigning responsibility for a security operation that went awry, ramified to separate those who favored a strong defense policy from those who were in favor of greater efforts toward rapprochement with the Arabs. (Those taking the latter position tended to follow Lavon in the affair, for reasons that had little to do with the original dispute.) It was as a result of the Lavon affair that a minority, following Ben-Gurion, left Mapai and formed the Rafi party. Alterman, although never in the Knesset, was a member of the circle around Rafi.

Gradual disillusionment and the crisis of the war seem sufficient to explain conversion in many cases, but the notion of marginality (described by Menachem Dorman as "walking in the political desert") was raised as an additional factor by several of the Movement's intellectuals in speaking about themselves or others in the Movement or both. Yisrael Harel, through 1969 editor of *Zot Haaretz*, the Movement's ideological journal, speaking of labor members of the Movement, noted: "No one in the Movement is in the establishment in their own parties. This they all have in common."[8] Eliezer Livneh, once a major ideologist for Mapai, had fallen out with the party on a variety of personal as well as ideological grounds years earlier, and in the years before the war had leaned towards Mapam's position on the Arab question. Yisrael Harel said of him, "Until he became part of this Movement he was nowhere, from the time Mapai left him and he Mapai. Even in Mapai he had been marginal to the real seat of power."[9] Isser Harel, first chairman of the Movement's Executive, had been the first director of Israel's security services; but he had resigned over a disagreement with Ben-Gurion. Hillel Dan, its second chairman, had been director of the Histadrut's building enterprise Solel Boneh; but he had been forced out of his position in a decentralization drive. The experience of marginality after an important, even a central, position had once been enjoyed may have prepared the way in some cases for the process of disillusionment which in turn facilitated conversion.[10]

Actually, all those who joined the Movement belonging to labor parties cannot be considered converts; those who came from the Kibbutz Hameuchad had traditionally subscribed to the values of an entire Jewish Land of Israel. The Kibbutz Hameuchad was the kibbutz movement that served as the chief power base of the Achdut Haavoda party, which in 1965 merged with Mapai to form the United Labor party. As noted in the previous chapter, Achdut Haavoda (along with Hashomer Hazair, which acted from different assumptions) refused to agree to the United Nations partition plan and urged instead a U.N. trusteeship over the entire country. This position arose out of the tenacious commitment of the Achdut Haavoda leadership to the idea of an undivided Land of Israel. Menachem Dorman, for years an ideologist of the Kibbutz Hameuchad, said of Yitzhak Tabenkin, for decades its leader:

Among all the people in Israel and in the labor movements, I don't know a single one for whom the idea of the completeness of the land is so central, almost a religious principle, as for Yitzhak Tabenkin. . . . With the Revisionists it was different because they did not think of a whole Israel acquired by working on and settling it—this the Revisionists never had. . . . Tabenkin went all the way. He would not accept the partition proposals. The division of the land is not the way to a state, he said, and historically he was wrong in that. . . . But in a wider perspective he was right, for he said a partition won't lead to peace. He said, you must have the whole country. Zionism needs an undivided Eretz Yisrael—from the geographic and all points of view, Zionism can only be fulfilled there. It can't be divided any more than a body can. This was his fanatically held central belief and he was right.[11]

Tabenkin's perspective had remained sufficiently normative within the Hameuchad that on the last day of the Six-Day War its secretariat passed a resolution calling for a massive settlement effort in all the conquered territories by the kibbutzim. The agreement of the other kibbutz movements was sought, in order that a united front could be presented to the government, but the others refused.[12] Finding that widespread support was lacking, the Hameuchad movement as a whole gave up; only those who joined the Land of Israel Movement (among whom were the two sons of Yitzhak Tabenkin) continued to press for settlement of the territories.

Apart from the converts with backgrounds in the labor parties—and even there the Hameuchad segment must be considered traditional bearers rather than converts[13]—adherents to the Land of Israel Movement came from three major sources, each traditionally opposed to a partitioned Land of Israel: the former underground organizations (Irgun and Lechi); the religious leadership; and the Canaanites.

While most of those active within the pre-state underground organizations had transferred their allegiance to Herut and then, after its merger with the liberals, to Gahal, there were former leaders who became disaffected with the party's management. Others, like Lechi's Eldad, considered Herut too accepting of the existing situation. One of the Movement's original nuclei was an ideological circle around Samuel Katz, before his break with Begin a member of the high command of the Irgun and then a member of Israel's Knesset for Herut. Professor Eri Jabotinsky, son of the Revisionist leader, had also been a member of the first Knesset for Herut and also left after a quarrel with Begin. Others had been members of the Irgun or of Lechi but had not remained active in the Irgun's political offshoot. Two men who backed the Movement financially, Dr. Reuben Hecht, a wealthy industrialist, and Joshua Bension, a bank manager, had been members of the Irgun. Uri Zvi Greenberg, although never a member of the underground, had written poetry which inspired both groups.

Students of social movements have traditionally pointed to their inclusiveness, and it is thus interesting that those who identified with Gahal, many of whom might have seen no conflict in belonging to the Land of Israel Movement as well, voluntarily stayed away or were warned away. Even Katz was uneasy about joining, despite the fact that his tie with Herut had long been severed. "I came into the Movement with some reluctance because of my background, and I told others to stay away. I just came to see that the Movement stuck to the point. And on the whole there has been no need."[14] The most important reason that figures identified with Gahal stayed away from the Land of Israel Movement was their fear that converts from the labor parties could not be attracted to or remain within a movement identified in any way with Gahal, and their presence would thus destroy the the Movement at the outset. But there was a secondary reason summed up by Knesset member Dr. Benjamin Halevi, a former member of Israel's Supreme Court and an exception in that he belonged to both Gahal and the Movement (He had joined the latter before joining Gahal): "Gahal's attitude is patronizing. They feel that suddenly all these people say what we've been saying all along. To tell Begin to join sounds to him absurd. It's nice you think that way, but don't teach your elders."[15]

On the other hand, some of the Movement's leaders from the labor parties made a conscious effort to bring in individuals identified with positions more extreme than Gahal's. Dr. Israel Eldad asserted his doubts concerning the wisdom of joining the Movement. "Shiloah asked me to join the Movement. I wasn't so sure if I should. One reason some others haven't joined is because of me and Uri Zvi Greenberg—our company is 'fascist.' If I was sure those others would join I would leave, and I said this to Shiloah. Because it's not so essential for us to be there; it's our thought anyway. But Shiloah said no, the greatness of the Movement consists in combining extremes from right to left."[16]

Leaders from the religious parties or individuals prominent in religious organizations constituted another major source of adherents to the Movement; with these, too, no problem of conversion was involved, for those who joined could see themselves as carrying on the traditional position of the religious Zionist party. In the last chapter the steadfast opposition to partition proposals at the various Zionist Congresses by the religious (Mizrachi) party was noted. From a religious perspective, the right and duty of the people of Israel to dominion over the Land of Israel was unquestionable. The only debate concerned whether domination must be pursued as a *prelude* to the redemption of Israel, or whether domination could only be established in the messianic redemption. Persistent adherence to the latter view led to refusal to recognize the state, as in the case of the religious sect Naturei Karta. On the other hand, as was seen in the previous chapter, the Mizrachi party, however reluctantly, did accept the U.N. partition plan; thereafter, the National Religious party became virtually a permanent part of the ruling government coalition, and its electoral strength provided the Labor party with the majority it never obtained on its own. The basic bargain was that the National Religious party acceded to the Labor party's policy in foreign and domestic affairs; in return, the Labor party had to accept a larger measure of conformity to Jewish religious law on the part of the state and its citizens than it wished to do.

For those affiliated with the religious parties, the choice was between the pragmatic orientation of the leaders of the National Religious party on the one hand and, on the other, affirmation of the religious basis of the people of Israel's right to the entire Land of Israel. A generational gap developed, with the younger group within the National Religious party opposing the pragmatic older leadersihp and providing recruits for the Movement. Adherents also came from the religious kibbutzim, from the religious university Bar-Ilan (its then rector, Professor Harold Fisch, joined), and from the yeshivot (religious schools).

The Canaanites were the third major grouping with traditional allegiance to the ideology of an Israel with boundaries beyond those of the partition state. But the Canaanites, unlike all others associated with the Movement, operated from an anti-Zionist perspective. The Canaanites were a small group of intellectuals whose greatest impact was in the 1940s and 1950s, and they sought to dissolve the connection between the state of Israel and the Jewish people. The appeal of the Canaanite ideology, which for a time caused considerable concern to traditional Zionist leaders, lay in its explanation of the widespread feeling among Jewish youth in Palestine, and later in Israel, that a national identity was being born which was not simply a Jewish identity. Furthermore, in some of its offshoots especially, the Canaanite movement also represented an attempt to find a solution for the objective problems of the Jewish state as an alien entity in a hostile Arab world.[17] The Zionist solution was to seek an ever larger Jewish population to defend itself against an ever bigger and more hostile surrounding Arab population. The Canaanites proposed the integration of Israel with neighboring peoples to create a new Hebrew nation. It was the task of the new Hebrew nation to help the Arabized peoples of the region to shake off the pan-Arab yoke. In the Canaanite formulation, Israel had abandoned the Maronites, the Druze, the Alawis, the Cherkess, the Kurds, the Bedouin, the Mutawalis, and others by insisting upon a Jewish conception of national identity, which kept any sense of shared history or fate from developing among other peoples in the region.

The Canaanites called for a two-stage plan in the realization of their goal of Eretz Hakedem ("the Land of the East"). First must come a *Brit Canaan* ("a Covenant of Canaan"), to include the Maronites of Lebanon, the Druze, and Bedouin. This union would, in turn, become the basis for the unification of all the inhabitants of Eretz Haprat ("the Land of the Euphrates") in a kind of Hebrew United States stretching from the Tigris River to the Suez Canal. (See Map VII.) After the Six-Day War, the slogan became "From a Greater Israel to Brit Canaan to Brit Hakedem."

While it was a foregone conclusion that the Canaanites would welcome the extension of Hebrew sovereignty over a greater part of Eretz Hakedem, only some of the Canaanites felt it possible to work with Zionist groups seeking the extension of specifically Jewish sovereignty. Yonatan Ratosh, the founder of the Canaanites, for example, made no attempt to combine with "Jewish" groups. On the other hand, Aharon Amir, a disciple of Ratosh, immediately following the Six-Day War converted his ideological circle into a "Committee for Action to Retain the Territories," attracted non-Canaanites to it, and joined with the Land of Israel Movement. According to Amir: "With the war, I saw a spontaneous occasion to keep all this, to solve the refugee problem. A chance to integrate the Arabs as far as possible into Israeli society. An opportunity to help achieve the de-Zionization of the state on a secular, non-denominational basis. Abba Eban said after the war that the choice was to be great or to be Jewish. Eban chooses a Jewish nation, I choose a great one."[18]

While converts thus constituted a relatively small proportion of the Land of Israel Movement, it is important to recognize that in the public perception of the Movement, converts appeared to constitute the overwhelming majority. This was because in the public perception only the former underground members were seen as maintaining traditional roles. The unification of the labor parties and the long association of the National Religious party with the labor parties in government coalitions had resulted in the public's identification of both the Hameuchad movement and the religious leadership with government policy; traditional positions in the pre-state period were forgotten, and all identified with government policy at the present moment were perceived as converts. On the other hand, from the standpoint even of the genuine converts—those from labor backgrounds other than the Hameuchad—the normative character of the ideological position taken by the Land of Israel Movement, emphasized in the previous chapter, became extremely important. Labor members, like other members, were able to see themselves as carrying forward the ideology of traditional Zionism, abandoned under pressure of events but capable of being renewed under pressure of events more favorable to its implementation.

While converts may not have been the largest segment of the Movement, they had an influence transcending their numbers and determined the first formulation of ideology, boundaries of membership, and strategy. The first test of power within the Movement came early, with the need to establish an ideological platform. Students of social movements have often assumed that movements arise and then develop an ideology to provide an appeal to the widest variety of constituents. In the case of the Land of Israel Movement, however, the conflicts and resultant compromises over ideology created the Movement. The outcome of the conflict over ideology defined, not only the key issues, but the composition of the Movement itself—who could remain within, who would have to leave, and who could not enter.

The conflict was precipitated by the need to define the Movement's aims. The beginning of the proposed manifesto of the Movement read: "Zahal's [Israel Defense Force's] victory in the Six-Day War placed the people and the State within a new and fateful period. The whole of Eretz Yisrael is now in the hands of the Jewish People."[19] But this was clearly a formulation unacceptable to the Canaanites. To say that the Land of Israel was in the hands of the Jewish people struck at the heart of Canaanite doctrine, with its insistence that the Jewish people as such had nothing to do with the Land of Israel. A compromise formula, deleting the reference to the Jewish people, was worked out. However, the next day Moshe Shamir said that he had been unable to sleep, for they had sold the Jewish people to the Canaanites. The Jewish people were restored to the manifesto, which then again read as indicated above.

The formulation also served to exclude some potential adherents among religious groups; their objection was to the phrase "the whole of Eretz Yisrael." To view the borders following the Six-Day War as the "whole of Eretz Yisrael" was clearly to take an idiosyncratic position. Transjordan was not in Israeli hands, although it had been part of the territory of the twelve tribes. The manifesto's position, then, while appearing maximalist both within Israel and abroad, actually represented a compromise made at the insistence of labor members. Their argument was that by defining the present boundaries as ultimate ones they offered the basis for arriving at a peaceful solution with the Arabs, who had no reason to make peace if they were threatened with the loss of further territory.[20] The ideological platform of the Land of Israel Movement was thus designed, not to maximize its appeal to all possible population segments, but to maximize the chances of appealing to a specific population segment: those adhering to the dominant labor ideology.

While Canaanites were unable to put their signatures to the Movement's manifesto, they wished to remain in the Movement to work with it on a practical basis. Again, it was the labor members who found this unacceptable. Isser Harel, first chairman of the Executive, put the issue bluntly by saying that the Executive of the Movement would have to make a choice between the Canaanites and the members from the Kibbutz Hameuchad. The ouster was formally accomplished through the Executive's decision that membership was possible in either the Land of Israel Movement or the Committee of Action for Retaining the Territories, but not in both. A number of peripheral members of the Committee of Action decided to remain in the Movement, but those who espoused the Canaanite ideology chose the Committee. From a social-psychological perspective it is interesting that the opposition to the Canaanites came from labor members and not from religious leaders. In fact, the Canaanites worked more easily with the religious groups than with any other, and acording to Aharon Amir, there were religious members in the Movement who wished to make him its Executive Director.[21] The reason, as Amir himself recognized, was that the Canaanites offered less of a threat to the religious groups, who had no problem about their identity and could exploit Amir as readily as he could exploit them, than to the secular Zionist groups who were deeply threatened by a nationalist view that broke their own less clearly defined link to Jews all over the world. Religious member Harold Fisch noted: "Amir was looked upon as insufferably right wing with his naked nationalism. . . . It didn't worry me. I can work with Marxists or pagans."[22] The upshot, however, was that while the Movement's broad basis of recruitment remained unprecedented on the Israeli scene, labor members drew a boundary. The Movement's tolerance extended only to all shades of Zionists.

As highly valued members, adherents from labor backgrounds were also able to determine the strategy of the Movement. It was at the insistence of labor members that the Movement quickly defined itself as an ideological movement directed to the persuasion of decision makers, rather than as a mass movement aimed at mobilizing the maximum number of adherents to put direct pressure on the government. Once again the Canaanites precipitated the initial conflict, for from the beginning the Committee for Action to Retain the Territories adopted an activist course. On July 11, just a month after the war, it called for a public demonstration in Jerusalem to protest the government's plan to hand Government House back to the United Nations. In August 1967, the group went to the airport to demonstrate against the United Nations envoy, who had come to investigate Israeli actions in regard to the unification of Jerusalem. The Canaanites urged an activist approach upon the Movement as a way to aid those seeking to reestablish Kfar Ezion, a religious kibbutz outside Jerusalem that had been overrun by the Jordanians in 1948. When permission was refused by the government, the settlers decided to organize an illegal return and Amir's group urged the Movement to participate. A number of labor members objected to the Movement's use of illegal measures. This particular conflict evaporated when Prime Minister Levi Eshkol decided to allow the settlement just prior to the proposed illegal sit-in, but a secondary reason for labor opposition to the Canaanites became fear of the activist tactics in which the Canaanites were likely to involve the Movement.[23]

The problem of strategy was heightened as it became increasingly clear that the Movement was not, as it hoped, helping the government act as the government itself wished to act, but was a true opposition group. Members from the Kibbutz Hameuchad were particularly insistent that the Movement address decision makers primarily, rather than the general public. Partly this was because these members viewed themselves as a part of the government (The Achdut Haavoda party, for which the Hameuchad served as a core, had been an integral part of the ruling United Labor party since the merger of 1965); but partly, too, the reasoning was pragmatic. Moshe Tabenkin said:

With us the government's power is greater than in any other democratic state. . . . The only way to influence the government here is through political parties. To get what you want, you must make your party act. Here you may struggle to carry out your ideals within the labor party, but you must be *within* it. You are not going to achieve anything if you base yourself only on your programmatically defined position. . . . If you create a party based on ideology maybe you can get 5 to 6 percent of the voters—nothing. But if you participate in the labor movement then those 5 to 6 percent can swing a lot of weight. . . . If you enter alliances with factors outside the party you weaken your position inside because your adversaries within the party say "What kind of party loyalist are you?"[24]

On the other hand, if persuasion of the decision makers failed, the Movement was then left with no alternative strategy. Israel Eldad was sharply critical: "So in that case, if we are not supposed to be a party or an opposition, so what are we supposed to do? Hold prayer sessions? Rallies? No, they said, be 'a moral force.' Make the Movement a political force through *shtadlanut*—be a representative to the powers that be—interceders. Go from minister to minister in the government; tell them to make a settlement here or there. I don't agree. It hasn't worked."[25] Another member, sociologist Aharon Ben Ami, summed up the dilemma of the Movement: "They [members of the Achdut Haavoda] wanted a center for disseminating ideas. . . . We had the choice of sacrificing the left to build a mass movement to put strong pressure on the government, or making the decision that we valued the left so highly that we would only do what their members agreed to. We chose the second."[26]

The structure originally established by the Movement did not fit the developing conception of the Movement's role. Initially, when the Movement believed its function was to rally mass support for a government-desired policy, it embarked upon a series of public meetings and devised a structure consisting of a *hanhala* or executive, composed of 15 members, a *moetza* (Council) of 60 members, and a *moetzet peilim* (Council of Activists) of 220 members. The hanhala was intended as an excutive body and the moetza as a policy-making body; the moetzet peilim, as the core of active followers, was to meet monthly. But if the Movement was a center for the dissemination of ideas, not for action, the separation of a policy-making body from a small executive to carry out policy made little sense; the Movement had one function and needed only one group to perform it. Accordingly, in 1968 the hanhala and moetza were merged, becoming an enlarged hanhala of 21 members drawn from all parts of Israel. The moetzet peilim became simply the moetza and thereafter met approximately eight times a year. The function of the moetza became essentially to serve as audience for the Movement's leaders and to allow adherents a sense of participation in the Movement.

The chief "actions" taken by the Movement were publication of the bimonthly *Zot Haaretz* (This is the land), meetings among the Movement's intellectuals themselves, meetings with government leaders, and meetings of the moetza. There was one exception to the Movement's avoidance of action that might embarass the government: the Movement became involved in the initial settlement of Hebron in the spring of 1968, a settlement which, if not illegal, was still clearly disapproved of by the government. Actual settlement was carried out by a group of religious Jews under the leadership of Rabbi Moshe Levinger. Hebron, of course, was the first capital of David and is, after Jerusalem, the city with the densest religious and historic associations for Jews. The city had remained a Jewish religious center until the massacre of its Jewish inhabitants by the Arabs in 1929. The would-be settlers turned to the Land of Israel Movement which, on these grounds, considered Hebron a prime target for settlement. When Movement intercession with cabinet members proved unavailing to secure permission for settlement, the Movement provided funds for the would-be settlers to rent the Park Hotel in Hebron for the Passover period—after which they refused to leave. Fearful of public reaction, the government did not remove them by force, but provided alternate accommodation in the military compound.[27]

For members of Hameuchad background in the Movement, the settlement of Hebron posed an acute dilemma. A cardinal principle of the Hameuchad was *hagshama atzmit*, meaning fulfillment through one's own actions, a sort of "put your money where your mouth is." The Hameuchad traditionally looked to voluntary rather than state action for settlement of the land. Moreover, the Hameuchad criticized the Movement for having failed to produce large numbers of volunteers for settlement in the territories, on the assumption that the very existence of such willing individuals would put pressure upon the government to create settlements for them, and the settlements would in turn make return of the land to Arab rule impossible. The settlement of Hebron fulfilled the principle of hagshama atzmit, and Hameuchad members thus could scarcely oppose it. They went to a fellow member from Achdut Haavoda in the cabinet, Yigal Allon, and persuaded him to visit the Hebron settlers in the first week of their stay. Pressure grew upon the government to establish a Jewish city in Hebron, and Kiryat Arba, the alternative Biblical name for Hebron, was established, now numbering several hundred families.

The settlement of Hebron was a major victory for advocates of an undivided Land of Israel. Against its will, the government was forced to underwrite settlement of Jews in a heavily occupied Arab area. The implications extended beyond Hebron to the entire province of Judea. Aware of this, the peace movement demonstrated, held meetings, and ran ads in the newspapers against the government's decision to build Kiryat Arba. As a result of the experience with Hebron, the government passed an ordinance providing that it was illegal to settle in the territories without permission. Subsequent attempts at settlement prior to 1973 by groups at Battir or Nablus (ancient Shechem) were terminated by forcible removal. These did not involve the Movement. Even in Hebron, the Movement's attempt to hold a meeting there was treated as provocative and was forestalled by the military government.

Labor members succeeded in maintaining their control over Movement strategy only so long as they were united. The elections of 1969 produced division among them and thus acute strain for the Movement. Some Labor members wanted a moratorium on all criticism of the government for the election, and they won official Movement adherence to this position. But other labor members wanted criticism maintained, and some even wanted the Movement to create a political party to run in the elections. In the last weeks before the election, some members sponsored Israel Eldad on a ticket called the Land of Israel party.[28] Movement members opposed to the creation of a political party by the Movement thus found that the worst had happened. Despite its decision to take no part in the elections, the Movement was identified with Eldad's ticket, since it not only bore the Movement's name but espoused the Movement's program. In what was widely interpreted as an effort to help Eldad's candidacy, a number of Movement members published an advertisement enumerating the short-term goals of the Movement: extensive agricultural and urban settlement, economic integration of the territories, and the introduction of Israeli law within them. The failure of the government to carry out any of these tasks was noted, and the advertisement concluded by appealing to voters to cast their ballots only "for those lists which explicitly support the policy outlined above and whose candidates have no reservations of opposition to it." In effect this "Declaration to Voters," which was signed by a number of members affiliated with labor—including Haim Yachil, Nathan Alterman, Eliezer Livneh, Moshe Shamir, and Menachem Dorman—was an appeal to voters not to vote for the Labor Alignment. Although this declaration was signed by individuals and did not carry the Movement's imprint, others from labor (particularly Hameuchad members) were extremely angry at what they regarded as a betrayal of faith by fellow members; some, without actually leaving the Movement, absented themselves for some months from its activities.

Once the elections were over (Eldad's list did not win a single Knesset seat), although direct conflict among members died down temporarily, tensions remained acute for those simultaneously seeking to play the roles of "insider" and "outsider" in respect to the government, and in fact worsened. This was because the Movement now found itself with a number of members in the Knesset, elected for their first terms. Isser Harel was elected on the State List; former Supreme Court judge Benjamin Halevi for Gahal; Rabbi Moshe Neriah and Avner Shaki, a professor of law, for the National Religious party. The number was sufficient that Land of Israel members and sympathizers from the various parties organized themselves informally within the Knesset to put pressure on the government to live up to its pledge in regard to creating settlements in the territories. Individuals

who had been sympathetic to the Movement in the Sixth Knesset now
drew closer. One of these was Mordecai Surkiss of the Labor Alignment (Mapai origin). Given the Israeli electoral system of elections of
"lists," those in the labor and religious parties were acutely vulnerable,
should they overstep the boundaries of permissible dissent, to party
sanctions. On the other hand, the Movement could scarcely view with
equanimity members voting for measures directly counter to its ideological position. What was the use of possessing power if one did not
exercise it or, worse still, used it against one's convictions? In the
event, sanctions were employed against recalcitrant labor party members both inside and outside the Knesset.[29] For religious party members the situation was easier; while the religious party, as a member of
the ruling coalition, was obliged to ensure that its members voted
with the government, the party was split down the middle, and this
split made it difficult for the party hierarchy to punish disobedient
members.

Ultimately, disagreements on strategy produced the long-feared defections of labor members. The Movement was able to survive these
defections easily because they were a product of the split, already
evident at the time of the elections, among labor members themselves,
and did not pit labor against other segments of the Movement. The
critical issue arose when Gahal left the Government of National Unity
in 1970 on the issue of acceptance of the American proposed cease-
fire on the Canal in the context of the Rogers Plan and then proposed
a combined front with other political parties and the Movement in a
"Committee against Withdrawal." Begin proposed that Yitzhak Tabenkin, the venerable ideologist of the Kibbutz Hameuchad, act as
chairman; but Tabenkin refused, the traditional gap between the one-
time Irgun leadership and the Hameuchad remaining in his perspective too large to be bridged. Arguing that the Movement would become merely a front for Gahal, a number of members—the most influential of whom were the Tabenkin brothers and Benny Marshak, a
one-time leader of the Palmach—left the Movement to form a purely
labor committee to advance the ideas of the Movement. Other labor
members of the Movement found no difficulty in the alliance with
Gahal, the years of Movement activity having served as socialization
for most adherents into a perspective in which traditional factionalism
was no longer important.

The departure of those leaders whose opposition to direct action had
been sharpest, and who had been most vigilant that the Movement not
overstep the boundaries of ideological statement, did not permit the
Movement to change its character. Labor and religious party members within the Movement still operated under severe constraints; the

central purpose continued to be the development of an ideological position; the basic strategy was still, to use sociologist Lewis Coser's typology, one of "boring from within." In the words of Isser Harel, "The Movement is not a party or an organization—it is an idea."

Since the statement of ideology was clearly the Movement's central purpose, it is necessary to examine in some detail the nature of the ideology advanced. Once the initial conflict had been resolved with the acceptance of the manifesto defining the existing boundaries as final ones and the title as that of the Jewish people rather than the state of Israel, conflicts over ideology all but disappeared. Thus the central task of the Movement was the one involving least controversy. Even those labor members most eager to avoid embarrassing the government through action were quite prepared to countenance statements of position which were radically at odds with the government's position. The decision not to seek either power or mass support, in fact, permitted fuller and freer ideological statement, for there was not the limitation attendant upon appeal to a large and varied constituency.

In respect to the statement of ideology a curious situation developed reversing what had emerged as the normal one, in which labor members exercised control over the activities of the others; here, the traditional bearers of the ideology of an entire land found it necessary to act as a check upon the labor converts.

In one sense, all members of the Movement advocated a radical ideology in that they included the Sinai peninsula in the definition of a whole Land of Israel. Sinai or parts of it had in the ancient period occasionally and for brief periods come under Hebrew sovereignty, and the Ten Commandments had of course been given while the Children of Israel wandered within it; yet, in Jewish traditional perception Sinai called up the period of the wandering in the desert and was not part of the Holy Land, which the Hebrews entered only on leaving Sinai. Even in the versions of the divine promise it was by no means clear that Sinai was included, and many interpretations suggested that the "River of Egypt" was Wadi El Arish, which runs through the Sinai. Certainly Sinai was never part of the British Mandate; even the Revisionist party and later the underground organizations, which claimed the entire territory of the original Mandate before the excision of Transjordan, never asserted that Sinai was or should be part of Israel. But for a number of the Movement's founders Sinai assumed crucial importance, and claim to it became a central rationale for the Movement. Isser Harel said: "There was virtual unanimity for keeping Jerusalem. The same applied, for different reasons, to the Golan Heights

and to the Gaza Strip, the retention of which was considered necessary and justifiable even by Mapam—the most unassertive and yield-
ing of Israeli political parties; Gahal clamored for Judea and Samaria
to be incorporated in the state of Israel—but there was an urgent need
for somebody to stress and to drive home the paramount importance
of retaining the Sinai; not because of sentiment but because control of
the Sinai Desert was an indispensable guarantee of our security."[30]

Sinai posed the greatest problem for religious members, for whom
traditional legitimations were indispensable. Religious members noted
that the medieval poet and scholar Judah Halevi had included Sinai
within the Holy Land, and some referred to the interpretation of the
borders of the Promise made by Bar-Deroma, whose territorial definition was the most sweeping. (See Map I.) Rabbi Moshe Rom, a yeshiva director who served as a member of the Movement's hanhala, observed that, according to some religious authorities, it was unacceptable to incorporate within the country territory outside of the Holy
Land until the entire core area was in Jewish hands. According to the
principles of the Ramban (Rabbi Moses ben Nachman, 1194–1270
A.D.), which Rom applied to this case, Sinai in 1956 would not have
been an acceptable acquisition for the Jewish state because Judea and
Samaria had not yet been taken. However, after 1967 it became so,
with the acquisition of the western bank of the Jordan. Rabbi Rom
asserted that, since wars of conquest were mandatory in Jewish tradition in order to achieve the Holy Land, it was unthinkable to return
Sinai to foreign rule after it had been won in a war for survival.[31]

If in one sense all members of the Movement were radical in ideology, in another sense all were traditionalists. In the previous chapter
it was noted that the Zionist claim was ultimately a religious one; and
despite the fact that most of the Movement's members were not religious, the Movement's manifesto was couched in religious terms. It
said: "The whole of Eretz Yisrael is now in the hands of the Jewish
people, and just as we are not allowed to give up the *State of Israel,*
so we are ordered to keep what we received there from *Eretz-Yisrael.*
We are bound to be loyal to the entirety of our country—for the sake
of the people's past as well as its future, and no government in Israel
is entitled to give up this entirety." (See Appendix I.) Implicit here is
the notion that a power higher than state sovereignty limits the power
of the state, and that the land belongs, not to the citizens of Israel, but
to the entire Jewish people. Since the Jewish people is not represented
in the government, the state cannot act in its name. Interestingly,
religious members of the Movement affirmed their belief that, while
many critics of the Movement saw religious legitimations as a smoke-

screen for nationalist assertion, all members of the Movement belonged to it essentially for religious reasons, although they took refuge in security and other arguments.

Religious members talked frankly in terms of redemption. Religious member Moshe Moskowitz asserted: "I believe this country is in one of the stages of redemption. The redemption of the land and people go together. We keep getting parts of the land; slowly more and more is added. . . . What guides the Jewish people cannot be explained in terms of the general history of nations. The only question is how much suffering goes with this process. But I do not doubt that the land and the people will find their mutual redemption."[32]

Those from Irgun backgrounds emphasized the historical claim. They pointed out that, not only had the Jews occupied Palestine for 1800 years, but they had never ceased to maintain their link with the country; and that Jewish settlement, albeit on a small scale for much of the recent period, had been continuous for 3500 years.[33] The British government, through the Balfour Declaration, and the international community, through the League of Nations, had recognized the peculiar bond between the Jews and Palestine in establishing the Jewish National Home in territory which included all of western Palestine. They argued it was impossible to maintain the legitimacy of the old borders if the legitimacy of the new was denied. If Jews had no title to Hebron, the first seat of David's kingdom, they had no right to Tel Aviv, a stretch of sand that had been in Philistine hands throughout much of the ancient period.

Others raised existential arguments, and these too had their roots in Zionist ideology. Jabotinsky, for example, had argued before various British commissions in the 1930s that, although rival claims to Palestine might find legal or moral support, only the Jewish people had the right given by overwhelming need. Only for the Jewish people, he argued, was Palestine not only the sole possible basis for national identification but the sole avenue for physical survival: "When the Arab claim is confronted with our Jewish demand to be saved, it is like the claims of appetite vs. starvation."[34] The Hameuchad's Moshe Tabenkin argued similarly: "Today the Jews demand an equal right to exist, and this is the foundation of their right to Israel. . . . The historical tie to the land becomes a force, in fact the only force, which can bring forth the energies to resist the destruction of this people. . . . We have come back because we must escape destruction. That is the great force of our demand, which also has great political force because no one else can offer us any other solution. . . . Their tie to this land is the only weapon Jews have to fight for their existence today."[35] Religious member Harold Fisch pointed out that an existential emphasis had the additional virtue of giving Sinai and the Golan weight equal to that of the West Bank. On existential grounds they could be seen to ensure the future of the state, just as the West Bank symbolized its past."[36]

All these were, of course, traditional legitimations; radical formulations came from those labor members who did not see themselves primarily as bearers of a pre-state Zionist position. Thus, while religious and historical legitimations were generally perceived as producing extreme demands, actually these legitimations served as a brake upon claims. For if history and religion determined boundaries, there was no freedom to fashion borders in accordance with quite different principles, such as security or economic viability. For some of the labor converts, security became the basis of legitimacy, and then the borders of Israel became a much more open question. Zvi Shiloah was the most outspoken proponent of the need for a new vision of Israel's boundaries:

I have not based my views on a historical conception of borders, because there have been many boundaries and all of them are historical. We need a geopolitical conception. We need a conception of a "great Israel" extending from the Mediterranean to the Persian Gulf. . . . The concept of space has not yet been grasped in Israel. . . . We must separate the Arab territories from one another. We must develop the geopolitical vision to recognize that it is essential to control large spaces, so that people cannot talk of Israel as a small obstacle in the Near East. The unity of Arab states is in any case a fiction, but once Israel becomes a big wedge between them, even the fiction disappears.[37]

Shiloah's conception could not be advanced publicly by the Movement, since it was committed by its manifesto to the existing borders; but his position was widely known (Shiloah wrote a book to detail it) and was shared by others of the labor converts.

In the pages of the Movement's journal *Zot Haaretz*, it was even possible to find members arguing against traditional legitimations, and the traditionally oriented reacted sharply to check the spread of radical formulations. For example, in *Zot Haaretz*, geographer Elisha Efrat urged that the Movement was mistaken in urging the retention of territories because of historical and religious associations. What was crucial about Hebron was that it was the agricultural center of the Judean mountains; relevant about Shechem (Nablus) was that Samaria, of which it was the major city, was the geographical center of Israel; and what made the annexation of East Jerusalem essential was that a capital city needs open spaces around it.[38] Eldad quickly attacked Efrat:

Anyone who negates, as Dr. Efrat does, the historic-nostalgic basis [of our demand for an entire land] what then is he doing here, precisely in this land, in the first place? . . . One cannot exchange Jewish existentialism for an Israeli existentialism, for Jewish existence is the underpinning for Israel. . . . If Hebron will remain in Israeli hands, it will not be because of the geopolitical grasp and economic education of the secular Zionists, but by dint of the group around Rabbi Levinger which was attracted to Hebron because it was the city of the fathers. . . . And at the head of his opponents stand realistic people like the economist Professor [Don] Patinkin, who should really be expected to understand the economic importance of the Hebron district for Jerusalem, or the historian Professor [Joshua] Prawer, who brilliantly dissects the reasons for the failure of the Crusaders, who did not settle on the land, and left it and the central mountain district in the hands of the Arabs, while he himself with all his "wisdom" recommends to us today, the Jews, to commit the same mistakes.[39]

Eldad was unusual in regarding the security argument, which others in the Movement saw as a useful supporting legitimation, as actively dangerous. "Even the best among us, those taking a clear Zionist, national, patriotic stand, they too in their arguments against retreat produce the argument of security needs, a smooth and dangerous argument. It is a snare and a trap and a door to pressures from outside and to the weakening of inner self-certainty. The 'security' of our ownership of Eretz Yisrael is beyond all questions of security.' "[40]

The Movement was on its strongest ground in affirming the legitimacy of Israel's claim to the territories taken in the Six-Day War. This may seem surprising since the government's position, summed up as "territories for peace," implicitly assumed that the territories belonged to the Arabs and were only being held as bargaining counters by Israel. Nonetheless, the Movement carried forward traditional Zionist assumptions, and the government, as an avowedly Zionist one, was in no position to counter claims to legitimacy with any confidence. The issue between government and Movement was fundamentally tactical, with the government arguing that while Israel might have the right to the territories (or at least to the West Bank and Golan) it was neither desirable nor possible, at this juncture of history, for Israel to keep them. The government concentrated on the issue of tactics and argued that the Land of Israel Movement, far from being conservative as it perceived itself, was actually offering a radical, even anti-Zionist, program.

The Movement's members argued that the Movement was conservative—that it not only carried forward traditional values, but recommended traditional patterns of action. Moshe Tabenkin argued: "If someone says we have no right to Judea and Samaria because there is an Arab majority there, then there was no moral basis in the past for our settlement. In my opinion, those in the kibbutz movement who are against settling the territories have the burden of explaining why it is now not permissible and in the past it was. Why was settling Mishmar Haemek socialist implementation, and doing the same thing in the Jordan Valley today fascism?"[41]

Government spokesmen countered—ironically in view of the Movement's expulsion of its Canaanite members—that the Movement itself was Canaanite, for it would destroy the Jewish character of the state by incorporating a huge Arab minority, destined because of the higher Arab birth rate soon to become a majority. Thus opponents argued that the Land of Israel Movement, in the name of implementing Zionist values, would destroy the fundamental Zionist value of Jewish sovereign self-determination.[42]

In reacting in turn to this criticism, the Movement was forced into a much more fundamental critique of the government than it had originally intended, for at issue was no less than the central conception of the nature of the state. The goal of Zionism had been the establishment of a state and the normalization of the position of the Jews in a state like any other. If that goal had been achieved with the establishment of the state, then the Land of Israel Movement was radical, seeking a drastic change in boundaries and a transformation of the population structure. But if the goal had not been achieved, if Zionism was still a movement in the process of implementation, if the partition-state was only a stage of the Zionist movement, then it was the government that was radical, abrogating Zionism's ongoing task by treating itself as the final fulfillment of a task for which it was truly but a humble, if powerful, tool. Tabenkin's statement, quoted above, reflected the Movement's attitude; implicit here is the view that statehood had changed nothing and that, if settlement in all parts of the Land of Israel had been in accordance with Zionist ideology then, it was no less proper now. For the government, statehood had changed everything, and what had been permissible under the British Mandate in the territory of the Jewish National Home was scarcely permissible now when boundaries had been established (even if they were not recognized) and the territory involved belonged to a foreign nation (even if occupied by Israeli forces.)

The Movement explained the government's loss of a sense of Zionist purpose on both structural and psychological grounds. On the one hand, in the Movement's view, the experience of statehood had led Israel's leaders to forget Zionist goals. Israel Eldad wrote:

Precisely those people who from the point of faith and ideals were furthest from the concept of a "great State-Zionism," and in the past derided those who wanted a state . . . it was precisely those individuals who reached rulership—state budgets, flags, ceremonies, international and national receptions of which they never dreamt in their little Zionism and "furrow after furrow." They became intoxicated with this statehood, and it became for them the total vision. This is the satiety which blinded them, which blunted their sensitivities, which made "Israel" the essence and the Land of Israel "foreign territory." . . . For years one had to fight that Zionism should be "state-oriented." Today the great amazement and paradox is that one has to fight that the state should be—Zionist.[43]

In addition, there were psychologically crippling problems at the heart of the Zionist movement.

The existence of the partition of the country is a function of the division of the existential soul of Zionism in its different layers. In these layers, from the beginning, there was a deep fragmentation, with guilt feelings towards the cosmopolitan ideals of socialism and liberalism, which were to liberate the world from nationalism—maybe even from the plague of the nation-states—and which would liberate the Jews entirely from their separate unique existence. . . . This is a typical schizophrenia. We have guilt feelings that we presumably have betrayed these universal ideals by turning to Zionism, which is of necessity "reactionary" for it is a return to sometimes irrational roots. . . . Had it only at least been possible to implement "utopian Zionism" in "ways of peace" through convincing the Arabs that we bring blessings to them too, and socialist liberation and progress! But in vain! To go on with psychological language, what is left is frustration—the feeling that perhaps Zionism is after all a reactionary movement.[44]

In the perspective of the Land of Israel Movement, Zionism's goal was indeed statehood and normalization of the Jewish condition; but these goals had not yet been achieved. Zionism had as its goal the ingathering of all the Jews of the world, with the exception of a small number who would be assimilated and lose their identity in their countries of origin, and this goal had clearly not been realized, Israel having little more than a fifth of the world's Jews living within her borders. Zionist faith was thus the answer to the "demographer-Zionists," as they were scornfully called by Movement members, for the Movement, in its official position, advocated granting full rights to the Arabs of the new territories once they were absorbed into Israel.[45] Given this position, ingathering of the exiles became a crucial condition for implementation of the Land of Israel Movement's ideology; this fact was recognized in the Movement's manifesto, which said: "A great Aliya [immigration] from all the diasporas of the Jewish people is the fundamental condition for preserving the national character of Eretz Yisrael." But, the Movement argued, all the world's Jews could only be ingathered into an undivided Land of Israel. The twin goals of Zionism were thus inextricably connected: the settlement of the entire land required the aliya of the world's Jews, and the world's Jews need the entire land to provide them with the conditions making settlement of millions of additional immigrants possible.

For the Movement there was no option. Menachem Dorman said: "The choice is not really in our hands; there is no alternative of going back to the old boundaries. We are condemned to be strong. . . . One thing all members of the Movement have in common is a sense of strength, and this is not chauvinism or overbearing pride, but comes from a feeling that either the state of Israel will be strong or it will not exist."[46] Returning the territories in exchange for peace, the government's avowed policy, was seen as an illusory alternative. In the Movement's view, the only path to peace was through power, not concessions. The Arabs would establish peace with Israel, not when their good will had been won by Israeli demonstrations of her own good will, but when they no longer saw the possibility of destroying her. Return of the territories would, by restoring Israel to the old vulnerability, merely increase Arab hopes for success in a renewed conflict. If Israel did not assert her will upon the region, the region would assert its will upon Israel by destroying her.

The Movement thus confronted the government, not only on the issue of the nature of the Israeli state and the role of its government in relation to Zionism, but on the issue of the role of the state in relation to the world balance of forces, the extent of the state's power, and its freedom to shape reality. For the government, Israel continued to be a small state subject to severe external constraints, ultimately without the ability to exert her own will against world powers that would in the end not countenance the expansion of the state of Israel into the borders established in 1967. For the government the territories *could* only be used as bargaining counters; temporarily held, they might buy permanent advantages. For the Movement, external constraints could be overcome; the argument was essentially, in respect to both the Soviet Union and the United States, "it depends on us." Eliezer Livneh said: "Without United States pressure, retreat is inconceivable. But it has come to the point that, even with United States pressure, retreat is inconceivable."[47] The Movement argued that the government had not adjusted to the change in power relations following the war—to awareness that Israel was now the strongest power in the region—and had thus failed to adjust its ideological perspectives to its power resources. A number of articles in *Zot Haaretz* in the first years sought to explain that the United States in fact wanted Israel to remain in the post-1967 boundaries to block Soviet expansion, but was inhibited from saying so openly by the necessity of maintaining dialogue with the Russians and of not taking a position more militant than that taken by Israel.[48] When the United States produced the Rogers Plan, calling for restoration of the old borders with "insubstantial changes," it became difficult to argue that the United States wished the present borders retained. In that event, the Movement argued, Israel—which provided the only impediment to Soviet domination of the Middle East and ultimately to its control of East Africa and India—must save the West against the West's own will.[49]

Sociologist Lewis Killian has pointed out that an ideology includes a double vision of the future: an image of heaven and of hell. In the case of the Land of Israel Movement, there were double visions of both, for the Movement, with its strong religious component, had both sacred and profane images of the future order. From the standpoint of religious members, the Movement had millenial overtones. In origin the millenial conception is Jewish, although a number of students of social movements have pointed to the importance of millenial conceptions in all western movements, including such explicitly anti-religious ones as communism and nazism. In the original Jewish vision, the millenium would see Israel given dominion from "sea to sea and from the desert to the ends of the earth." It was noted earlier that for some religious Jews restoration of Israel to its land could occur only in this revolutionary millenary period, while others argued that dominion must first be restored by the Jew's own efforts, and that only then could God's redemptive design for mankind be fulfilled. The religious members of the Land of Israel Movement, of course, fell into the second group and saw the events that had produced Israel's conquest of the Holy Land as stages in the divine redemptive process.[50]

For the secularists within the Movement there were several visions of an ideal future. For those within the Movement who remained dedicated to the vision of a just society based on equality of labor, the future order would implement that vision. Moshe Tabenkin said: "If we settle the land there will be labor hegemony, for the settlement effort is dictated by labor and precisely my way of life will win out."[51] Others had a more strictly political vision of the future order, which would be based upon Israel's dominance in the region. This vision had, in fact, much in common with that of the Canaanites: a "United States of the Middle East"; but whereas the Canaanites wished to unify the region in terms of a melting-pot interpretation of United States society, with Israelis constituting the "Anglo-Saxon core" to which others would assimilate, the proponents of the vision within the Land of Israel Movement had in mind a pluralistic interpretation of that society, in which each group maintained its separate identity. In a Middle East which had lost its monolithic Arab character through liberation of various nationalities within it (e.g. Maronites, Kurds, Cherkess), Israel's integration became possible.[52]

The vision of hell was common to all members and followed Israel's retreat from the territories—a retreat which the religious members saw as being in contravention of divine command, and which secular members perceived as contrary to elementary political sense. In a typical scenario, this one written in 1969, a writer described Israel's retreat in return for Arab agreement to minor border changes and a signed "peace document."

We will of course be careful in the formulation of the peace treaty. Our legal experts will take care to insert the proper paragraphs, which will secure our rights under any contingency. After that, we will touch our glasses with Gunnar Jarring, or whoever will replace him. And then will begin the retreat: in return for promises and the securities of the peace treaties we shall withdraw from our fortifications on the banks of the Suez and retreat to the old border. . . . We shall rid ourselves immediately of Judea and Samaria with their Arab inhabitants who threaten Israeli demography. The political border between Jews and Arabs will be the old one, with minor changes in favor of the Jews. But the Arabs will not be the same Arabs they were before the retreat, nor the Jews the same Jews. Along the line Jenin-Tulkarm-Ramallah and from Bethlehem southward to Aqaba will sprawl the irregular Arab force for the liberation of Falastin from the Zionist affliction. Encouraged by its first success, reinforced by 2,000 youth with political and military experience who returned from Israeli prisons, this will be a force which thousands of students, young workers and farmers will rush to join. . . . Not many days will pass, and the war of annihilation against the Jews will receive a momentum it never had before.[53]

Equally serious would be the effect of these events upon the Israelis themselves: "After they had been seduced in a critical moment to give up part of the land of their fathers in return for the illusion of an imaginary peace, they will see themselves after a few months cheated and bereft. They will still have an excellent army and the mighty God in heaven. Both had given them the miracle of victory and they had squandered its fruits. . . . As the Six-Day War lifted them to the height of human and civic morality, the retreat will throw them into the abyss of demoralization."[54] Disaster certainly, perhaps even annihilation, would be the outcome of failure to implement the Movement's ideology.

Since a movement will define its goals as just, desirable, and achievable, it must have an explanation for the failure of society to implement them, and a focus for the hostility such failure produces in those who believe in the ideology. Eric Hoffer has stressed that a movement can do without belief in a God, but not without belief in a devil.[55] The devil can be an objective force impeding a movement's success or, as is frequently the case, a scapegoat may be found.

In the case of the Land of Israel Movement, the search for devils was inhibited by a tendency to blame the entire nation for its loss of moral will and fibre. On the other hand, the leadership was viewed as far more culpable than the common people, who were seen as being realistic and possessing the requisite moral fibre, if not misled by their leaders. And it is interesting in view of the inward orientation of the Movement that the individual who began to take on the role of the devil, representing all that was worst in Israel's moral and political leadership, was the man who symbolized both in his personal style and in his assigned role the outward orientation of the state—Israel's Foreign Minister, Abba Eban. Repeatedly, Movement members referred to Eban as a "foreign stone." (Eban means "stone" in Hebrew.) This could not be explained by his South African birth, since most of Israel's leaders were foreign born; Golda Meir herself spoke Hebrew with a broad midwestern American accent that aroused no sense of her foreignness. What seemed foreign about Eban, then, was clearly his style rather than his accent or place of origin. It is hard to imagine him in an open shirt without tie, long the standard uniform of Israeli politicians, and his accentless Hebrew sounds literary and artificial to the plain-spoken Israeli. While most of Israel's politicians from the labor parties spent at least some years on a kibbutz (and many of the Movement's members had kibbutz backgrounds as well), not only had Eban never been a kibbutz member, but it proved difficult even to imagine him as one. For the Movement, Eban, the man, embodied the style of Jewish representation it felt must come to an end: representation by the individual acceptable to the non-Jew, rather than by the individual more typical of the Jewish community. According to Eldad: "Eban is not a liberated Jew, not a free Israeli, but an emancipated Jew whom circumstances compelled to become a Zionist. There are Jews upon whom Zionism is compelled. For them Zionism is an historical road accident."[56]

But Eban's role as Israel's representative to the outside world was also crucial in his identification as the man chiefly responsible for Israel's failure to adopt the Movement's ideology. As Foreign Minister, Eban presented Israel's position to foreign governments and interpreted their position to the Israeli government. Furthermore, as a result of the allocation of responsibilities within the Cabinet, he was also responsible for information policy abroad. The Movement felt that Eban misrepresented Israeli government policy in such a way that foreign governments were in effect told Eban's policy, and that he in turn misrepresented the positions of foreign governments. Eban became responsible for the Rogers Plan; his presentation of Israeli policy had led the U.S. State Department to assume that Israel could again be prevailed upon to restore the pre-1967 boundaries without substantial change.[57] His responsibility for information policy made Eban all the more central a target, for information policy involved the official legitimation offered by Israel for its presence in the territories. Israeli information policy treated the territories frankly as "occupied" rather than "liberated," and their retention was excused on the grounds they were being held until the Arab states should be willing to sign a peace treaty with Israel. In the Movement's view, of course, it was crucial that Israel stress Israel's *right* to the territories; the Movement argued that, even from a purely tactical point of view, it was folly to portray the state as an occupying power without rights, for in effect Israel then put herself in the dock, playing into the hands of Arab propagandists.

Yet the identification of Eban as the devil preventing the implementation of the Movement's ideology was hindered by doubts that he in fact exercised independent power. Some members argued that he was simply a government mouthpiece. If he was weak there was no point devoting a great deal of attention to him, and in part the fact that so much attention continued to be devoted to him was a function of Eban's own hostility to the Movement. For example, Eban wrote of an ideological article by the Movement's Eliezer Livneh that it "could not have been written or published a few years ago except by a professional humorist with a gift for parody."[58] Yet sharp as the feeling was against Eban, as both the symbol of perspectives and the architect of policies deemed destructive of the state, the Movement, despite ongoing pressure by elements within it, steadfastly refused to so much as pass a resolution condemning him, and calling for his resignation. Here again, key labor members argued that direct condemnation of a central figure of their own party constituted unacceptable "action" by the Movement as against appropriate "persuasion" of decision makers. When the Beersheba branch of the Movement published a long direct attack upon Eban (and upon the Movement itself for failing formally to condemn him), *Zot Haaretz* and Movement members in the Knesset dissociated themselves from the pamphlet.[59]

The Movement never found another devil to equal Eban, although the peace movement as a whole—collectively called "the defeatists" by the Movement—was a major target, and within it "the professors," a group of academics coming especially from the Hebrew University in Jerusalem, were the object of special bitterness. Of course the peace movement was not in power; the peace movement did not create Israeli policy. What could be argued concerning its members was that they symbolized the very worst tendencies in Israeli society, by their presence put pressure on the government to do even less toward implementing the Land of Israel Movement's ideology than it might otherwise have done, destroyed the belief of youth in the justice of the Jewish claim, and undermined the entire legitimacy of Israel's position in the territories by, in the Movement's view, fabricating a "Palestinian identity" to which the West Bank and Gaza, at least, could then be said by right to belong. This last was particularly important for, as we have noted, the government was hesitant to attack the Movement squarely on the issue of legitimacy; and cabinet members, for the most part, were as opposed as the Movement to the creation of yet another Arab (Palestinian) state. For the Movement, it should be stressed, the villain was not Palestinian nationalism but the idea of it as advanced by Jews. Although the Arabs in general, and especially the proponents of pan-Arabism, were in an obvious sense the enemy, they were not the villains in the Movement's analysis. On the contrary, the Arabs were seen as Israel's best friend, saving her through their intransigence from her own moral weakness.

In short, the alternative ideology the Land of Israel Movement offered to decision makers was clear-cut and relatively simple, with defined short-term and long-term goals. In the short term the Movement advocated settlement, both agricultural and urban, on a vastly increased scale in all the territories, the introduction of Israeli law into them, and their administrative unification with Israel. In the long term the Movement urged full legal and formal incorporation of the territories into Israeli, just as had been done—and done alone—in the case of eastern Jerusalem. The Movement provided a comprehensive series of justifications for the course it recommended, drawing from traditional Zionist ideology, and it urged that its program was not merely capable of fulfillment but was without realistic alternative if the state was to survive.

4
The Peace Movement

Although the peace movement can be viewed as a counter-movement, it seems clear that it would have developed even if the Land of Israel Movement had never been formed. For the peace movement the Six-Day War provided the opportunity to solve the problem of Israeli-Arab relations which had bedevilled the Zionist movement since its initial triumph with the Balfour Declaration. While the Land of Israel Movement saw in the Six-Day War the opportunity to realize the territorial aims of traditional Zionism, the peace movement saw in it the chance to realize Zionism's aspirations for the Jewish state to achieve an accepted and respected place in the region and the admiration of the world as a state embodying the highest ideals of law and justice.

When the Six-Day War broke out, there was near unanimity among those who were to become part of the peace movement that the war was necessary, inevitable, and thus—from Israel's point of view—just. Immediately before the outbreak of the war, the left-wing journal *New Outlook* called for exploration of all diplomatic avenues and backed Foreign Minister Abba Eban's effort to give international diplomacy every chance to open the blockaded Straits of Tiran.[1] Nonetheless, there was the conviction that the Arabs had precipitated the war and that Israel's ultimate decision to make a preventive strike was the proper one. This conviction contrasted with the uneasiness within Israel's extreme left wing after the Sinai campaign of 1956, primarily because of the identification of Israel with the "imperialist" actions of England and France. In the view of Israel's left wing, the task of the state was somehow to free itself from its image as a colonialist implantation in the Middle East, and with the Sinai campaign Israel had succeeded only in reinforcing that identification.

But while the Six-Day War was seen as a just one, the result of the war, ironically, was to make Israel overnight an "unjust" society, a state with the very characteristics of which it had so long wrongly been accused. In the view of those who were to join its peace movement Israel now was indeed colonialist and imperialist, for she ruled over a large hostile population, while her borders were tripled in size and thus proportionately even more swollen than her population. This situation was intolerable to those who became active in the peace movement. As one writer put it: "There is another reason why I do not want to hold onto these territories. *I don't want to be a colonialist!* . . . If we hold on to the territories, we shall enslave the people living there, since practically all the inhabitants do not want to live in the State of Israel or in a protectorate, and they say this even today, while still under the shock."[2]

Yet this very situation held a promise as well as an unbearable threat. The new borders and the new population, rightly used, could become the vehicle for finally achieving peace; the war thus became an unexampled opportunity for abruptly reversing past trends. The war, far from constituting the opportunity to realize the territorial aims of Zionism, as the Land of Israel Movement saw it, was seen by the peace movement as the opportunity to prove finally to the Arabs that their vision of Zionism as inherently expansionist was wrong, and that Israel on the contrary was a state which genuinely yearned for peace with her neighbors and was willing to prove it by total forfeiture of territorial claims, even in a just war which had been forced upon her. In one formulation: "The borders we should insist on are those which existed on June 5; we want the State of Israel as it was then, with borders of peace that mean security."[3]

The peace movement drew for membership upon traditional groupings which maintained perspectives that made it highly probable they would seize upon the Six-Day War as an event which made possible the realization of long-held goals. There were few prominent converts in the peace movement. While well-known individuals from Mapam crossed over to the Land of Israel Movement, there were no prominent members of Gahal to lend comparable drama to the peace movement by crossing over to it. To be sure, individuals prominent in the dominant Labor Alignment gradually became associated with the peace movement, but the process was slow and there was not—at least in public perception—the impact of a sudden complete turnabout in ideological conviction of a number of leading intellectuals.

Predictably, Mapam was the single chief source of the peace movement's leadership. But just as Gahal, despite its well-established commitment to the ideology of an undivided Land of Israel, was unavailable after the Six-Day War as an avenue of protest against government policy, so Mapam, which had joined with the Labor party in a coalition government as early as 1965, was unavailable to those seeking an institutionalized avenue of criticism.

The Hashomer Hazair, which at the founding of the state became the basis (with the Achdut Haavoda) of the Mapam party, in its origin had been a romantic Jewish European youth movement. In the early period there was a quasi-religious search for a communal world soul and a conception of modern man choking in a mechanistic civilization.[4] From the beginning the Hashomer Hazair was deeply concerned with the problem of reconciling its universalist with its nationalist ideals. This the movement did through arguing that Jews would make their universalist contribution through nationalism. "There are still Zionists, too, who do not understand that the nationalism of the modern Jew does not predicate his seclusion from the future problems of mankind but rather prepares him for a nation which will take an active part in the solution of these problems. This is the main and deep significance in progressive Zionism. This is the Zionism we believe in, it is for this Zionism that we strive."[5] The youth of the Hashomer movement who came to Israel felt that the society they created "should serve as an example of social justice and of a new morality."[6] Their efforts were heavily concentrated upon the building of miniature "just societies" in the kibbutzim; those of the Hashomer Hazair were always deliberately kept relatively small and were concerned with the formulation of an ideology to be accepted by all members. At the Hashomer Hazair's world convention in 1927, a majority wished to resolve that the kibbutzim of their federation in Palestine provided the only way for realization of the Hashomer Hazair's ideals, but a compromise was reached so that in the end the resolution said that the Hashomer Hazair considered these kibbutzim as "the main form and manner of realizing its ideals in Eretz Yisrael."[7] These kibbutzim might seem to others to be mere small isolated communes, remote from the concerns of the rest of the world, but not so in the perception of their members. As one observed, "I saw the 'Shomer Colony' in Palestine in the form of a citadel set high up on a hill. As the sun sheds its rays on all the surrounding country, so would be the effect of this citadel on the outside world."[8] Indeed, the Hashomer kibbutz was seen as the "cornerstone and prototype of a new social order" that would educate the worker "in self-government, in creativeness, and in brotherhood."[9]

Not until the mid-1920s in Palestine did the Hashomer Hazair take a sharp leftward turn, increasingly looking to Marxist class war doctrines as economic crisis in Palestine discouraged members concerning the possibility of building a socialist society on agrarian communes. The ideological crisis that seized Hashomer Hazair in the late twenties and ended with many members defecting, either to Palestine's Communist party or to the ideologically similar Poalei Zion Smol, preoccupied the party's leaders to the point that only in the mid-1930s did they turn their attention to the problem of relations with the Arabs. The other Zionist parties had sought to deal with this problem since the riots of 1929 and were especially concerned with the concrete challenge of establishing representative institutions in Palestine.[10] This "reform," sought by the British in the wake of the riots, was of course deeply threatening to the Jewish minority in the country. When the Hashomer Hazair did turn its attention to these problems, it rejected the basic assumption of the larger Mapai party that only a change in power relations could create the basis for understanding. (That assumption, incidentally, has continued to characterize the ruling Labor party until the present day; the belief is that only when Israel is strong enough that the Arabs lose hope of destroying her will they be willing to make peace.) Hashomer Hazair argued that what was essential was, rather, to change the structure of Arab society—on the theory that the true interests of the Arab masses did not conflict with Zionism.[11] Instead of seeing the conflict as one between rival nationalisms, Hashomer Hazair saw the Arab peasant as the victim of a kind of false consciousness instilled in him by the dominant effendi class, yet capable of being taught to see his true identity of interests with the Jewish worker and to join with him in a united front against the common enemy: the exploiting class. To the members of the Hashomer Hazair it was an article of faith that "the day will yet come when this alliance will break down the walls of hate and murder erected by muftis and Arab effendis as well as the boundaries that have been set up by British imperialism."[12] The realization of Zionism was only the beginning. "We are socialists who believe in a movement that cannot be satisfied merely with formal attributes of nationhood but look toward solving the needs of the suffering masses. We feel that in this part of the world known as the Near East, the socialist order of justice toward which we strive will be advanced through the realization of Zionism."[13] Class war, of the Jewish as well as the Arab proletariat, would usher in the society of workers and agricultural laborers, equal productive citizens of the classless society.

The goal of the Hashomer Hazair was a just society rather than a just state. Presumably, the just society can be built in a variety of political frameworks; to alleviate Arab fears, the Hashomer Hazair proposed a bi-national state and guaranteed permanent equality of representation to the Arab population in institutions of government—despite the fact that the movement, which was unwilling to abandon the principle of Jewish immigration, assumed that eventually there would be a Jewish majority. Hashomer Hazair continued to advocate this policy and oppose partition up to the founding of the state.

Mapam, the second largest party in the first Knesset, steadily lost strength. Its position was eroded by the problem of maintaining its leftist ideology, which called for identification with Soviet policies, considerably past the point at which the Israeli consensus recognized that the Soviet Union was committed to an anti-Israel policy. (Achdut Haavoda left Mapam on this issue in 1954.) Mapam continued to look upon itself as the guardian of Arab rights, seeking an end to limitations upon the freedom of Israel's Arab citizens and calling for more perseverance and imagination on Israel's part in reaching accommodation with Arab demands. Once Israel had been established, Mapam abandoned its bi-national proposal; no longer ready to give up Jewish sovereignty, Mapam looked for accommodation through Israel's willingness to make concessions to what it defined as justifiable Arab concerns, such as giving land-locked Jordan access to the Mediterranean and making maximal efforts to solve the refugee problem.

Moshe Shamir's description of the Hashomer Hazair as "schizophrenic" may, as the analysis of a renegade from the movement, be suspect. Nonetheless, maintenance of a Zionist ideology in combination with a radical-left ideology (in a world in which radical leftism has identified Arab nationalism as progressive and Zionism, in view of its conflict with it, as retrogressive) involved a high degree of ideological tension. The difficulty of interweaving the conflicting strands meant that young people who had been socialized into the ideology, given a crisis such as the Six-Day War, could easily draw upon one strand and criticize the other in terms of it. While some, like Moshe Shamir or Avraham Yaffe, crossed over into the Land of Israel Movement, a larger number gave priority to the radical-left definitions of their ideological background and became part of the peace movement.

The dilemma of Mapam became acute before the elections of 1969, for it then had to decide whether to unify with the other labor parties, to dissociate itself completely from them and go into opposition, or to choose the alternative it ultimately did take—to align itself without actually merging with the United Labor party, composed of the former Mapai, Achdut Haavoda, and Rafi parties. In protest against this choice, a small segment of the Mapam leadership, chief among them Jacob Riftin, broke away to form *Brit Hasmol* ("Federation of the Left"), which then constituted one of the groupings of the peace movement. More significant, more than one-third of Mapam's Central Committee, 239 of 433 members, voted against the proposal for alignment. the division within Mapam was as much tactical as ideological:: Could Mapam accomplish more to achieve its ideological aims through working within the government, or could it achieve those aims better as an opposition party? Those in favor of the union insisted that the party's effectiveness would be much greater if it held a share of power; those opposed argued that Mapam would not have sufficient ministers to shape cabinet decisions and that, on the contrary, by giving up the necessary role of ideological critic, Mapam would leave the way open for the "weeds of the cosmopolitan left" to expand their following, that is, the two communist parties of Israel and the frankly anti-Zionist groupings.[14]

Even after their defeat, most of those who opposed Mapam's decision remained within the party, but the considerable dissatisfaction with that decision, both within the party institutions and in the kibbutzim of the Kibbutz Haartzi Federation, especially among the kibbutz youth, constrained Mapam to embark upon the uncomfortable course of openly criticizing the government while participating within it; indeed, the widespread dissatisfaction kept the party from imposing sanctions on members who criticized the government far more vigorously than the party leadership thought defensible. Youth from the kibbutzim of the Hashomer Hazair constituted the leadership of Siach (Smol Yisrael Chadash—the Israeli New Left), one of the larger groupings within the peace movement, composed largely of university students who saw themselves also as part of the worldwide student revolution of the 1960s.

"Traditional" recruits to the peace movement came also from the academic faculties of Israel's major universities, especially the Hebrew University of Jerusalem. Known popularly as "the professors," a number of those who joined were real converts to the peace movement, men who had been politically inactive or had been affiliated with the dominant Labor party; but in the public perception professors, especially professors at the Hebrew University, were natural bearers of the peace movement's ideology because of the association of the university, first with the Brit Shalom (founded in 1925, it included a number of professors at the university, especially those of Central and West European origin; and it was supported by Judah Magnes, president of the University), and then with the Ihud. For the intellectuals of the Ihud, philosopher Horace Kallen noted, "peace and harmony with the Arabs were, so to speak, the categorical imperative."[15] Martin Buber saw accommodation with the Arabs as a Jewish *religious* challenge, *the* divine challenge posed in the modern period for Jews within the Holy Land.[16] Toward the end of the mandate period the Ihud suggested that radical concessions be made to Arab demands, including sharp limitations upon Jewish immigration (something which the Hashomer Hazair was unwilling to do).

In size no larger than an ideological circle, the Ihud was important both because of the intellectual stature of its members and because it was the only Zionist grouping which consented to permanent minority status for Jews within Palestine. The Ihud's intellectuals, most of them of German and American origin, espoused no ideology of the left; the just society which they sought was built upon the satisfaction of the aspirations of Palestine's peoples, whatever form national self-determination should assume. Themselves attached to the values of liberal rationalism, the members of the Ihud hoped the societies which emerged in Palestine would be built upon these values. The Ihud remained in existence after Israel's War of Independence, and a small circle of Ihud members published a paper called *Ner* ("The Lamp") in which they spoke out concerning the plight of the Arab refugees, restrictions on Israeli Arabs, and the search for peace. Of the old academic circle of the Ihud, most had died; only Ernest Simon, professor of education at the Hebrew University, represented direct continuity with the old Ihud.

The peace movement's professors, heavily concentrated in the social sciences as were their forebears in the Ihud, were guided less by left-wing ideologies than by conceptions of justice and models of rational problem solving and conflict resolution. They feared the possible consequences for Israeli democratic society of rulership over an unwilling national minority which, in view of the differences in birth rate between Arabs and Jews, was a potential majority. And familiar with models of conflict resolution, despite their recognition of the irrational character of Arab hostility, the professors hoped that significant first steps by Israel to break the circle of suspicion and hatred could lead to a lessening of hostility by the other side, corresponding steps to reduce conflict by the Arabs, and eventually a gradual end to the conflict, According to Joshua Arieli, a professor of American history at the Hebrew University, "it would seem reasonable that the government of Israel would seek alternative proposals which might mean less than peace—if they bring a de-escalation of regional tensions and point towards a way to resolve the conflict."[17] The professors were not numerous, but they were influential within the movement because they were articulate—they wrote extensively both in Israel and abroad. Moreover, precisely because they were not for the most part carriers of leftist ideologies, the professors were able to give the peace movement, so heavily concentrated in leftist groups, a broader ideological base.

Another small but potentially significant source of adherents to the peace movement was at once traditional and ideologically surprising: those for whom religion was the mainspring of commitment. From the religious viewpoint, of course, there was no question of the Jewish title to an undivided Land of Israel, and the Land of Israel Movement in fact failed to win some religious support by refusing to state a claim beyond the boundaries achieved in the Six-Day War. On the other hand, within the religious Mizrachi party in the Zionist movement there had always been a minority which urged maximum concessions and consistently favored the partition proposals which the majority within the Mizrachi party rejected. Those who served as chief exponents of this view in the pre-state period were attracted to the peace movement. Notable here were Moshe Unna, a member of the National Religious party in the first six Knessets, and Pinchas Rosenbluth, director of the religious division of Mikveh Israel, the first agricultural school in Palestine. Moshe Haim Shapira, who represented the National Religious party in Israeli cabinets until his death in 1970, had been one of the group within Mizrachi favoring partition, and had been in the small minority in the People's Council—Moetzet Haam—that voted against the declaration of Israeli statehood when United States opposition was apparent.

In the pre-state Mizrachi party theirs had been a lonely position. Rosenbluth observed that he, Unna, and Shapira, as delegates to the twentieth Zionist Congress, had unsuccessfully sought permission to register a religious minority vote for the Peel partition proposal and that Rabbi Meir Berlin (later Bar-Ilan), the head of the party, had refused, treating such a vote as a religious sin.[18]

Part of the opposition of these men to the prevailing religious definition of the situation was simply pragmatic. Rosenbluth noted that Bar-Ilan had acted as if the entire country were "in his pocket" at a time when British control made any such assumption an absurdity. But beyond pragmatism or even timidity (of which some of the religious members of the government were accused), these men shared a fear of repeating historic experience. The two disastrous wars against the Romans had been the work of religious zealots unwilling to compromise religious principles. The potential for unleashed religious fanaticism was viewed with the deepest alarm by some religious leaders.[19] After the establishment of the state, it was Shapira and others with a marked willingness to compromise who were to dominate the National Religious party until after 1967, when they were challenged by a youthful right wing which was almost as numerous.

Rosenbluth and Unna also defended their position on specifically religious grounds. Pinchas Rosenbluth said:

The Jewish idea requires not just following certain verses in the Bible, but that every generation direct its own life. . . . Every generation must find its meaning in the Jewish heritage. We cannot disregard the Arab population, for the Arabs have rights. . . . These promised frontiers, what are they? They are different in the promise to Abraham and in Numbers: they changed at different times. But what is written is not so important, the oral law is what is decisive. There is an interesting passage in the Talmud. . . . The example is given where a horse is sent to the doctor and since his place in the stable is empty, a bull is put in there. The horse returns and the question becomes, Who should be there? Rashi says Israel was expelled from Palestine and returns, and God does not know what to do.[20]

Three major arguments were advanced. One was that the highest Jewish value was Jewish survival, and that if holding territory—even rightfully Jewish territory—endangered the existence of the nation, from a religious point of view, the territory would have to be relinquished. Second was the argument that sovereignty over the Land of Israel was a political rather than a religious issue. Most religious leaders felt that it was contrary to Jewish religious precepts to relinquish any part of the Land of Israel. But religious members of the peace movement saw the state of Israel as a secular state; the land was holy no matter who ruled over it, and who ruled over it was thus a matter of political importance but religious indifference.[21] Finally, although these men were Zionists, they accepted an argument that had long been employed by religious anti-Zionists, who had insisted that the redemption of Israel could never be accomplished by the secular socialists who predominated in the Zionist movement. They pointed out that the divine promises concerning the Land of Israel were conditional upon people keeping the *mitzvot* (religious commandments), and it could scarcely be argued that a state of universal adherence to the mitzvot had been achieved. The widespread identification of the results of the Six-Day War as miraculous made these men profoundly uncomfortable. The prophets, they asserted, had not described the events surrounding the redemption like this; rather the political world, as it was known, would be abolished and Egypt, Assyria, and Israel would become brothers. The Six-Day War was a political necessity without religious significance, not a prelude to the end of days.[22]

Religious leaders prominent in the peace movement were few. But despite the small number active in the peace movement, the statement of ideology in religious terms was significant, for it provided the grounds on which Jews for whom the religious commitment was primary could accept retreat, particularly from the holy provinces of Judea and Samaria (the West Bank), as permissible, even desirable. The view that redemption, and thus the restoration of an entire Land of Israel to the Jewish people, would occur at a millenial period through God's direct intervention and not through the actions of men, continued to be basic to the Aguda party in Israel, which represented a more extreme religious perspective than the National Religious party, and in the pre-state period had been bitterly hostile to Zionism as a subversion of the divine intent. As a result, while the National Religious party affirmed its refusal to participate in a government that returned the provinces of Judea and Samaria to Arab rule, the Aguda party became a potential ally for the Labor government, should terri- torial concessions, in its judgment, become desirable on the West Bank.

There were others who joined the peace movement: journalists, en- tertainers, Israel's younger generation of writers, and students. Many of these had no formal affiliation but signed protest statements, wrote articles, and on occasion joined in demonstrations. A few of the more prominent journalists associated with the movement, including Amos Kenan and Uri Avnery, had flirted with Canaanite ideology.[23] While this might seem an odd background for members of the peace move- ment, given the Canaanite conception of an "Eretz Hakedem" in lands stretching from the Euphrates to the Nile, and while current Canaan- ites did not join the peace movement, Canaanite ideology might serve as socialization toward a non-Zionist perspective. Once Canaanite mythology concerning the reconstruction of an ancient pre-Jewish "Semitic" empire was discarded, what remained could easily be dis- satisfaction with the present legitimations of the state, and a search for a new way of achieving a modus vivendi in the region. This was, after all, the problem the Canaanites in their own way addressed. But most of the artists and journalists who were attracted to the peace movement had no such background; thus, why they were drawn to the movement, in the absence of traditional links to the perspective, remains in need of explanation.

What seems to offer the most satisfactory explanation, although ad- mittedly we tread here on speculative ground, is the sociological con- cept of reference group. Sociologists disagree, to be sure, concerning precisely what the term should denote; for some the notion of "non- belonging" is central; for others reference groups include all those to whom an individual compares himself whether they are or are not membership groups. According to yet another interpretation reference groups need not be existing groups at all, but can be any collectivity, real or imagined, whose perspective is assumed by the actor.[24] The concept of reference group has not been raised in connection with the Land of Israel Movement for good reason: reference groups, at least reference groups of the sort that played a role in the peace movement, were simply unavailable to the Land of Israel Movement.

Although the varying attitude toward the territories can be seen as developing autonomously from different interpretations of the Jewish —and Israeli—experience, both the Land of Israel Movement and the peace movement were forced to confront world attitudes, for ulti- mately Israel was dependent upon the aid of outside powers.

In the analysis of the Land of Israel Movement, it was in the interest of the free world to have the strongest possible Israel. Israel was seen by the Movement as protecting the strategic southern flank of NATO from an otherwise uncheckable Soviet penetration of the Arab world and through the Arab world of Africa and India. Failure to support Israel was viewed as leading to calamity, not just for Israel, but for the West as a whole. The failure of the West, given this conception, to recognize its interests[25] (and the Land of Israel Movement perceived, albeit more slowly and reluctantly than the peace movement, the increasing international isolation of Israel) reinforced existing perspectives in the Movement that saw the West as blind, disintegrating, and morally bankrupt. The most systematic critique of the West in these terms was produced by Eliezer Livneh in his *Israel and the Crisis of Western Civilization.* Livneh approved Austrian historian Friedrich Heer's analysis of the holocaust as the central truth of European history, and argued that the destruction of the Jews involved the complicity of virtually all western societies, both the Axis powers and those who fought against them. Livneh points out that aid to the Jews was quite independent of what side a country was on; that of the three countries which made genuine efforts to save their Jewish populations (Finland, Bulgaria, and Denmark), the first two were allies of Germany; and that the country most hospitable to Jewish refugees during the war was Spain, whose regime was condemned by those who considered themselves the standard-bearers of western values. For Livneh, behavior toward the Jews is a touchstone of the condition of Western civilization, and he sees the post-World War II period as a mere philo-Semitic internezzo preluding new terrible dangers. Abundance, urbanization, technology have produced only greater dissatisfactions; classical liberalism has collapsed, leaving in its wake libertinism, the absence of all restraints, and the lust for violence as collective catharsis.[26]

But this kind of radical critique of the West, couched in terms of Jewish interests and values, had no resonance outside Israel. It did not even resonate among western Jews, themselves largely caught up in the leftist critique which was preoccupied in removing what in Livneh's perspective were the remaining restraints. The Land of Israel Movement spoke the language of those most discredited in the West at the end of the Vietnam period and its aftermath. Both the language of geopolitics and the language of a civilizing mission, which were natural to the Movement, were, temporarily at least, wholly unacceptable to opinion makers in western countries, most importantly in the United States.

The critiques of the Left and of the Land of Israel Movement have, to be sure, an important point in common; they both assert that the

West has power. But whereas for the Land of Israel Movement the defect was in the failure to use that power, in the perspective of the left the problem is the West's excessive use of power. Either the withdrawal of the West from many global positions is explained by the left as due to victories of the oppressed, or the reality of withdrawal is denied and the continued presence of the West, albeit in new (neocolonialist) guises, is asserted. In the perspective of the Land of Israel Movement the corruption of the Western tradition and will are such that, despite declared principles, the West will sacrifice allies and free peoples to tyrannies of the worst kind if bargains of expedience can be struck with totalitarian adversaries, with the result that position after position, both moral and strategic, is yielded until at last a point will be reached at which there is nothing left to bargain and the free world will be doomed in one way or another.

The critique of the Western world by the Land of Israel Movement, at least in its application to Israel, whether objectively right or wrong, suffers from the psychological disadvantage in comparison to the critique from the left that in terms of its own assumptions, explanation of Western attitudes becomes difficult. For since the assumption of the Land of Israel Movement, no less than of the left, is that the West has power, the logical inference is that a position is not relinquished unless there is strong pressure to do so. But if Israel was a Western bastion protecting Europe, why did no European country seem to view Israel in that way? The Israel of the post-1967 period could have received European support and the perpetuation of its new frontiers been seen as a strengthening of the Western position. But no Western country advocated this. The analysis was thus not convincing, especialy in the absence of any strong pressure upon the West (prior to the 1973 oil boycott) to sacrifice Israel; the Land of Israel Movement seemed to be arguing that the West was giving up a vital position for no reason whatever. The analysis of the Land of Israel Movement therefore found itself without intellectual validation outside Israel, and this affected its power to convince the public within Israel as well. Believers in the ideology were not dissuaded; their belief in the decline of the West was merely confirmed by each successive indication of Western readiness to see Israel weakened. But there were no outside individuals and groups whose values or standards could be taken as a frame of reference by members of the Land of Israel Movement; thus, the reference group of the Movement necessarily became an "internal," indeed a "vanished" one—the Zionist leaders of a past era whose vision was finally capable of being implemented.

For the peace movement, on the other hand, numerous reference groups were available, for its analysis resonated everywhere in the

West, and not merely in left-wing groups. Indeed, many of the left-wing groups within the peace movement had the problem of rejection by their "normal" reference groups, for the more radical left-wing groups outside Israel in the aftermath of the 1967 war tended to brand all Israelis as "imperialist tools" and "colonial settlers" without making finer internal distinctions. In an open "Letter to All Good People" journalist Amos Kenan recorded his outrage in semi-humorous fashion: "I am for Cuba. I love Cuba. I am opposed to the genocide perpetrated by the Americans in Vietnam. I want the Americans to get out of Vietnam immediately. But I am Israeli, therefore I am forbidden to take all these stands. Cuba does not want me to love her. Someone has decided that I am only permitted to love the Americans. . . . I am not permitted any longer to toast justice with a glass of champagne. I am not permitted to eat caviar and denounce the Americans. . . . I am also finally and absolutely forbidden to sign petitions of all sorts for human rights, for the release of political prisoners from the jails of reactionary regimes. I am not 'In,' I am 'Out.' For me the party is over. Period."[27] For some of the left-wing intellectuals of the Israeli peace movement the structure of expectations imputed to some audience became that of an imaginary audience, the "better possible social judges" of whom James wrote. Kenan professed allegiance to "maybe a leftist entity, maybe an ideal, I don't know; an idea is much more than a group or a party, and I don't have to take existing groups as the final word on any idea."[28] Others turned to vanished reference groups; the model cited by Jacob Riftin, who led the group which broke away from Mapam to form the splinter Federation of the Left, was the old Hashomer Hazair of the 1920s, and the leadership of the Soviet Union in the period of Lenin.

On the whole, however, flesh-and-blood outside reference groups were available to the intellectuals of the peace movement, even if some shifts in reference groups occurred under pressure of circumstances. For Mapam the Soviet Union had been the traditional reference group ("the second fatherland"),[29] and although no substitute of comparable substance was found, "progressive circles" such as those surrounding Sartre in France replaced it as a normative touchstone. Maki, the Israeli Communist party, had as available reference groups the communist parties of European countries such as Sweden and Holland which did not follow the Soviet line. Israeli's small War Resister's League was linked with divisions of the same organization in western countries. Siach, the New Israeli Left, had as its reference group radical student movements, especially in Europe.

Groups in Israel with a commitment to the values of the peace movement, then, found no lack of outside validation of their position;

indeed, the validation was found chiefly outside the boundaries of the state, since within Israel the movement's following was not large. And, given the almost uniform commitment outside of Israel among the politically most variegated groups to the values of the Israeli peace movement (for there was no serious body of opinion that argued that Israel should retain all the territories or even most of them), it could be expected that those groups most open to external reference groups would be most likely to adopt the perspective of the peace movement, even if they had no traditional allegiance to the ideas it advanced. Professors, journalists, writers, artists, entertainers, students are particularly open to the communication channels built up by associational rather than communal structures, such as the social worlds of the theatre or the fraternity of historians. Those in the intellectual and artistic professions in a country like Israel, at once small and seeking western standards of excellence, inevitably turned to the intellectual and artistic world of Europe and the United States for styles and fashions. The standards absorbed are in the first case those pertinent to performance in the specific associational role; yet political, intellectual, and artistic standards necessarily are intermixed, for standards are not abstract but are embodied in significant others. An "intellectual" or "theatrical" culture, for example, at any time involves an entire web of perceptions, by no means limited to a specific set of skills.

In the post-1967 period the associational worlds to which Israeli journalists, artists, professors, and students were exposed were more apt to encourage identification with the peace movement than they would have been a few years earlier. As a result of the Vietnam war, western intellectuals and artists had moved from an attitude of indifference to politics, sufficiently characteristic after World War II for some to argue that the "end of ideology" was at hand, to an orientation that celebrated the virtues of "progressive third-world" nations seen as battling the imperialist industrial superpowers. While in these circles there continued to be a certain sympathy for Israel as long as she could be defined as a small democratic nation, there was criticism of her in the unfamiliar role of occupier of Arab lands and ruler of conquered peoples. For those for whom associational structures tended to assume more importance than communal structures, then, insofar as those associational structures transcended state boundaries, the analysis of the peace movement could be expected to assume particular force; not surprisingly, Moshe Dayan's son Assaf, an actor, called himself a "Moked man" (one of the two political parties associated with the peace movement) and announced his belief that the territories should be returned to the Arabs.[30]

Unlike the Land of Israel Movement, the peace movement never achieved unity. There were two reasons: one was the difference in basic framework in terms of which the problem was seen and the other was the impossibility of arriving at a common recommended program of action. The peace movement represented a set of common orientations to the problem of Arab-Israel relations, but it offered no single clear-cut course of action to decision makers. Part of the difficulty was that the left-wing groups—and the peace movement was overwhelmingly concentrated within them—saw the Jewish problem in terms of more general categories, specifically as an aspect of the class problem. Matspen, the most extreme of the left-wing groups, saw Zionism as reactionary, preventing the unification of the downtrodden classes of all the societies of the Middle East, Israeli and Arab. Such Zionist groupings as the Federation of the Left and the Israel Communist party (Maki) insisted that national self-determination could be combined with class struggle. Siach, the student grouping, shared the vaguely anarchistic romantic conceptions of the New Left and was impatient with all traditional formulations of the class struggle. Those who considered themselves communists could not easily ally themselves with avowed socialists; and even among socialists differences that might seem to an outsider a matter of nuance were the basis of serious divisions, for the leftist groupings were essentially sectarian in character. Thus, for example, in 1970 Jacob Riftin differentiated his Brit Hasmol from Siach:

Siach is anti-Soviet although there are those within Siach who do not go along with this general line; Brit Hasmol's attitude is independent. We can criticize the Soviet Union, but between criticism and total negation there is a big difference. . . . Besides, we are much more class-conscious than Siach. . . . They call themselves the *New* Israeli Left, but we are against this. We know there is something new, but there are also old things. The point is that besides Cohn Bendit and Marcuse there was Lenin and Rosa Luxembourg and Mao Tse-tung, and you can't act as if world revolution started with the student rebellion in May in Paris. There are good and bad things in the old left; but the same is true of the new, with its worship of violence and power apart from any revolutionary strategy. We don't oppose all they do; they can run around naked and grow their hair long, but it should also be possible to be dressed.[31]

The "bourgeois" sections of the peace movement had rather different ideals of justice and freedom, and even within them there were important divergences. For Uri Avnery with his party (Haolam Hazeh) built around the magazine that served as the Israeli *Playboy*, "freedom" was a libertarian ideal, freedom of the individual from repressions, offering self-expression to all; but the economic structure of society was a matter of indifference, and indeed socialism was if anything suspect as regimenting rather than freeing the individual. (From the standpoint of some of the puritanical leftist sects, Avnery's libertarianism was an outrage, an expression of capitalist decadence.) For the professors, committed on the whole to liberal rational ideas of justice, part of the left was morally unacceptable. Professors Joshua Arieli and Jacob Talmon refused to participate in a proposed "peace front" for the elections of 1969, on the grounds that they could never join with Moshe Sneh of Maki because he had justified the Doctors' Plot.[32] (This was the fictitious plot, supposedly conceived by a number of Jewish doctors, to murder Stalin; the men thus accused were saved only by Stalin's death. Sneh had justified it at the time, being then an orthodox Communist.) The preoccupation with moral statement could also interfere with unity. Ernest Simon said of Simon Shereshevsky, who dominated the remnant of the old Ihud: "You can't sit on a committee with Jeremiah the prophet."[33]

The problem of program interfered with unity no less than the problem of divergence in basic ideological vision. There was unanimous agreement that Israel should make an enormous moral effort, some grand gesture for peace, but there was no consensus what that gesture should be. Some wanted to return all the territories; but some wanted to keep only Jerusalem, some the Golan, some Gaza, some all three, and some proposed yet other territorial changes (Sharm el Sheikh, the Latrun area, etc.). Even those who agreed on proposed boundaries might disagree on how to go about relinquishing the territories. The ultimate moral gesture might have been simple unilateral return of the territories to Arab control, but virtually no section of the peace movement was prepared to recommend such action. While morality and justice made it clear that the territories, or the overwhelming majority of them, could not be kept by Israel, morality and justice provided no guidelines on the means by which the return should be accomplished; indeed, morality and justice could be interpreted rather diversely on this question.

There was general consensus that Israel's keeping the territories would be an affront to all basic moral values, whether Jewish, Zionist, socialist, humanitarian, or liberal. Professor Arieli wrote: "It is in our most vital interest to find as quickly as possible a way towards a settlement which would enable us to return the occupied territories to their inhabitants, as the rule over another people against its will undermines the very moral basis on which the state of Israel was established."[34]

The goal of Zionism had not been to make Israel a nation like all the others; the goal had been the prophetic one of making Israel a light unto the nations. What was permitted to other nations was thus not permitted to Israel. Gabriel Stein, professor of chemistry at the Hebrew University, calling for a vast Israeli effort to solve the problem of the refugees, conceded that in no comparable case had a country repatriated refugees: "Our decision to behave otherwise springs from two considerations: the first reason is that the Israeli people does not wish, and does not have to behave like every other nation. . . . We should be interested, without taking into account how other countries behave, and for the sake of our own consciences, in doing everything possible that is good and right and humane without endangering ourselves."[35] If Israel was to be a model to other nations, her image in the world was a matter for serious concern. Objecting to what he felt was Israeli insensitivity to this matter, Professor Talmon wrote: "World opinion that watched our national endeavor with sympathy and came to our aid would shake its head and ask: 'Is this that Jerusalem that was built on righteousness?' Let us not make light of world opinion."[36] Similarly, religious member Pinchas Rosenbluth insisted: "It is an important Jewish principle . . . that what people say is important. If we ignore this we desecrate the name of God in the eyes of the world."[37] Even on strictly pragmatic grounds Israel could not afford to ignore world public opinion, for in the end she would be forced to do what morally she should do of her own accord. Moshe Unna remarked that Israel was learning that what others said of her did matter, for the opinion of other nations was a political factor.[38]

For the sake of her own soul, for the sake of her world image, for the sake of future peace, Israel must make a dramatic move that would finally convince the Arabs that she genuinely repudiated all intentions of territorial expansion. There was one proposal that aroused greater enthusiasm within the peace movement than any other; indeed the peace movement may be seen as originating with it: the proposal for a Palestinian state to be created by Israel in the West Bank and Gaza. It is easy to see the reason for the enthusiasm of proponents. While all other solutions—except unilateral withdrawal, which was essentially without supporters—required Arab cooperative action of some sort, and Israel had no control over the behavior of Arab states, the proposal for an Arab state on the West Bank and in Gaza appeared to be capable of realization by Israel alone. It had the additional virtue of seeming to eliminate the source of the entire Arab-Israel conflict. As members of the peace movement saw that conflict, it was rooted in two nationalisms—Jewish and Palestinian, the second developing in large part in response to the first—competing over a single homeland. The Land of Israel Movement, in contrast, saw the conflict as one between Jewish and *Arab* nationalism; in that context, of course, the Palestinians were a relatively insignificant factor. Jewish national aspirations had been satisfied through the creation of the state of Israel; but Arab Palestinian aspirations, although destined by the U.N. partition plan of 1947 to find fulfillment in part of Palestine, had been tragically balked. If the national aspirations of the Palestinians could now be fulfilled through Israeli action in setting up a state for them on the West Bank and in Gaza, the entire reason for the conflict (given the peace movement's analysis, and a rational model of human action) would evaporate, and the Palestinians, from serving as the source of enmity between Israel and the Arab states, would become the bridge to peaceful relations with them. Since the new state at the outset would be federated with Israel—at least this was the plan as initially formulated and as it continued to be advanced by most advocates—and thus have a common defense policy, the danger of the new entity simply becoming another hostile Arab state would be eliminated.

Despite the superficial attractiveness of the scheme, there were serious reservations about it even within the peace movement on the grounds that it was impossible to implement, offered no solution to the problem even if it could be implemented, and was morally suspect. Even though Israel controlled the territories militarily, the cooperation of their Arab residents was necessary for the establishment of any sort of political entity. One member of the peace movement wrote: "Some people on the West Bank told me: 'Even if we dared to come to an agreement with you, we would be branded as traitors and our agreement wouldn't be worth anything—even if we are the real parties to the case. Go and speak to Cairo, to Amman, to the Arab countries.' "[39] Even if a leadership ready to accept Israeli terms could be found, some within the peace movement feared that making peace with the Palestinians might not necessarily mean making peace with the Arab states, and in that event Israel would have accomplished nothing of value. Haim Darin-Drabkin, one of the original signatories immediately after the Six-Day War to a proposal for a federation of Israel with a West Bank state, even in signing appended his reservations concerning the plan: he thought a federation with Jordan best and only if this was impossible should a federation with the West Bank alone be considered. In Drabkin's view, "To a great extent the prospects for realizing the federal project will also depend upon reaching agreements with the neighboring countries. In the absence of any such agreement to end hostilities, it will be almost impossible to establish an island of tranquillity in a sea of hatred."[40]

For some in the peace movement any type of federated state, whether the partner was the West Bank, Jordan, or even Lebanon, was feasible only as an end product in the peace-making process. Once the Middle East had been at peace for a period of time, once friendly relations between Israel and the Arab nations were firmly established, then federation, with its inevitable partial relinquishment of sovereignty, might be considered. But to impose federation as a means of reaching peace upon deeply hostile and suspicious states was impossible.[41]

Equally important, many within the peace movement found the plan morally wrong. To some the plan for a Palestinian state sounded suspiciously like a plan for a puppet state. Moshe Sneh of Maki argued: "We are for the right of the Palestinian people to national self-determination. Haolam Hazeh says we must recognize the rights of a Palestinian entity—that the people of the West Bank *should* establish a Palestinian state, federated with Israel. That's not self-determination."[42] Some within the peace movement felt the move would actually worsen Arab-Israeli relationships, as expressed in the following statement: "The program for a separate Palestinian state only pours oil on the fires of hatred and damaged national pride, and stiffens Arab resistance to any negotiations and political settlement. No matter how honest the intentions of its partisans are to shorten the road to peace, objectively they are adding obstacles and making it longer."[43]

For some, the very arguments used by proponents strengthened suspicions of the plan. Professor Shlomo Avineri of the Hebrew University, writing in favor of a Palestinian entity, said that such leading figures within the Israeli cabinet as Defense Minister Moshe Dayan and Deputy Premier Yigal Allon had advanced proposals that in effect supported the concept. To opponents this was proof, not of the merit of the idea, but that such an entity was merely a cloak for Israeli domination, a device to continue the military occupation under a fairer name.[44]

In lieu of the creation by Israel of a Palestinian state, then, some within the peace movement simply argued for Palestinian self-determination—whatever that might turn out to involve. According to one writer, "The most moral action for Israel is to make a declaration of intent toward the Palestinians recognizing their absolute right to self-determination."[45] But this statement of intent lacked the advantage of being capable of immediate implementation—presumably that absolute right would be honored at some future time when a peaceful solution had been arrived at with the Arab states. Leaders within the peace movement offered a plethora of proposals, but apart from the Palestinian state proposal these aroused little echo, even among other members of the peace movement. There were proposals for confederation with the state of Jordan; detailed programs were drawn up for a bi-national state in which Jews and Arabs would have equal representation (e.g., if the Prime Minister was a Jew, the Minister of Defense would have to be an Arab and vice versa); a policy of a sliding scale was advocated whereby Israel would retreat in a series of steps in return for step-by-step Arab concessions (e.g., for a declaration of an end to the state of belligerency Israel would relinquish a certain amount of territory); a policy of giving up territories in return for agreements "in principle" by the Arab governments was offered; a number of proposals were offered for exchanging the territories for security arrangements, including international guarantees, international police forces, and demilitarized zones.[46] There was an almost universal feeling in the peace movement that more could be done for the refugees. Some urged ambitious resettlement schemes to solve the problem, at least in respect to the substantial proportion of refugees now in Israeli hands; others urged more modest pilot schemes.[47]

Some in the peace movement, a small proportion and considered marginal within the movement, insisted that to achieve peace Israel must offer more than territorial concessions and refugee resettlement schemes. They argued that it was illusory to believe the Arabs could be satisfied unless the very nature of the state was changed. They insisted that the Arabs were deeply suspicious of Israel's proclaimed tie to the Jewish people and looked upon the state's asserted mission as a homeland for all Jews as proof of its inevitably expansionist character. To ease Arab fears, they said, the Law of Return, the basic law of the state, incorporated into the state's Declaration of Independence and embodying the basis of the Zionist drive to statehood, would have to be repealed. According to one professor:

Utopian or messianic Zionism, which is the only kind that still exists today, I regard as intolerable. It is a danger to the Israeli state. I see any demands of or on the Jews of the diaspora as immoral. No one has any duty to the State of Israel or any right to demand to come here. The only justification I saw for Zionism was to save those Jews in the diaspora who needed a haven. This was Herzlian Zionism and this is why I was a Zionist. . . . Now we have messianic Zionism starting with Ben-Gurion and going on with Golda Meir. For them, rather than seeing Israel as a place to save the Jews, they come with demands on Jews to save Israel. . . . If we say millions of diaspora Jews should come to Israel, how should they [Arabs and non-Jews] know our Zionist leaders don't mean it seriously? The only reason can be to annex still more territory. Messianic Zionism creates among non-Jews and Arabs the feeling that Israel is an imperialistic state, not satisfied with its borders and making space for millions of Jews. So long as Israel has anything to do with official Zionism, it is impossible to obliterate the image of

Israel as an expansionist state. Since I don't think any Arab can want to make peace with an expansionist state, there is no chance for Arabs to come to a serious agreement so long as the image of Israel as expansionist remains, which it will so long as that image is fed by talk of Zionism.[48]

He thus proposed the voluntary limitation of Israeli sovereignty in an area vital to Zionist ideology, in order to win Arab agreement to Israel's existence. Such limitation involved the sacrifice of the state's central legitimation—to serve as a homeland for the entire Jewish people—and for the majority of the peace movement's members this was an unacceptable sacrifice. On the other hand, there was a certain amount of sympathy within the peace movement for the view that Zionism as an ideology had persisted beyond the time appropriate to it, and that it now interfered with Israel's task of integrating herself into the region, since Zionism continued to identify the state primarily with the interests and needs of people in other parts of the world, particularly the western world. It was argued that some "Zionist" peace groups merely paid lip service to Zionism, the term retaining for them a positive emotional tone. In some cases there was disagreement over whether an individual or group was actually Zionist or not. Uri Avnery, who wrote a book entitled in the English edition *Israel without Zionists,* was variously accused of being a Zionist masquerading as an anti-Zionist and of being an anti-Zionist covering up his real views to gain votes.[49]

With all the variety of proposals advanced, there was no confidence within the peace movement that peace as the Israeli government understood it, in the sense of peace treaties and normal relations between states, was attainable through implementation of any one of them. Many argued that all the most generous actions by Israel could achieve was to start a process of reconciliation at the end of which peace might lie. According to Brit Hasmol's Jacob Riftin,

We say that to expect peace and direct negotiations from the Arabs is absurd. Why should they want peace? After the Six-Day War the prospects were diminished. There is a long history of conflict here between the Jews and the Arabs, and they are deaf to each other. To say we can have a peace treaty with them is absurd. I'm not against peace—I'm willing to pray for it —but it's not realistic. We say we must find a compromise to stop the fighting. . . . All we say is that between the certainty that the war will go on for years and involve ever-widening groups—the Soviet Union and even China —and the chance for peace, we say the chance is worth taking. . . . More than a chance we don't promise.[50]

Those who insisted on the need for much more radical concessions were not sure that the abandonment of Zionism would suffice. The professor who assailed "messianic Zionism" offered what in his own view was a rational solution; yet there was always the possibility that reason might not provide a foundation for the relations between states. He also insisted: "The only rational steps I can see are to dissever any connection to the World Zionist Movement, to abolish the Law of Return or expand it to include all former Arab residents of Israel, renounce any annexation including that of Jerusalem—to go back to the old borders. . . . If the irrationality then continues, a psychoanalyst should treat it."

Yet, for all the uncertainties, most within the peace movement felt Israeli initiatives must be taken. Sensitive to pressures upon Israel from the outside and viewing them as likely to mount, viewing peace treaties as utopian at this stage, many within the peace movement argued that Israel should capitalize on her present favorable situation to obtain the best security bargain possible in exchange for territory. Journalist Amos Kenan said: "The big powers need an arrangement, not peace. And so we will get in the Middle East the kind of solution there is between East and West Germany, or North and South Korea, or what they hope to get between North and South Vietnam. It is an unsolved problem, but it rests in a kind of status quo, a state of expectation, until something happens or something dies, or something changes, and life goes on, that's all. It is not peace and not war; it is the modern solution."[51]

Some actually looked forward to a solution imposed by the great powers as the only answer. According to the professor who wanted to abolish the Law of Return: "I think rational people in the government are hoping for external pressure. The only way I can still see Golda Meir sleeping at night—not seeing that she had led Israel to the point of annihilation in a number of years—is through hoping that Russia and the United States will come together and enforce all the things I have mentioned—return of all or most of the areas, giving the refugees the right to return, and making sure that Israel no longer will have any possibility of expanding. The members of the Israeli government must somehow hope the great powers will save them from themselves." In the view of Ernest Simon, a major function of the peace movement was to prepare the people of Israel for the inevitable imposed solution: "The government does nothing to prepare public opinion, but to a certain extent we do prepare public opinion for the inevitable crisis."[52]

Thus, if retreat was moral and inevitable because of outside pressures, and if peace as the Israeli government defined it was unobtainable, it behooved Israel to use her present favorable position to obtain the benefits that would arise from generous actions still taken of her own will. These benefits could be in the form of security guarantees or Arab good will, but the "total peace to be implemented overnight" demanded by the Israeli government could not be achieved. Waiting for it would only bring new war and an imposed solution. And while an imposed settlement was not viewed as necessarily bad (Ernest Simon said, "better an imposed peace than free killing"), voluntary actions taken by Israel would serve her world image better and serve her better with her Arab neighbors.

Within the peace movement, in addition to the moral concerns, there was a sense of Israel's weakness, of her inability successfully to confront her Arab neighbors and the outside world; this sense was evident even before the Arabs demonstrated the strength of their oil weapon. Whereas the Land of Israel Movement argued that Israel could preserve her existence only through her own strength, the peace movement felt that only through Arab consent could Israel's existence be secured and, thus, that almost any chance was worth taking that might win that consent. This sense of weakness was perhaps given most explicit expression in the words and writings of Nahum Goldmann, president of the World Jewish Congress, who was a favorite of the peace movement although as a Swiss citizen living abroad he was not actually a part of it. In *Foreign Affairs* Goldmann wrote articles advocating that Israel's existence be guaranteed by both the great powers and the Arab states, under the condition that she be neutralized and perhaps ultimately demilitarized.[53] Here was the notion that by complete weakness and dependence Israel might be able to win consent to her existence. While most members of the peace movement were not prepared to offer a radical sacrifice of sovereignty of the type suggested by Goldmann, the sense that winning legitimacy in Arab eyes was Israel's only possible salvation was common in the movement.

The absence of unity did not in itself hurt the peace movement; the chief damage occurred when member groups and individuals made abortive attempts at achieving unity, for unsuccessful attempts inevitably sharpened divisions and caused the additional embarrassment of giving them wide publicity.[54] Precisely because of the multiplicity of groupings, there was freedom to follow any tactics and to make any ideological statement.[55] No individuals had veto power over others, for a group did not have to fear that its raison d'être would be destroyed by defections undermining the claim to a broad base. It is no surprise, then, to find the peace movement engaging in more vigorous and varied activity than the Land of Israel Movement, including sit-ins and street demonstrations inviting arrest, a style which is by now familiar in the United States but which had the shock of novelty in Israel when the peace movement began to employ it.

And yet ultimately the peace movement, no less than the Land of Israel Movement, found itself constrained to serve as an ideological movement, seeking to persuade decision makers through elaboration of an alternative ideology and to change public values. In this case the constraints lay in the problem of audience. In the peace movement's own estimation, it had the support of perhaps 5 percent of the Israeli public, and most of this support was for what was perceived as the most moderate section of the movement. Any group which attacked basic Zionist legitimations could expect virtually no audience at all, for such an attack deeply threatened the public's self-definition. Within Israel Zionism might be ridiculed, shrugged off, dismissed as the obsession of an older generation; yet for all that it remained central to the nation's vision of itself. The people of the state of Israel still thought of that state as a homeland for the Jews of the world whenever they should wish or need to claim it. The implementation of the ideology brought considerable internal strain, felt especially in the great immigration from the Arab countries in the early years of the state, and again in the wave of Soviet immigration still in process, for the problems of absorption were severe and produced widespread resentment among native Israelis. No doubt the external threats to the state made the public more willing to tolerate difficulties, for the compensation of large-scale immigration was clear: increased ability of the state to hold its own against such threats. But whatever the reasons, the only Jews in Israel who had thus far failed to agree on the basic conceptions of Zionism were the Canaanites, some Communists,[56] and the ultra-religious Mea Shearim sect which refused to recognize the state at all.

The abandonment of Zionism, then, was an ideological alternative to be sure, but one without an audience. Those who wished to make such radical criticism had the choice of making it—in which case, like the radical left group Matspen, they abandoned the Israeli audience for one abroad (Most of Matspen's members were in Europe or the United States, and Israelis heard of their activities through the foreign press); or of muting the critcism within Israel to maximize audience and making the criticism more explicit for foreign audiences. Thus, for example, Uri Avnery's book, entitled *Israel without Zionists* in the United States, in Israel became *War of the Seventh Day.*

For most of those within the peace movement, Israeli sovereignty was not negotiable. But, disagreeing among themselves as to what program of action would be best suited to achieving peace, they found it easier to unite on what should *not* be done than on any positive steps. Israel should not alter the status of the territories she had occupied in any way. This should be the practical demonstration of Israel's intent to return all or almost all of the territories. But what then? And suppose the Arabs made no response? Many in the peace movement were ready to go no farther than a statement of intent. Pinchas Rosenbluth said: "I don't have any illusions, but we must have our own program. It is not our program to annex territory. If the Arabs won't accept what we offer, we must defend our rights. In practical terms, then, perhaps I don't differ so much from the others."[57] But this was not far from the program of the government, especially its dovish wing.

Ironically, then, in view of its greater freedom of action, the peace movement had less freedom of ideological statement. While in the case of the Land of Israel Movement the inability to act served to strengthen the freedom to formulate ideology, for the peace movement the freedom to act placed constraints on the ability to speak out, for action required having at least some base of support and refraining from alienating that support through extreme statement. The peace movement thus depended on issues arising independently of its own actions, on the basis of which a broader public could be mobilized.

A variety of issues arose in the six years between wars: Jewish settlement in Hebron; the policy of destroying the houses of those cooperating in terrorism; the crackdown on terrorism in the Gaza Strip; the displacement of Bedouin by Jewish settlements in northern Sinai near Rafah; the attempt by the former Arab residents of the villages of Ikrit and Bir'am on the Lebanese border, removed to other areas within Israel during the War of Independence, to resettle them; and others.[58]

The only one of these issues to assume major proportions was the so-called Goldmann affair of 1970. Nahum Goldmann, the President of the World Jewish Congress, long a source of irritation to the Israeli government because of his public pronouncements concerning the need for Israel to make greater concessions, was allegedly approached by a chain of authorized intermediaries concerning Nasser's desire to talk to him, if he should come with the "knowledge" of the Israeli government. The Israeli government refused to sanction the meeting, and the peace movement thus was able to cast doubt on the credibility of the consistent government claim that it was ready to seek peace through all available means. In protest, intellectuals and students staged a sit-in in Golda Meir's garden; this was the first time the peace movement used this type of protest. But the action which received the greatest publicity was a letter sent by 54 young men at a Jerusalem high school to the Prime Minister in which they asserted that they felt doubts about their ability to fight in the army. The letter was seen as especially significant because the signers included the son of Yitzhak

Sadeh, leader of the early elite military formation of labor Zionism, the Palmach, and the son of Victor Shem-Tov, a minister (for Mapam) in the Israeli cabinet. The outcry over the Goldmann affair died down when Nasser denied he had ever made the overture and it began to appear as a false rumor. While many continued to believe that it had been genuine and that Nasser had disclaimed his overture only because of the sudden publicity, once the offer had been denied it was difficult to maintain public indignation.

Not long afterward, the United States came forward with a proposal for a cease-fire combined with a renewal of the Jarring initiative within the framework of Security Council Resolution 242; the Israeli government accepted. Gahal withdrew from the Government of National Unity in protest, and with this a good deal of the force of the peace movement's criticism was dissipated. Here was an announcement of intent to return territories under conditions that would ensure Israel's security. The peace movement was not satisfied, to be sure: a year after the cease-fire one member noted that, while the government had eliminated the extremists (with the departure of Gahal), it continued to show "lack of flexibility and imagination which makes abortive all efforts for a total or even a partial settlement of the conflict."[59] But the casualties had stopped at the Canal with the cease-fire; thus public anxiety, and hence public readiness to be mobilized, was much reduced.

Like the Land of Israel Movement, the peace movement provided a vision of heaven and hell, the first if its ideology was implemented, the second if that of the Land of Israel Movement won acceptance. And as in the case of the Land of Israel Movement, the image of hell was clearer and found wider acceptance than the vision of heaven. For the more conservative wing of the peace movement, heaven was restoration of the old society, which was seen as approaching or at any rate striving for the ideal order, before it had been burdened with territories and foreign peoples. Professor Joshua Arieli wrote of pre-June 1967 Israel: "It was a vital democracy, effervescent, and in some respects exemplary and singular. Among the democracies of the West it was perhaps the only one which knew how to incorporate political and personal freedom with far-reaching equality, and to base both on a feeling of commonality, on common targets and purposes, and on the identification of the individual with the whole. Prominent in it was the readiness of the individual to serve the community; an active citizenship which aspired to put the concerns of all over those of the individual; and a readiness to mobilize the strength of society in voluntary ways for the achievement of a daring, universal, even utopian vision."[60]

At the other extreme the anti-Zionist Matspen looked forward to a heaven which appeared one version of the Arab guerilla movement's utopia, as Israel became a "democratic, secular" state, presumably with a Moslem majority, in which Jews became equal citizens in the same sense as in the United States. For others in the radical wing of the movement, the idea of heaven was one of a multi-communal society built upon disparate religious and ethnic communities in which each would retain its separate character and autonomous political expression with sovereign power over its own members.[61] For the ideologists of the left, so heavily concentrated in the peace movement, heaven necessarily involved a transformation of the social order of all states in the region, with the perfect classless society to be created in each of them. This was not a strong overt element in the ideology of the peace movement, even in the formulation of left-wing members, because the emphasis was on Arab right to self-definition and self-determination, and even the creation of social revolution was seen as imperialistic if recommended or initiated by Israel. At the very minimum heaven was a state of peaceful relations with the Arab states, in which the desire for national self-determination of the Palestinians was fulfilled, and the will to Jewish self-determination was honored in turn. For all the peace movement's rejection of the Land of Israel Movement as "messianic," there clearly were millennial aspects to the peace movement as well.

Yet even the most conservative section of the peace movement was not wholly satisfied with Israel as it existed prior to 1967; it had merely been on a path which could lead to a just society before it was derailed by the war into becoming a society of occupiers and colonizers. While the left-wing members of the peace movement, regardless of their attitudes regarding Zionism, were critical of what they viewed as Israel's increasingly "capitalistic" structure, this was not the area of Israeli life emphasized by the peace movement as a whole. The very fact that the peace movement was so heavily concentrated in the extreme left made left-wing members anxious to avoid identifying the peace movement itself with a left-wing critique, for the need was to broaden the base of support. But one area on which all members of the peace movement—including religious members—could agree was the need to separate church and state, and membership in the peace movement overlapped to a large extent with membership in the League against Religious Coercion. In terms of the assumptions of neither radical socialism nor liberal rationalism could a society be considered "just" in which fundamental personal decisions (marriage and divorce, for example) were limited, even determined, by a religious law upheld by the power of the state. The issue transcended the power of a religious bureaucracy, for involved more fundamentally were issues of

Jewish and Israeli self-definition and the extent to which the state of
Israel was linked to or could be separated from the Jewish people.

The vision of hell was the same throughout the movement. Joshua
Arieli provided a scenario to follow upon implementation of the goals
of the Land of Israel Movement:

[This implementation] would have led to an immediate condemnation by
the United Nations, the imposition of sanctions, and perhaps even the expulsion of Israel from the United Nations. . . . It is reasonable to assume that
the Security Council would have charged the powers or part of them to
force Israel to retreat from the territories and compel its wishes on her. . . .
Let us assume Israel could resist all this. . . . Then she could adopt the position of Rhodesia, fortify herself in her isolation, and survive. . . . Then the
question must be asked—how would the state of isolation, of unceasing war
in its borders, influence the regime and image of Israel? It is not difficult to
predict the result of such a state of affairs. We would turn into a besieged
state to which fighting and war are the natural form of life, fully employed
in defending itself and in guarding its very existence. In such a situation, the
society and regime of Israel would change into emergency forms.[62]

Arieli asserted that he already detected symptoms of a siege mentality
in Israel and a paranoid conception of the world. Ran Cohen of
Siach offered a similar vision: "All this will compel us, whether we
want to or not, to become a true warfare state; a state that sees in the
mobilization of its resources for war a glorious mission; a state which
will link its future with the devil provided he will supply her with
arms; a state in which there will be no right of appeal, thought or
struggle for anyone who does not fall in step with the line of the
'besieged people.' Such a state, no matter how committed and dedicated to democracy our people may be, will of necessity be ruled by
generals (politically) and by fanatic fascists (spiritually)."[63] Israel
was thus seen as ultimately being annihilated or, if she survived, as-
suming a shape in which her continued existence had no worth.

In seeking to locate the forces which prevented implementation of
its ideology, even less than the Land of Israel Movement for whom
Eban became to some extent the embodiment of folly, was the peace
movement able to find a suitable single target. The government's policy was not sufficiently opposed to that of the peace movement to
make even a figure like Dayan a suitable devil; he was identified, after
all, with the liberal policy Israel followed in dealing with the Arabs of
the territories, and only gradually began to favor Jewish settlement on
the West Bank. Gahal's Begin was a possible target, but he never dominated policy and after 1970 was out of the government altogether. For
the peace movement the basic problem was the moral corruption of
the public through the "mystical chauvinism" which the Six-Day War

was supposed to have released in the population. Ernest Simon described this as a "primitive synthesis of the faith of the fathers with the sentimentality of the sons." Pinchas Rosenbluth called it "a dangerous mixture of religious mysticism and chauvinistic nationalism."

Interestingly enough, if the professors so prominent in the peace movement were seen as villains by the Land of Israel Movement, the poets, heavily concentrated in the Land of Israel Movement, were marked out by the peace movement. Amos Elon, one of Israel's younger generation of writers, observed: "But from the poets one hears recently about territory only. Nathan Alterman went furthest when he wrote that a Munich is possible not only between nations, but between a nation and its past. And this political fog is not untypical of the ideas current among many of his writing colleagues. . . . How long will it take before the politicians of the various parties will be induced to use the emotional power of these slogans? . . . As one who always preferred poets to politicans, I pray that the politicians should this time be wiser than the poets."[64] Actually, just as there were many professors sympathetic to the Land of Israel Movement, so there were poets favorable to the peace movement. The gap, as Elon himself noted, was generational. "It is important to note that among the writers and poets of the Land of Israel Movement there is not a single one of the writers of the younger generation who were educated and grew up in the period of the state."[65] Nonetheless, the writers of the Land of Israel Movement had greater prominence, and just as to the Land of Israel Movement it appeared especially wrong that the guardians of the nation's intellectual heritage should undermine the moral basis of the state's legitimacy, so it appeared especially evil to the peace movement that the nation's poets and writers, guardians of its sentiments and molders of a nation's perspective on itself and reality, should forsake "reason" and "morality" for "mystical chauvinism."

In summary, then, unlike the Land of Israel Movement, the peace movement could offer no single ideological alternative coupled with a clear-cut program to implement it. This inability existed partly because of the disagreements within the peace movement, split on attitudes regarding both socialism and Zionism, and partly because of the difficulty of formulating a program of action. The Land of Israel Movement's program depended only on action by the government of Israel. There might indeed be problems flowing from outside reaction to those actions; but, given willingness to confront these, the program itself lay purely in the power of the government. This was not the case with the peace movement: barring willingness to engage in simple unilateral withdrawal, any Israeli action depended upon Arab cooperation.

Nonetheless, the peace movement did provide an alternative to government policy in advocating a whole new set of orientations. The government would have to give up more than it wanted and receive less in return. The peace movement urged that Israel make a firm commitment to borders at least approximating those which existed prior to the June War; and it demanded that Israel show willingness to make a variety of concessions, not merely territorial, but ranging from modifications of its definition of peace to modifications of the Zionist character of the state.

5
Undermining Government Consensus

The presence of the Land of Israel Movement and the peace movement as competing ideological alternatives initially strengthened the government. Considered individually, each might have been expected to weaken the government, but the impact of their combined existence was rather to weaken each other. The Land of Israel Movement especially, which boasted of a broad intellectual base and the participation of leaders associated with the main stream, including famous writers, poets, and intellectuals, was distressed to find itself defined within a relatively short time as "fanatical" and "sectarian." The peace movement developed more slowly because its position was so close to that of a clear majority within the government. But the peace movement also found itself successfully defined by the government as "irresponsible" and "extremist." And precisely because the perspectives of the peace movement and the government were so close, the peace movement found itself with less public support than the Land of Israel Movement, which could look upon all of Gahal's voters as essentially supporters of the Movement.

The government was enabled to brand the movements as irresponsible extremes so quickly because the very presence of both as competing ideological alternatives gave the government the tactical benefit of sheer centrality. The government drew strength from the combined attack, for it was enabled to point to the opposite sins of which it was accused, and thus to demonstrate its own "moderate" and "moderating" position. In effect, then, the criticism of one group contributed to cancelling out the criticism of the other, and each heightened the marginality of the opposing movement instead of weakening the position of the government, whose ability to resist both groups as impractical extremes was enhanced.[1]

It is interesting to note that the government seemed to be equally opposed to both movements, despite the fact that from a practical standpoint the Land of Israel Movement could have been viewed as a useful tool. The peace movement's insistence that the government was not doing everything necessary to achieve peace had the undesirable effect of fostering the impression abroad that Israel could be pressured into further concessions; at the same time, from the government's point of view, the peace movement heightened the force of the external constraints by converting them into internal ones—i.e., undermining morale at home. But a strong Land of Israel Movement could strengthen the government's hand in relation to international pressures, for the government could represent to foreign statesmen the danger that the alternative to meeting its own minimal demands was the accession to power of militant groups. And indeed the Movement's leaders, after experiencing the blow of learning that the government hoped to use the territories as a basis for bargaining to secure other ends (such as recognition and peaceful relations) nevertheless hoped that for the above reasons the government would lend at least tacit support to their efforts.[2]

But if in the short run the presence of the opposing movements strengthened the government, in the long term their articulation of ideological alternatives weakened it severely. The government commanded the pragmatic center and had broad public backing for its policy, but that policy in the end had to show some signs of being itself pragmatic—of working in the real world. After the 1967 war, it is important to note, there was virtual unanimity on the government's policy of "territories for peace," the Land of Israel Movement being the *only* group which disagreed with it; Gahal, which participated until 1970 in the Government of National Unity, subscribed to the policy as well. There was a great deal of disagreement as to which territories should be given up in exchange for a peace agreement. Gahal was willing to make concessions only in the Sinai peninsula (but apparently far-reaching ones there), while others in the government were prepared to return most of the West Bank in addition. But this disagreement did not interfere with the consensus in the early period following the war, since the policy met with no Arab response and there was thus no need for definition of what different partners to the consensus meant by its terms. Not only did the very broad consensus hold that territory could serve as bargaining counters for peaceful relations; equally important, the consensus held that not *all* the territories were negotiable, that some would have to be kept permanently by Israel. Again, there was a wide divergence on what territory was nonnegotiable, but even Mapam, the most concession-minded of the parties in the National Unity government, insisted specifically in the aftermath of the war upon keeping the Gaza Strip and Jerusalem.[3] And, also important, whatever the disagreements concerning what territories should be kept and what returned, there was virtual unanimity—and within the government total unanimity—on what should be obtained in return. All agreed that peace meant a state of normal relations between nations, open borders, free passage of nationals, exchange of ambassadors, and trade relations, and that it should be established by means of a formal peace treaty.

But the years went by without any indication that the government's policy was in fact practicable. The first major blow to the policy came shortly after the war when at Khartoum in August 1967 the Arab states announced their three "nos"—to recognition of Israel, to negotiation with her, to peace with her. This left the government of Israel in the position of negotiating with itself, and in the first few years the government was clearly engaged in drawing hypothetical maps, in the event that negotiations with the Arab states should begin. The problem with these maps, however, was that none of them—even if a majority in the government might agree on a formulation (and it did)— could be openly affirmed as the government's territorial offer to the Arabs. There were various reasons for this. One was the presence of Gahal within the Government of National Unity. Since Gahal was fully committed to the retention of Judea and Samaria, any official statement by the Israeli government indicating readiness to relinquish any part of the West Bank would have brought down the National Unity government. But even after Gahal left the government in 1970, the difficulty of stating a territorial position remained, partly because the National Religious party remained an essential part of the government coalition and that party was bound by party convention resolutions to assert Israel's claim to Judea and Samaria. But more important, the government was afraid that by publicly asserting a territorial position, Israel would be providing what was from her point of view a minimal demand for territory, a demand which would at once be treated outside Israel as a maximal position to be a starting point in any future negotiations, rather than an end product of negotiations as Israel intended.

The government, then, had a map and could not say so. When Golda Meir in effect outlined the map in an interview with the *Times* of London on March 13, 1971, she caused an uproar in the Knesset.[4] The map had actually been in semi-official existence (as the party's so-called oral doctrine) since the Labor party convention formulated its platform for the 1969 elections.[5] (The term "oral doctrine" had overtones in Israel that it does not have in English: Jewish law consists of the written Torah and the oral law—both of which are equally binding.) More serious, the government had a map upon which it could not act, at least not vigorously and unambiguously. If Israel was planning to keep certain territories she could have made a public commitment to such action. This was done in the case of Jerusalem, which was incorporated into the state right after the war by the Knesset.

If the Israeli government, as the oral doctrine indicated, was equally committed to retaining the Golan, Gaza, and Sharm el Sheikh (including part of Sinai) these could have been incorporated into Israel, Israeli law introduced into them, and residents within them given the right of Israeli citizenship. But Israel could not do this because the essence of its position was that new borders would be negotiated with the Arab states and a full peace treaty follow upon this process. If Israel unilaterally annexed the areas, there would be no agreed-upon borders to arrive at in negotiations. Since Israel, in demanding that the Arabs lay down no pre-conditions, herself kept insisting that she would come to the bargaining table without pre-conditions, clear *faits accomplis* had to be avoided; this was particularly important because Israel could not afford to antagonize the United States, which foresaw only minimal border changes in a future settlement. The government then established settlements in the Golan, in the Jordan Valley, and on the southern border of the Gaza Strip, and it began development of a town called Ophira at Sharm el Sheikh but without changing the legal status of any of these places or making an all-out settlement effort in any of them.

Nor was the oral doctrine completely convincing. What about the future of Hebron? The Ezion bloc and Hebron (both in the province of Judea) had been settled by Jews in defiance of government wishes, although the government had then underwritten both. The government was unwilling to state that Hebron was irrevocably part of Israel in a negotiated settlement, yet the urban quarter of Kiryat Arba was expanded and it was difficult to envisage Israel returning it to Arab rule. A new road was built connecting Kiryat Arba to Jerusalem which avoided all Arab settlements. Presumably this action created the possibility of returning Hebron to Arab rule while keeping the Jewish "upper Hebron" territorially connected to Israel. But a potential Arab province of Judea assumed an increasingly odd shape with Jerusalem incorporated into Israel, Kfar Ezion creating a bulge within it near Bethlehem, and the land between the Judean watershed and the Dead Sea-Jordan rift valley reaching beyond Hebron in the south of the province presumably also committed to Israeli rule. An Arab Judea would be an enclave within Jewish territory. (See Map VIII.)

The government became increasingly vulnerable to attack by the competing movements against which it had originally mobilized such overwhelming consensus. In the absence of any progress or even apparent hope of progress in reaching agreement with the Arab states, the government's policy could be portrayed as a policy of doing nothing at all, which could easily be equated with having no policy at all. The government's official position began to sound like a broken record

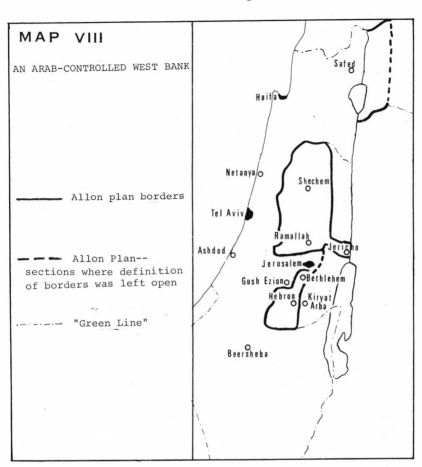

MAP VIII

AN ARAB-CONTROLLED WEST BANK

——————— Allon plan borders

━ ━ ━ Allon Plan--
sections where definition
of borders was left open

.—.—.—.—.— "Green Line"

Safed

Haifa

Netanya

Shechem

Tel Aviv

Ramallah

Ashdod

Jericho

Jerusalem

Gush Ezion   Bethlehem

Hebron   Kiryat
Arba

Beersheba

—there was no going on from it. Abba Eban announced after Gahal left the government that Israel was prepared to make concessions that would "startle the world,"[6] but it continued to seem inadvisable to spell them out. Both the peace movement and the Land of Israel Movement could argue that they offered alternative programs of *action*. The Land of Israel Movement, of course, urged the government to incorporate all the territories and embark upon a full-scale program of Jewish settlement. The peace movement insisted that the government could search far more vigorously for ways to give the territories back, to the Palestinians of the West Bank if not to Jordan. They argued that it was the government's false conception of peace as necessitating an abrupt about-face by the Arabs rather than as requiring a prolonged process of reconciliation passing through various stages of mediation, compromise, and partial agreement (indirect talks, an end of belligerence, temporary arrangements, international guarantees, etc.) that made progress impossible. Slowly these ideas began to crack the government consensus, weakening cohesiveness as cabinet members and individuals in key party posts began to argue with each other on the basis of the ideological alternatives offered by the movements.

It can of course be objected that, since the ideas offered by both the Land of Israel Movement and the peace movement were essentially traditional perspectives within Zionism which had been adapted to the current situation, the split within the government would necessarily have developed—even had these movements not existed—once it became clear that the government's policy was unworkable. That individual members of the government were sympathetic very early to the perspective of one or the other movement is clear. Dayan, for example, who was to move closest to the perspective of the Land of Israel Movement by 1973, was not converted by the Movement to the idea that the provinces of Judea and Samaria should remain part of Israel. The day before the Six-Day War ended, Dayan appeared in a taped television interview from Tel Aviv shown on "Face the Nation." Emphasizing that he spoke as an individual, Dayan said: "I don't think that we should in any way give back the Gaza Strip to Egypt or the western part of Jordan to King Hussein."[7] Arie Eliav, who was to become the Labor party leader first to be identified with the perspective of the peace movement, wrote his pamphlet *New Targets for Israel* in 1968, which suggested that he had not been converted by the peace movement. Nonetheless, it would be a grave mistake to dismiss the movements as unimportant because others independently developed similar beliefs, and to say that the failure of the government's policy must necessarily have brought the ideas of these individuals to the fore. Part of the function of the movements was in fact to bring home to government members that the policy of "territories for true peace" was unworkable, that it was not simply a policy that could be translated into action if the government was patient a little longer.

Labor Zionism, to be sure, had traditional figures like Berl Katzenelson and Yitzhak Tabenkin who placed great emphasis on the wholeness of the land, but Labor—as the dominant party adapting to the realities of the situation—had become the party that identified itself with partition as a solution, the party calling for compromise with the Arabs based on territorial concessions of Jewish rights within the area of historical Palestine. This orientation was reflected in the Israeli government's insistence prior to the outbreak of the 1967 war that it had no territorial ambitions, a position maintained after the dramatic successes of that war in the willingness to return territories for peace. The ideology that called for the maintenance of territorial claims to all of Palestine had become wholly identified with Herut, and the ideological bitterness with which Herut was viewed on a variety of grounds made its nationalist ideology—which became the chief identifying characteristic of Herut as the differences on economic issues were muted—wholly repugnant to the Labor party. It was psychologically impossible for labor simply to adopt the ideology of Herut. The Land of Israel Movement was thus extremely important in putting the ideology of Labor's chief ideological opponent in a non-party framework, thus serving as a sort of half-way house that eased the transition both for those who adopted the ideology and for those who, though never adopting it, were put in the position of having to accept programs of action based on it.

But beyond this, the Land of Israel Movement formulated ideological alternatives with a clarity and energy that Gahal did not match. Through its journal *Zot Haaretz* and the writings of member intellectuals in Israel's newspapers and journals of opinion, the Movement provided an ideological underpinning for the view that the territories should be retained by Israel. Perhaps the reason Gahal did comparatively little along these lines was that Herut, its major component, had asserted that the entire Land of Israel (including the East Bank of the Jordan) belonged to Israel for so long that events which gave Israel a good part of that land (and additional territory in Sinai) merely seemed confirmation of what were from the standpoint of Begin and his associates old beliefs. Only in the Land of Israel Movement did the perspective find new bearers who felt challenged to justify their views through creation of an ideological structure and conversion of a larger public. The task of ideological construction was something that individuals within the government, constrained by their formal allegiance to the government's policy, could not do, however sympathetic they might be to a different ideology. And yet when such government figures made statements in sympathy with differing policies it was essential that the public be able to relate them to a set of ideological justifications.

Furthermore, both movements indicated to members of the government that there was a reservoir of support for these ideologies outside of the frameworks in which they were traditional. In the case of the Land of Israel Movement, support for the ideology was expected in Gahal and in the National Religious party, which was divided on the issues involved. But if the support were to be confined to these sources, it would be insufficient as a basis for public policy. Dayan might have bolted to Gahal, with whose views he was in sympathy following the 1967 war, were it not that he knew Gahal had never offered a credible challenge to the Labor party's rule and that he knew Israelis did not vote on the basis of personalities, even very popular ones. This last knowledge came from bitter personal experience, for prior to 1967 Dayan had spent years in the political desert in the Rafi party, led by the most illustrious political personality of them all, David Ben-Gurion. The Land of Israel Movement, by drawing from all parties, suggested that there was potentially much wider support for its position, given leadership from within the government. Dayan was a practical politician, and he found himself in the position of pressing his views almost singly against the great weight of opposition of his colleagues. He could take the risk of putting the full weight of his prestige behind implementation of the ideology only if he believed there was a chance for realization of his aims.

In the case of the peace movement as well, the availability of formulated ideological alternatives was crucial to those within the Labor party who in some instances may have come independently to similar conclusions. As in the case of the Land of Israel Movement, the peace movement showed there was a reservoir of energetic support for alternate policies beyond the tiny institutional structure provided by Haolam Hazeh and beyond the Communist Rakah party, which drew its overwhelming support from Arabs protesting the existence of Israel. Arie Eliav, for example, was an ambitious practical politician who was not going to take the lead in advancing alternate policies if he felt the major support for them was in Israel's Arab population. But the peace movement, with its ability to draw on quite a broad constituency under favorable circumstances (as in the Goldmann affair, for example) proved that potential support for alternative policies, given appropriate leadership, was much larger.

Paradoxically, although the government found itself slowly implementing the programs of the Land of Israel Movement prior to the October war of 1973, the impact of the ideas of the peace movement was greater upon members of the government. This is not really surprising: the perspective of the peace movement was much closer to that of the government consensus, since the peace movement essentially urged that greater flexibility could bring progress toward peace. Attacked for rigidity, the government's response was to intimate that it did indeed have indirect contacts which were exploited on all possible occasions with the Arab states. This was presumably true (In Ben-Gurion's period unofficial contacts were maintained; Golda Meir herself had once secretly negotiated with Abdullah, finding her way to Amman disguised as an Arab),[8] but the assertion only served to confirm the peace movement's assumption that in spite of their overt position the Arabs were ready to talk. Presumably, then, the government did not talk seriously enough, did not show sufficient readiness to make necessary concessions.

There were three elements in the official Israeli government position, on any one of which (or all of which) modifications were possible: the method by which negotiations were conducted, the amount of territory negotiable, and the state of relations that would follow negotiations. Israel demanded direct face-to-face negotiations; the peace movement argued that indirect mediated contacts must be employed at least as a preliminary. Israel refused to specify what territory was negotiable (it asserted that "everything" was negotiable but that under no circumstances would the country return to the old borders); the peace movement urged that the government specify what it was prepared to return and that the offer be more generous than the government apparently had in mind. Israel demanded full peace treaties to replace the state of belligerence; the peace movement argued that intermediate "stages to peace" would be necessary. In the long range, perhaps more important than the peace movement's impact on the elements of the government's negotiating position was its influence on the way in which key government figures defined the nature of the Arab-Israel conflict. To the government, the conflict was one between Israel and the Arab states, and the Palestinians were refugees to be settled on a permanent basis in these states when peace came. But the peace movement, by its great emphasis upon the Palestinians, produced a changed perception of the conflict among some government leaders. The problem of the Palestinians ceased to be seen as a refugee problem and became, rather, a national problem; thus the solution lay, not in making accommodation with the Arab states, but in satisfying in one way or another the national aspirations of the Palestinian people.

The process of attrition among decision makers is most easily documented in the case of Mapam, whose ministers participated in the government under the terms of the Labor Alignment and which was bound by government policy. Mapam was under obvious and direct pressure from the peace movement, for the majority of the movement's leaders had Mapam backgrounds and direct links with the membership, often within the Hashomer Hazair kibbutzim from which Mapam's leadership was drawn. The tendency toward radicalization, which had plagued the leadership in the late twenties and early thirties, reasserted itself, putting pressure upon the leaders to accommodate or face serious defections. Thus, far from becoming more stringent in its demands between 1967 and 1973, Mapam called for greater concessions. The only party within the government prepared openly to draw maps, Mapam included the Gaza Strip in its 1967 proposal as part of Israel. By 1970, political resolutions passed by the Mapam Political Committee called for taking back the 1948 refugees in exchange for the incorporation of Gaza; in 1973, the fate of Gaza was to be decided by Israel's security needs, the will of the inhabitants, and the needs for the solution of the refugee problem. (The latter two considerations scarcely forecast its incorporation into Israel.) In 1967, Jerusalem was declared an unqualified part of the state of Israel (with various religions given autonomy in maintaining the holy places); in 1973, Mapam was ready to recognize the rights of the city's Arab population to specific "municipal arrangements" as a national minority with the right to choose between Israeli and Jordanian-Palestinian citizenship. Moreover, while in 1967 Mapam called for replacing the cease-fire agreements with lasting peace agreements, in 1970 the idea of indirect talks was accepted; and by 1973 Mapam was prepared to see Israel conduct negotiations "either for comprehensive permanent peace or for partial agreements, interim agreements." And while in 1967 Mapam called for a peace agreement with "the State of Jordan," by 1973 Mapam was talking of the right to "self-determination of the Palestinian-Arab people."[9]

Although Mapam was aligned with the Labor party and had members in the cabinet, it had been consistently pro-Arab within the Israeli context. But a similar development occurred within the center of the Labor government, in the traditional Mapai group which formed the core of the United Labor party. The most outspoken here were not members of the cabinet, but individuals with major positions in the labor party hierarchy. Arie Eliav, who became the chief spokesman of the "doves" within the Labor party, served as a member of the Knesset and held the post of Secretary General of the Party from 1970 to 1972. His *Land of the Hart,* published in 1972, which expanded his earlier pamphlet *New Targets for Israel,* was treated—perhaps wrongly—as a manifesto of the peace movement coming from a central government figure. For actually, as Eliav himself pointed out, while his territorial proposals were presumably more generous than the government's (unannounced) intentions, his chief departure was in the matter of tone rather than in any ideological substance.[10] Even more than many in the peace movement, Eliav was optimistic about the future of Israeli-Arab relations, for he was confident that once Israel had made a full and specific statement of her generous intent, peace would come; this very optimism permitted him to maintain a definition of peace every bit as rigid as that of the government. And while Eliav was in accord with the peace movement in emphasizing the Israel-Palestinian conflict as the central problem, he was no more willing than the government to set up an independent Palestinian state on the West Bank; he insisted with Golda Meir that there was room between the Mediterranean and the desert for only two states, Israel and a Palestinian-Arab-Jordanian one.[11]

Eliav obtained open support from two other central labor figures: Yitzhak Ben-Aharon, then Secretary General of the powerful Histadrut (General Federation of Israeli Workers), who came from an Achdut Haavoda background; and Avraham Ofer, a member of the Knesset for Mapai known for his work in party organization, who after 1973 was to serve in the Rabin cabinet. In some respects Ben-Aharon went further than Eliav, arguing for unilateral Israeli withdrawal if a negotiated settlement could not be reached: "I think someday we may conclude that it would be better if a certain segment of the population and a certain area were not subject to our rule and authority, without receiving a counter-signature on the matter. From this standpoint perhaps there is something in the saying of certain comrades that there is a kind of peace that is not countersigned."[12]

Eliav's activities went beyond ideological statement. He unsuccessfully sought to organize a revolt within the party against the passage of the 1973 platform by the Labor party convention, proposing his own alternate platform which was essentially a statement of intent to return virtually all the territories in exchange for a binding peace.[13] Eliav succeeded in gaining some 10,000 signatures from the general public for his platform, but he made no headway within the Labor Party Secretariat, which voted 78 to 0 for the policy on the territories hammered out in the so-called Galili compromise. Eliav, who abstained from the vote, read a statement asserting that the Galili document was "born to the crack of the whip of threats" and went "against all that I understand to be the values of the Labour Movement." Eliav declared himself the emissary of those "in this hall and land whose souls weep in silence because of this document."[14]

Within the Israeli cabinet, apart from the Mapam ministers, a group of ministers within the Labor party itself moved steadily closer to the peace movement, notably Israel's powerful Minister of Finance Pinchas Sapir, Foreign Minister Abba Eban, and Minister of Education and Deputy Prime Minister Yigal Allon. These men never openly associated themselves with the peace movement (although both Eban and Allon were clearly wooing its intellectuals in the period before the outbreak of the October war),[15] but increasingly found themselves taking its positions. All three regarded the territories as a burden, and in the minds of all three the demographic problem seems to have been uppermost, the fear that the Arab population would soon equal or outstrip the Jewish population in an expanded Israel. And yet it is interesting that none of them suggested that Israel keep Sinai, where there was no problem of Arab population; the issue of moral rights to territory was inextricably bound up with the demographic issue, and there was no separating them.

It must be stressed that the relation between these ministers and the peace movement (which regarded them as "passive" exponents) was an uneasy one. None was quicker and more explicit in affirming determination to return as much of the territories as possible than Pinchas Sapir: on the other hand, Sapir remained far from the peace movement, many of whose members held as an ideal an ultimate integration of Israel within the region (while maintaining its Jewish identity), in that he would have liked to rope Israel off from the rest of the Middle East, just so long as these countries would not make war upon her. And Eban seems to have retained faith in the original government formulation despite the passage of the years. In 1970, three years after the war, Eban affirmed its sound logic: "We want to give the Arab states two impressions: the impossibility of changing the present situation without peace, but also the authentic possibility of changing it, with peace. We thought they would explore a peace settlement—the expectation has not been fulfilled. Our error was not of basic appraisal but an unduly sanguine view of time."[16] And three years after that, only two months before the Yom Kippur War, Eban was still arguing that Israel's policy stood in no need of change, and that more time was indispensable for inducing change in the attitude of the Arab states by lopping off options "that are sterile or unacceptable."[17] But in the meanwhile Eban was prepared to state clearly to the inhabitants of the West Bank, "Your political destiny does not lie with Israel,"[18] and was thus willing not only to make the statement of intent called for by the peace movement but also to agree that a policy of "stages to peace" might be a rational approach, with each stage bringing the solution to a specific problem.[19]

Allon's relation to the peace movement was the most curious of all. His background was the Achdut Haavoda, whose ideological leader had been Yitzhak Tabenkin. Allon had accused Ben-Gurion of neglecting opportunities during the war of independence to conquer Judea and Samaria and in a 1959 book, *A Curtain of Sand,* Allon wrote:

If indeed the Arab rulers once again force upon Israel a total war, the existing borders will no longer bind the Israel Defense Forces in its operations and the state in the shaping of its future borders. However, here too one must distinguish between areas which were once an inseparable part of a whole Israel—in its historical borders—and territories which belong historically to the Arab states. . . . What is the difference in principle between Nazareth, which was not included in the State of Israel according to the partition plan of the U.N.—and was included as the result of the war of defense—and Jericho, for example, which is held to this day by an invading Jordanian army? . . . There must be no return to the unreal and artificial frontiers of today. If the war should break out again, there is no returning to the historical mistake which was made in the War of Liberation and afterwards in the Sinai War. No longer should the war be stopped before full victory is achieved, the completeness of the land and peace treaties which will ensure normal relations between Israel and its neighbors. . . . If Zahal [Israel Defense Forces] should cross the borders of the divided land, it is forbidden to retreat again but we must aspire from then on to stabilize the borders, which from the historical, economic and security aspect are the most natural.[20]

According to Israeli journalist Shabtai Teveth, Allon and Menachem Begin were the most vigorous in demanding that the Old City of Jerusalem be taken, while Dayan and others in the cabinet still hung back at the beginning of the 1967 war.[21] Yet after the war, which brought under Israel's dominion areas "once an inseparable part of Palestine," Allon took a very different position from the one he recommended in his book. True, he did not recommend total withdrawal; the Allon plan, which the government implemented, called for a string of Israeli paramilitary settlements in the uninhabited Jordan Valley and envisaged this territory, comprising roughly a third of the land of the West Bank, becoming part of Israel in an ultimate peace settlement. Allon was the first of Israel's cabinet ministers to visit the settlers in Hebron, openly identifying with them, although the settlement of Hebron was bitterly attacked by the peace movement. Allon specifically assailed what he perceived as the extremists of the peace movement, insisting that Israel had not chosen the reality she faced and that reality could not be changed by "the babble of righteous people and pacifists."[22]

Allon's position seems to have been that Israel could not despair of peace, that she must prepare for it and foster the complex process that would lead to it, and that territorial compromise was central to its achievement. Allon was sensitive to the issue of historical rights; he said that if he argued for territorial compromise it was in spite of historical rights and for the historical target of peace. Allon became increasingly sympathetic to the peace movement on the matter of Palestinian national rights; he observed that, regardless of the absence of a specifically Palestinian nationality in history, such a national entity was taking shape before Israel's very eyes.[23]

Ranged against these men and taking an outspoken position that brought him increasingly close to the ideological alternative offered by the Land of Israel Movement, was Moshe Dayan. For a variety of reasons, to be examined shortly, Dayan was far more successful in implementing his views than the relative isolation of his position would suggest. While Dayan's inclination from the beginning was to keep the provinces of Judea and Samaria within Israel, only gradually did he seek to make it government policy. In August 1967, at a burial rite for those killed during the War of Independence whose graves were transferred to the Mount of Olives in the newly united Jerusalem, Dayan addressed our "brothers who fell in the War of Liberation" in terms that indicated his views were not based primarily on security considerations, but on a conception of Zionism that showed him in spiritual fellowship with the Land of Israel Movement: "We have not abandoned your dream and we have not forgotten your lesson. We have returned to the Mountain, to the cradle of our people, to the inheritance of the Patriarchs, the land of the Judges and the fortress of the Kingdom of the House of David. We have returned to Hebron and Shechem, to Bethlehem and Anatot, to Jericho and the fords of the Jordan at Adam Ha'ir."[24] (The reference to the "Mountain" is to the hill country of Judea and Samaria, for early Israel, unlike modern Israel, was not primarily a country of the coastal plain.)

In the months and years that followed, Dayan repeatedly associated himself with the government's position of "territories for peace," but it became increasingly apparent that Dayan's definition of negotiable territories was not that of the majority within the government, and more and more Dayan became willing to state his position without insisting, as he had done earlier, that he was expressing his personal views. Rather, Dayan embarked upon an effort to impose his views upon the government. Dayan frequently has been accused in Israel of wavering and inconsistency, of changing his position from month to month; and there is no doubt that it is possible to find contradictory quotations in his speeches. For example, in December 1970, asked if he preferred a larger bi-national Israel to a small one with a Jewish majority, he said he preferred a larger country for defense reasons "but if it threatens the essence of our Jewish state, then I prefer a smaller one with a Jewish majority."[25] Not only did this statement contradict Dayan's more frequently expressed attitude toward the future of Judea, Samaria, and Gaza (where the "demographic threat" was concentrated), it also contradicted the basis upon which Dayan customarily argued—namely, the fulfillment of the historic task of Zionism.

Furthermore, under attack for particular statements, he frequently denied that they meant what they clearly seemed to mean. And as the play of international forces upon Israel changed from month to month, Dayan's uncertainty was further heightened, for the possibility of an enforced big-power settlement loomed sometimes larger, sometimes smaller. His attitude toward the possibility of a settlement with the Arabs wavered. And it is also clear from his speeches that Dayan was not sure about the nature of the central values held by the people of Israel, and to what extent those values were in conformity with, or could be shaped in conformity with, his conception of proper national goals.

In spite of all this, Dayan's overall position developed with sufficient consistency that it can be traced with some confidence. Dayan seemed more inconsistent than he was because his position did not correspond precisely to any of the alternate ideologies that became recognized after the Six-Day War. Dayan was very close to the Land of Israel Movement's view (and that of Gahal and part of the National Religious party) concerning the West Bank, but he differed from the Land of Israel Movement in his attitude toward Sinai. Public confusion was further heightened because Dayan was virtually alone in failing to promise peace as a probable outcome of the policies he advocated. Dayan consistently pointed out that Israel's keeping the territories would lead to greater Arab hostility and increased likelihood of war.[26] In a country so urgently in search of peace it seemed a contradiction in terms that one could advocate a policy which did not hold out hope for peace, and these statements by Dayan were promptly but wrongly interpreted as arguments against keeping the territories.

Dayan's first major proposal at variance with government policy came in November 1968, when he urged that the territories be economically linked with Israel. Specifically, he argued that the southern region of the province of Judea should be linked with southern Israel through a common electricity system, water system, transportation network, and through agricultural planning, and marketing.[27] It could be argued—and was—that Dayan's plan did not necessarily require Israel's political control, for government policy demanded "peace" for territories, and economic links were part of the meaning of peace. Yet in that speech Dayan also said he did not want to see Gaza go back to Egypt or Hebron to Jordan, and he called for greatly expanded Jewish settlement of the Ezion bloc. What he urged, then, was a single economic region including the province of Judea, southern Israel, and Jerusalem, whose political future was unspecified but strongly implied.

A year later Dayan was urging that Israeli law be introduced into the territories.[28] This time Dayan was careful to say he was not proposing annexation, and he distinguished his proposal for the introduction of Israeli law in the framework of orders of the military government from imposition of Israeli law through the Knesset, which would symbolize a change in sovereignty. As for the present situation, Dayan objected that the maintenance of existing law constituted a striking expression of Israel's recognition that her presence was temporary. That same year Dayan called for four Israeli urban settlements in the Judean Hills adjoining the major Arab towns of Ramallah, Jenin, Nablus, and Hebron.[29]

Dayan concluded that Arab consent could not be won for borders that Israel would find satisfactory; thus, he said, the Israeli government formula calling for "secure and agreed borders" was contradictory: "secure" borders in Israel's definition could never be "agreed" borders in the Arab definition. Accordingly, at the 1969 convention of the Labor party, Dayan called for the phrase "secure, strategic" borders to be substituted in the party platform.[30] (In a typical Labor party compromise, both Dayan's phrase and the traditional phrase were included in the platform—Dayan's in the platform plank on security policy, the traditional one in the platform plank on foreign policy.)

More and more persistently Dayan called for accelerated settlement in the territories and the establishment of "facts" by Israel. Israel had to "give real content to the borders"[31] that even the majority within the Labor party agreed should be established. Formal annexation, Dayan asserted, was not important and would not (as the Land of Israel Movement argued) prevent pressure from the great powers for change; nor could the possibility of an agreement with the Arabs yet be wholly ruled out. Nonetheless, Israel must not just sit and wait: "What we do today in Ramat Hagolan in my opinion is much better than public announcements of annexation of the Golan plateau. Settlement and pioneering projects there carry greater weight than a legal announcement in the Knesset on annexation. It is my opinion that in every area we must examine what can be done and must be done now in order not to waste time and the governmental authority we now possess at a time when we do not merely lack an agreement with the

Arabs but even any discussions with them. In my view the solution lies in action, not declarations of annexation."[32] Six months later Dayan expressed more pessimism on the prospect of peace with the Arabs: "The time has come to accept their refusal to make peace, and to act accordingly."[33]

The succeeding years confirmed these views of Dayan; at the same time, the petering out of efforts by the major powers to find a common basis for imposition of a settlement made him more confident that Israel could in fact exert her will free of overwhelming external constraint. In 1971, after an official speech as a member of the government, Dayan asked for permission to speak as an individual. "I know there is a Security Council Resolution 242 and there is a Rogers Plan and there is a Dayan plan and there is an Allon plan and there are and will be other plans. But there is one thing bigger and greater than all of them and that is the people of Israel returned to their homeland."[34] Repeatedly Dayan returned to this theme, sometimes deliberately minimizing the role of security considerations in relation to issues of national identity. Asked in a radio interview to identify Israel's motive in settling Hebron, Dayan replied: "In Hebron we are seeking what we are seeking in Jerusalem—a homeland."[35] To the Army Command and Staff College, Dayan said impatiently that, more than four years after the Six-Day War, there was no justification for Israel's any longer spending 99 percent of her energy within the Green Line (the 1949 border): "We should regard our role in the administered territories as that of the established government—to plan and implement whatever can be done, without leaving options open for the day of peace—which may be distant."[36] And in 1972 Dayan said bluntly, "Coexistence of Jews and Arabs is only possible under the protection of the Israeli government and army. . . . The departure of the government of Israel and its army from the Strip and the West Bank means in fact also debarring Israel from these places."[37] (The official Israeli position was that Jewish settlements were possible in areas that might ultimately be returned, since in a condition of peace there was no reason why Jews could not live under Arab sovereignty.) Dayan urged: "We must persist in implementation of our vision and not be afraid of realizing Zionism, for it is in our hands to build our future."[38]

By 1973 Dayan was insisting that it was intolerable that "the government of sovereign Israel should restrict Jewish land purchases in Judea and Samaria."[39] As for looking upon Jewish settlement there as "temporary," Dayan replied, "If we wish to end it then we have to stop teaching the Bible."[40] Dayan warned of difficulties in the diplomatic arena, even warfare, if Israel followed the course he charted. But the emphasis would be on settlement, said Dayan, "leaving no room for a separate Palestinian state, a Jordanian Jerusalem Old City or a Syrian Golan Heights."[41]

Shabtai Teveth, in his biography of Moshe Dayan, interprets Dayan's position as growing from a belief he had developed prior to the 1967 war that the solution to the Arab-Israel problem could lie in a confederacy including Israel, Jordan, and the Palestinians of the West Bank. In Teveth's view, Dayan after 1967 was trying to develop a framework of this sort:

In Dayan's view, the two nations in the area formerly called Palestine could function within a single economy, even though they belonged to different cultures and sovereign states. The basic principle in his approach was neighborliness, or in his phrase, "a joint way of life." . . . Dayan saw the country as an integral part of a region and only its geographic and economic borders were identical. They contained two distinct demographic and cultural entities whose political demarcation did not follow strictly demographic lines. Thus an Arab from Jerusalem and an Arab from Nablus, though belonging to the same demographic and cultural group, could belong to different political entities. Both would work in the same economy but would vote for representatives in different countries and enjoy different civil rights. Dayan's overall aim was to blur the identification between the geographic and the demographic lines of demarcation. . . . The Jewish State Dayan envisaged was not defined by a geographical border but by demographic and cultural criteria. The same applied to the Palestinian entity, although he had not yet decided whether it should be a state in its own right or a part of the Hashemite Kingdom of Jordan whose inhabitants live in Israel.[42]

Yet it is difficult to see in what sense Dayan's proposals could be defined as establishment of a "confederation," for what Dayan was really doing was seeking to answer the demographic argument raised to such effect against the Land of Israel Movement by eliminating the conventional tie between citizenship and geographic place. The Land of Israel Movement did not differ with Dayan in its discomfort at the prospect of a large Arab minority, potentially even a majority. But since its members saw no possibility of separating the rights of citizenship from political sovereignty, they addressed this problem (when absolutely necessary, since they preferred to avoid it) in a variety of ways: by arguing that once Jewish sovereignty was clearly established large numbers of Arabs would leave; by asserting their faith in large-scale Jewish *aliya* from the Soviet Union and the West; by advocating postponement of citizenship rights for a certain period pending peaceful conditions in the area; by disputing the accuracy of predictions of Arab population growth; by minimizing the problems that would be caused by a very large Arab citizenry, to name a few. Dayan, however, suggested that the Arabs of the West Bank retain Jordanian citizenship while the land remained under Israeli sovereignty.[43] This was indeed having the best of both worlds. Left unanswered was the question of why Jordan would permit individuals who did not live in its territory to be voting citizens. Hussein continued to claim the West Bank after Israel's 1967 conquest and thus permitted continued citizenship where he ultimately hoped to reclaim territory. But once Israeli sovereignty appeared irrevocably established there would be no reason for Hussein to continue to offer citizenship to the inhabitants. Dayan's "solution" appeared to the Land of Israel Movement impractical; in fact the idea was idiosyncratic with him and had no following. In practical terms, then, Dayan's insistence that military control over the West Bank remain with Israel, that Israeli law be introduced in the West Bank, that the West Bank be economically integrated with Israel, and that Israelis have the right to settle anywhere in the West Bank meant that he took a position in respect to the West Bank almost indistinguishable from that of the Land of Israel Movement and merely offered yet another and rather bizarre suggestion for coping with the demographic problem.

As the time approached for adoption of a platform for the elections scheduled for November 1973, Dayan made a series of demands upon the Labor party with the implicit ultimatum that if his demands were not met he would leave the party. Dayan wanted expansion of Jewish settlement and industrial development around Jerusalem; a new seaport of Yamit in northeast Sinai east of El Arish; and, most far-reaching in implications, permission for Jews to buy land directly from Arabs in the territories. The upshot was a compromise platform, known as the Galili document after the cabinet minister who drafted it. The proposal for Yamit, which also aroused opposition on economic grounds (Sapir argued that investment in the project would undercut the development towns within Israel) was to be "studied"; the tempo of settlement accelerated and the "scope of settlement activities increased"; Israeli businessmen who invested in areas of Jewish settlement in the territories would receive special tax concessions; and on the most controversial question, the right of Jews to purchase land in Judea and Samaria, an elaborate provision hedged that right with sufficient restrictions that those in the cabinet opposed to such purchases felt they could live with it. "Only in instances in which land is required for constructive purposes—after its acquisition is examined from political and security standpoints and after it becomes apparent that it cannot be purchased for the Israel Land Administration (or that the administration is not interested in purchasing it)—will right of purchase be granted to companies and individuals. The committee of ministers will be authorized to decide on granting permission. The Land Administration will also endeavor to acquire land purchased by Jews."[44] But despite the restrictions—which meant that, depending upon implementation, in practice private individuals might *not* be able to acquire land—this provision of the platform had revolutionary implications for Israeli policy in the territories. Instead of a policy of confined "security" settlements established by government plan, the territories were potentially thrown open to the individual Israeli citizen for settlement and investment. Implemented in the West Bank, the obvious target area, that policy would mean the achievement of the goals of the Land of Israel Movement for the provinces of Judea and Samaria.

On the question of Sinai, on the other hand, Dayan was the first in the cabinet to propose territorial concessions in the absence of a peace treaty with Egypt. Even during the 1967 war Dayan initially had wanted to stop at the Mitla and Giddi passes, according to his biographer Teveth, saying, "What do you need the Suez for? It's political madness,"[45] and telling the cabinet, "Anyone with an ounce of sense should keep away from the Canal. If we reach the Canal, Nasser will never agree to a cease-fire and the war will go on for years."[46] The momentum of battle carried Israeli forces to the Canal despite Dayan's reservations, and the convenience of the Canal as a defense line kept Israeli forces there; but Dayan continued to view the closure of the Suez Canal as a situation which was intolerable from the Egyptian standpoint and must inevitably lead to war. However, Dayan believed, once the Canal was open Egypt might be able to live with an arrangement that gave her part of Sinai and left part in Israel's hands. If Egyptian interest in a renewal of war could be eliminated, Israel would not need to worry about Jordan and Syria. Thus, as Dayan saw it, territorial concessions to Egypt, even without formal peace arrangements, had the advantage of possibly postponing a confrontation with Egypt (Dayan argued for as long as twenty years), by implication giving this time to Israel to consolidate her hold over the other territories.[47] As early as 1969, Dayan said that when he talked of paying a price for a peace agreement it was from his point of view in connection with the Sinai Peninsula and not the West Bank.[48]

Thus in 1971, Dayan was anxious to follow up what had originated as an Egyptian suggestion for an interim settlement involving Israeli withdrawal from the Canal, even though Egypt had violated the provisions of the stand-still cease-fire to bring up missile sites only a few months earlier, an action which had led to Israel's breaking off negotiations under Ambassador Jarring. When Sadat sent his Russian advisers packing the following year, Dayan became even more interested in finding a modus vivendi with an Egypt that now seemed less threatening. In September 1973, immediately preceding the October war, reports were circulating that Dayan was proposing a plan for a partial settlement with Egypt that would divide Sinai between Israel and Egypt, and would allow Egyptian troops to cross the Canal, one of the sticking points in prior negotiations for an interim settlement.[49] In short, Dayan did not wholly adopt the ideology of the Land of Israel Movement, for the Movement was no more prepared to accept Israeli withdrawal in Sinai than in any of the other territories. Nonetheless Dayan was very close to the Movement in basic perspective. The chief difference was that Dayan, disagreeing with the Movement's assumption that as long as Israel remained in the existing borders the Arabs would not dare to make war, sought to find some way of taking Israel's major enemy, Egypt, out of the conflict, the better to achieve the goals of the Movement outside of Sinai.

Although Dayan's position was a lonely one within the cabinet, he was not completely without support even there. Former Rafi member Shimon Peres (to become Minister of Defense in the Rabin cabinet after the 1973 war) backed Dayan, as did Minister of Police Shlomo Hillel. And although the cabinet ministers representing the National Religious party were themselves relatively dovish, the party was committed by resolutions to its national convention in 1969 to implementing "our historic religious right over the promised land" and "extensive agricultural and urban settlement in the liberated territories."[50] The National Religious party was concerned primarily with Judea and Samaria, the core area of ancient Hebrew settlement and the holiest part of the Holy Land. Four years later, at its next convention, the political resolutions were stronger, the tone millenial in contrast to the sober words of 1969: "In full and unshakable faith in the fulfillment of the divine promise by the prophets of truth and justice that the people of God will return to the land of its patrimony to work and guard, to build and fructify it, to maintain a state of Torah and mitzvot in the borders promised to it by the Lord, the Mafdal [National Religious party] sees in this the beginning of the fulfillment of Divine Providence and a process on the path to the full development of the people of Israel in the land of its fathers."[51] And as part of the resolution, the convention voted that it would resign from any government that voted to return any part of the "inheritance of the Patriarchs" (Judea and Samaria) as part of a peace settlement. Dayan himself observed that his position was much closer to that of the National Religious party than to that of his own United Labor party.[52]

On specific issues Dayan also won support from Israel Galili, Minister without Portfolio in the cabinet and a close adviser of Golda Meir, and from the Premier herself. Both were prepared to see further settlement and wanted considerable modification of Israel's pre-war frontiers in any peace settlement. Golda Meir's attitude stemmed from a profound suspicion of Arab intentions and a determination to keep

Israel in as strong a defensive position as possible. On the other hand, Mrs. Meir clearly did not want to keep Judea and Samaria: "It is unthinkable that there should be under our rule a population composed partly of citizens of Israel and partly of non-citizens. . . . I don't want a bi-national state and I don't want to be obliged to count apprehensively every day how many Jewish babies have been born."[53]

The presence of sharply conflicting views within the government could not long escape public attention, for as the initial consensus broke down in the face of Arab refusal to negotiate, cabinet members and key government and party officials argued with each other openly. The ideological alternatives articulated by the Land of Israel Movement and the peace movement were in fact being publicly debated by cabinet ministers within the ruling Labor party, and the rift widened steadily over the years. The pattern established was one of challenge producing response, as Dayan would make a proposal leading toward incorporation of the territories and others would attack him. These ministers found themselves affirming the position of the peace movement, for while the government's stand was that the future of the territories should be discussed only with the Arabs in peace negotiations, the peace movement wanted a prior public Israeli commitment to large-scale withdrawal. Ministers who argued against settlement were in effect affirming their commitment to returning the territories.

The first public airing of the fundamental differences that were to threaten ultimately to split the Labor party came after a speech by Dayan in Beersheba in November 1968, in which he called for economic integration of the southern region of the West Bank with southern Israel. Sapir reacted sharply, warning that such a policy would have disastrous consequences: "I believe that integration means converting Israel into an Arab state,"[54] while Eban said it meant a policy of apartheid.[55] Asserting that he had no personal quarrel with Dayan, Sapir observed: "Maybe, Dayan as a sabra, has sentiments about Hebron. I do not have any such sentiments. . . . I do not see the great importance of cities like Hebron and Jenin. What do they have there? We also have grapes that ripen late in the season."[56]

While disparaging references to Israel's ties to Jenin or Nablus provoked little reaction in Israel, treatment of Hebron in these terms produced considerable public shock.[57] Hebron, it will be recalled, was the city second to Jerusalem in holiness to Jews and, like Jerusalem, had drawn religious Jewish settlers consistently from the ancient into the modern period until the massacre of the Jewish inhabitants by the Arabs in 1929. Sapir was thus in ideological company with the peace movement in attacking a historical basis for attachment to land not presently settled by Jews. (In Hebron, Jewish settlement had in fact

been renewed some months earlier with the "sit-down" settlement led
by Rabbi Moshe Levinger, which formed the nucleus for Kiryat
Arba). As for Dayan's proposal to establish quarters next to four West
Bank cities, Sapir objected: "Can anyone imagine the tragedy involved
in settling 40,000 Jews in Nablus and Jenin?"[58] Dayan retorted sharply
that insanity lay, not in settling there, but in leaving those areas.[59]

The dispute was out in the open now and was exacerbated with the
passage of time. Dayan pointed out that Israel lacked goals because
of the fundamental disagreement within the leadership.[60] At the
Labor convention in 1969 the apparently trivial change in wording
suggested by Dayan, from "secure and agreed" borders to "secure, strategic" borders as Israel's goal, produced a major confrontation between him and Eban. In an unscheduled address to the convention,
an angry Eban said it might be better if the party split now, for without Dayan it was still possible for Labor to receive the majority of
the public's votes.[61] In 1971, when Dayan said Israel should regard her
role in the territories as that of the established government, he produced a sharp reaction not only from the United States State Department (which objected that this was totally inconsistent with Israel's
acceptance of Security Council Resolution 242) but from Eban, Allon,
and Sapir as well.[62]

Dayan's attempt to meet the demographic argument by suggesting
that Israel retain the territories but that the Arab inhabitants continue
to have voting rights in Jordan brought predictably sharp attacks.
Eban retorted: "It would be portrayed as a denial of rights! We have
the territories—and they don't even become citizens. It would look
worse than the greater Israel policy [Land of Israel Movement] of
keeping the territories and granting citizenship and equal rights to
Arabs."[63] On the annexation of Gaza Dayan found support from Galili,
who told the Knesset in the aftermath of a dispute over the eviction of
Bedouins near Rafiah, "The Gaza Strip will not be separated anymore
from the body of Israel." Eban flatly contradicted this assertion, saying, "Since 1967 there has been no change in the status of Gaza or in
the position of the government concerning it."[64]

In November 1972, when Dayan again emphasized that Israel must
rule as the regular government in the territories, Sapir attacked the
"creeping annexation" of the West Bank, pointing out that the Arabs
would be close to half the population in a single generation. "Is this
the Jewish fate we aspired to?" he asked. From social, political, and
security points of view, argued Sapir, Dayan's policy represented a
grave mistake. To believe that raising the standard of living could
compensate for nationalist aspirations was to ignore the lessons of history.[65] When Dayan on October 17, 1972 said that the coexistence of

Jews and Arabs was possible only under the protection of the Israeli government and army and that withdrawal meant Israel could have no foothold in these places, Allon objected that if Dayan "also referred to the post-peace period or meant this as a substitute for peace, then what he said has great and far reaching significance."[66]

The conflict came to a new climax with the formulation of the platform for the 1973 elections, with a significant faction in the Labor party anxious to push Dayan out altogether while Golda Meir still headed the party and could be expected to lead it to victory even without Dayan's presence.[67] Dayan wanted to open up Judea and Samaria to purchases by Jews from Arab landowners, but Mapam threatened to break away from the Alignment if such a policy was followed, and within the Labor party itself there was sharp opposition. The compromise formula finally reached has already been described; once again the differences had been papered over and the Labor party managed to continue its "united" existence. But the public acrimony did not cease. When Dayan said that Israelis should cease studying the Bible if they had no desire to settle the West Bank, Eban in effect accused Dayan of "Hottentot morality." "Zionism, apart from its emphasis on territories and landscapes of the homeland, gives a central place in its consciousness to the aspiration for peace, and to repulsion from all superfluous domination of other people against their will. Let us recall David Ben-Gurion's definition: 'He who says I do not want others to dominate me, but I do want to dominate others—betrays a Hottentot morality.'"[68] Those opposed to Dayan within the government sought to equate a policy of annexation with one of neglect of Israel's social problems of poverty, inequality between Ashkenazic and Sephardic communities, etc. Abba Eban, for example, objected to the plan to expand Jerusalem in the direction of Nebi Samuel, arguing that Israel needed to abolish its Katamons (a slum district in Jerusalem) before building new Savyons (a wealthy suburb of Tel Aviv) at Nebi Samuel and that it was impossible "to foist the security policy of Gahal on the social policy of Avoda [the Labor party]."[69]

Perhaps nowhere was the ideological conflict within the Labor party more embarassingly visible than in the pages of *Ot*, a weekly political magazine published by the Labor party beginning in 1971. The editors represented the wing of the Labor party ideologically very close to the peace movement, and they published a series of articles attacking those within the government who had moved closest to the Land of Israel Movement, notably Moshe Dayan. But they also criticized Golda Meir and Israel Galili for their support of Dayan and their suspicion of unilateral Israeli concessions. Dayan and Meir understandably found this situation, in which their policies and actions were attacked by a political journal of their own party, unbearable; and they objected strongly to the magazine's editorial direction.[70] But what is most interesting about *Ot* is the way its contents reveal the fundamentally contradictory ideological positions which had found bearers in the Labor party. In an effort to provide a less one-sided forum, the editors published articles by such traditional labor party figures as Rachel Yanait (widow of Israel's second President, Yitzhak Ben-Zvi, and herself a member of the Land of Israel Movement). The journal, supposedly designed to reflect the policy consensus of the Labor party, instead revealed the deep split within it.

Since the majority of the Labor party leadership was clearly more in sympathy with Sapir, Allon, and Eban, it may seem surprising to find that the government was successfully propelled by the activist wing toward implementation of the ideology of the Land of Israel Movement. That this was what was happening was clear to all by the time the platform compromise was worked out for the 1973 elections. The peace movement was appalled by the direction of government policy, but it was no less convinced than the Land of Israel Movement (which was in fact perhaps less confident that it approached ideological victory) that this was where a policy of "creeping annexation" took the country.[71] The government's very disclaiming of the Land of Israel Movement was significant. Thus in August 1973, Israel Galili said that while Israel was of course settling territories not to leave them, it was important to stress that the government had not adopted the slogan "not one step."[72] Presumably, Galili felt it necessary to distinguish the government's policy from that of the Movement precisely because the two had begun to look so similar.

There were other indications of the shift in direction. Ben-Gurion in the immediate aftermath of the 1967 war had become an honorary father of the peace movement, a surprising development, since he had traditionally been associated with an activist position within the Labor party. In an interview with a Japanese television station, Ben-Gurion stated that all territories but Jerusalem and the Golan should be returned to the Arab states in return for peace. Ben-Gurion was without political influence in his retirement but, as the man who had been undisputed leader of the country for so many years, was a figure of importance. It was therefore significant of the change in sentiment that by 1972 Ben-Gurion had changed his mind and now talked of the need for energetic settlement in the territories.[73] Also of interest was the Knesset reaction to King Hussein's plan for a federation of Jordan with the West Bank subsequent to Israeli withdrawal. While

Allon commented favorably upon the plan, Israel's Parliament reacted by going on record that "The Knesset reaffirms and confirms the historic right of the Jewish people over the Land of Israel."[74]

There were compelling reasons for the apparent anomaly of a government's implementing a policy which a majority of its members opposed. In fact, the government was engaged in a simultaneous effort to try out on a limited basis policies that accorded with the program of the peace movement and policies that met with the approval of the Land of Israel Movement. The problem was that the first effort did not work, but the second did. And thus, however slowly the government moved in the second direction, each step constituted a definite commitment to that path, while all efforts in the other direction produced no result. The government rather quickly abandoned a strict interpretation of its demand for direct negotiations to produce a final and total peace. Its agreement to enter into the Jarring talks meant willingness to undertake indirect negotiations, even if direct negotiations were the subsequent goal. The acceptance of Security Council Resolution 242 by Israel in 1968—which Dayan called "a fatal mistake"[75]—marked an effort to move in the direction advocated by the peace movement. Although Israel's leaders persisted in emphasizing that the resolution called for withdrawal from "territories" rather than from "the territories" (leaving territorial acquisition open under terms of the resolution), in the minds of all countries other than Israel the resolution essentially called for Israeli withdrawal from the occupied territories. Any Israeli illusions on this score must have been dispelled when the United States advanced the Rogers Plan of December 1969, calling for only "insubstantial border changes" in the framework of a peace agreement. The Rogers Plan was quickly rejected by Israel, but the interpretation of Security Council Resolution 242 by Israel's only significant supporter on the international scene was now quite clear.

Despite this, only six months later Israel accepted an American proposal for a cease-fire agreement on the Canal to terminate the Egyptian "war of attrition" and for continuation of negotiations through Dr. Jarring within the framework of Security Council Resolution 242. That initiative collapsed when the Egyptians used the cease-fire to advance their missiles in violation of the agreement and Israel withdrew from the Jarring talks in protest. But within a matter of months Israel was engaging in talks once again, and was now ready to retreat from its long-held position that it would remain at the cease-fire lines until a peace agreement was reached. Israel was prepared to withdraw from the Canal in an "interim agreement" that would permit its reopening by Egypt, provided Egyptian armed forces did not cross it. On the issue of direct negotiations Israel also retreated, agreeing to

"Rhodes-style talks" on the pattern of the talks that had produced the 1949 armistice agreements, where ostensibly talks were held in separate rooms and positions were mediated through the U.N. representatives.[76] The government had in effect adopted the peace movement's program of "stages to peace" and agreed to indirect negotiations. There even were explorations of the peace movement's favored plan for a "Palestine entity," but here the reluctance of West Bank leaders to become involved in the creation of what would have been no more than a semi-autonomous province blocked progress.

The peace movement could and did argue that Israel did not go far enough. Israel, for example, refused Nasser's demand that Israel agree prior to negotiations to return to the old borders, even though for the first time the term "peace" was used in reference to what Egypt was prepared to offer in exchange. Whether further or better-timed concessions would have obtained a response must remain unknown,[77] but from the standpoint of the government, all efforts to pursue the path marked out by the peace movement through greater flexibility ended in complete failure.

One the other hand, all steps toward implementation of the ideology of the Land of Israel Movement had their intended results. Agricultural settlements were begun in the Golan, which the government had resolved would remain part of Israel. The Allon plan, which required keeping a section of land along the Jordan River on the West Bank, began to be implemented; this plan had the double virtue, from the standpoint of the government, of helping to promote Israeli security through giving Israel control of the Jordan and of involving no addition of Arabs to the Israeli population. At first para-military Nahal settlements were established, but the accepted procedure was to make them regular civilian settlements after the passage of a few years—and the years passed. By 1973, in the Golan, on the West Bank, and in northern Sinai a total of forty-four settlements had been established by Israel, and fifty were planned to be established by the end of the year.[78] In addition there was Kiryat Arba (upper Hebron), which the government was committed not merely to support but to expand. By the time of the October war, the government had undertaken to enlarge the boundaries of Jerusalem (without formal annexation) for the creation of a new industrial district as well as residential expansion.[79]

Plans afoot disrupted by the war would have involved the creation of further "facts." A new port of Yamit, Dayan's plan for the development of northern Sinai, was to be studied.[80] Plans existed for the Judaization of the Gaza Strip: the peace movement complained of maps showing fingers of land thrusting through the Strip which the Israeli government planned to acquire and settle with Jews.[81] Granting Jewish settlements in the occupied areas special tax status, a plan which became part of the Labor party's platform, would have accelerated settlement and investment in them. If the restrictions surrounding the sale of land by Arabs to Jews on the West Bank should come to be loosely applied, a point of no return could rather quickly be reached, at least in respect to the West Bank.

While Dayan's recommendations for action were never fully followed, many of them were partially implemented considerably after he made them. Israeli law was never introduced into the territories; no regional plan to link the towns of Israel with those of the West Bank was devised; and no Jewish urban settlements were set up on the hills beside the major West Bank towns (except Hebron). Dayan's proposal for the Jerusalem area—that Bethlehem be attached from the south and Ramallah from the north to form a "Greater Jerusalem"— was also not implemented. On the other hand, the economic integration between Israel and the West Bank which Sapir deplored proceeded steadily; a more limited expansion of Jerusalem was undertaken; and a basis for incorporation of the West Bank on a practical level was established with the adoption of the election platform of 1973.

The government embarked upon a policy which must lead to the very result the majority of its members deplored because it saw no options. A majority might have been content tentatively to explore the various lines of action proposed by the peace movement and, as these failed, simply to await changes in the Arab world. But pressure was placed on them by Dayan who, despite the small size of his following in the cabinet, wielded disproportionate power because of his personal popularity. Every poll conducted before the October war showed that Israelis had more confidence in Dayan's views on matters of security than they had in those of any other government leader. And since Gahal remained as the major opposition party articulating a policy to which Dayan's bore an increasing resemblance, there was the danger that Dayan might leave the Labor party, should his proposals meet with complete rejection, take with him most of the former Rafi segment of the Labor party, and form an alliance with Gahal in the elections for the Knesset. Further, since the National Religious party —upon which Labor traditionally relied for its working majority and thus its ability to govern—was committed by party resolutions to retaining the West Bank, the danger became that not only Dayan and Rafi would be lost, but the National Religious party as well. The formation of the Likud strengthened Dayan's hand, and members of the Land of Israel Movement regarded the chief importance of this joining together in an electoral bloc of the parties opposed to "renewed partition of the Land of Israel" as the strengthening of the hawks within labor.[82] The price of all-out opposition to Dayan within the party began to seem great indeed—the possible loss of power by the Labor party for the first time since the foundation of the state.

And yet the policy of annexation of the territories remained essentially a policy taken for lack of perceived viable alternatives: the government had embarked upon a program without accepting the ideology that underlay it. This fact was understood by the Land of Israel Movement and was a source of deep anxiety to it. For the Movement had not been successful in restoring what had once been a widespread belief among the Jews of Palestine, even while they were a small minority in the country, that the historic Land of Israel belonged to them. There was no real sense of legitimacy concerning the new borders, no transformation of consciousness to make Israelis view Hebron as indistinguishable from Tel Aviv. A soldier after the 1967 war voiced a sense of loss for the old Israel, saying that he felt Israelis had lost something very precious, their little country, and he felt no emotional ties to the broader areas Israel held today.[83] Sometimes the Movement was hopeful that this would change over time: "In twenty years the elementary attachment to Israel in her historical natural boundaries was shaken and for that reason only slowly does consciousness ripen concerning the necessity to keep the country in its entirety for settlement and newcomers. But the feeling is implanted more and more both in the people and the government and will win out."[84] A year later, the Movement was quoting the words of a member who had died, novelist Haim Hazaz, who had lamented that there had developed "a heresy in our Zionist essence concerning our right to this land that undermines us from inside and gnaws at us."[85]

This same problem troubled Dayan and seems to have been one root of his ambivalence concerning policy toward the territories. In a matter of months after the Six-Day War, Dayan was putting the question in the same manner as the Land of Israel Movement might have phrased it: "The question before us is not a question and solution of foreign policy but first and foremost a question of inner will and inner faith and the answers can only be given by ourselves. First and foremost is the question 'What are we and what do we believe in?' "[86] The erosion of legitimacy was Dayan's central concern, for this was "the axe swung against the roots of our labor."[87] Arguing against a member of the peace movement who had objected to talk of "liberated territories" when the inhabitants scarcely saw the Israelis as "liberators," Dayan said: "We do not refer to the Arab inhabitants [in speaking of the liberation of Jerusalem] but speak of ourselves—we have liberated ourselves from being cut off from Jerusalem. I am sorry if that which was central to the yearning for the return of the People of Israel to the Land of Israel is made illegitimate."[88] The Six-Day War had given Israel an opportunity. "It also imposed a test—concerning our belief in ourselves and our knowledge of what we want. If we believe and want it, the map of the Land of Israel can be determined by ourselves. If we are prepared for the political and military struggle and if we are ready to carry the full burden of the struggle I believe we can carry it through. It is in our power to withstand military tests and a political struggle, providing we can unite in seeing it the same way, the leadership and the public and the Jewish people."[89] But of course such unity did not exist, and Dayan was well aware of it. "What disturbs me is not knowing if we have the same faith we've had in the last fifty years—or rather in the last one hundred years—since Jews began to immigrate to Israel about a century ago. . . . What I am afraid of, and it would be a disaster, is that we are losing our heart, our faith."[90]

To Dayan it was clear that the course he advocated meant continued warfare with the Arab states and diplomatic isolation. Were the people of Israel ready to pay that price, and did they in fact place positive value on the achievement of the original Zionist vision? *Shivat Zion* ("the return to Zion"), said Dayan, is greater than the state of Israel.[91] (This was of course basic to the Land of Israel Movement's position that the state was only a stage and a means to the realization of Zionism.) Did the people of Israel see in the densely occupied town in the hills of Samaria a city called Nablus, or did they see in it the ancient Hebrew town of Shechem? And if what they saw was Nablus, could they be brought to see Shechem? Or was Zionism a completed movement as far as Israel's people were concerned, its existing achievements to be conserved, and change a threat rather than an acceptable challenge? And for all his proposals to avoid granting citizenship to Arabs of the territories, Dayan warned that keeping the territories must involve more than a will to expand the land of the state; it involved a transformation of attitude toward the Arabs of the territories. If Israel wanted to keep Hebron and Gaza, Dayan warned, her people must stop seeing them as enemies and come to view them as citizens, for otherwise the territories would ultimately be returned.[92] Certainly in his speeches, which often seem more an intellectual's uneasy probing than a conventional politician's words, there is an effort to define the nature of the problem for an Israeli public that tended to avoid the essentially moral issue which both the peace movement and the Land of Israel Movement addressed.

In a sense this uncertainty may seem surprising for the data from public opinion polls consistently showed a majority of Israelis (as the

TABLE I: *Willingness to Return Territories in Order to Obtain Peace*

Percentage of those not willing to return occupied territories

Area	February[1] 1968	April[2] 1968	November[3] December 1968	February[4] March 1969	March[5] April 1971	May[6] July 1972	October[7] November 1972
Golan Heights	99	98	94	97	92	92	93
Sharm el Sheikh	93	91	82	87	91	90	96
Gaza Strip	85	86	73	75	70	69	66
West Bank	91	92	73	75	56	47	58
Sinai Desert	57	66	46	52	31	36	41

Source: Israel Institute of Applied Social Research Survey VII, p. 72.
The range of possible responses varied in the following way:
1. (*a*) not to keep; (*b*) to keep;
2. same as above;
3. (*a*) not to keep; (*b*) depends on conditions; (*c*) to keep;
4. same as the third survey;
5. (*a*) to concede everything; (*b*) to concede only part; (*c*) not to concede anything;
6. (*a*) to return everything; (*b*) to return most of the areas; (*c*) to return only a certain part; (*d*) not willing to return anything;
7. source: *The New York Times*, April 19, 1973. The range of possible responses was not specified. However, the following information was included: 59 percent said that they were willing to return part of Sinai in exchange for peace without specifying which part; only 5 percent would give back most of the territory of the West Bank, and only 3 percent would return all of it.
From Abel Jacob, "Trends in Israeli Public Opinion on Issues Related to the Arab-Israel Conflict," *The Jewish Journal of Sociology*, vol.16, no. 2, December 1974, p. 194. Reprinted with permission.

accompanying table shows, in most cases a very large majority) in favor of keeping all the territories except Sinai, which was precisely the area where Dayan was in favor of major compromise. As Abel Jacob has noted, the apparent reduction in the proportion of those unwilling to return territory over time is an artifact of the questions asked and does not reflect a change in public opinion,[93] which remained stable and in some cases (Sharm el Sheikh for example) hardened against return.[94] Poll data of this sort underlay the Land of Israel Movement's conviction that one could trust the sound instincts of the "man in the street" and, coupled with the public confidence in Dayan, undoubtedly contributed to the government's reluctance to alienate him to the point where he might make an alliance with the political parties committed to keeping the territories.

On the other hand, neither Dayan nor the Land of Israel Movement leaders were overly impressed with the results of these polls, for the sentiments expressed contrasted with other sentiments and above all with overt behavior. At the same time that 95 percent were saying that they were unwilling to return "most" of the West Bank,[95] 80 percent were expressing their satisfaction with the government,[96] whose policy continued to be opposition to settlement there. And most important, the public continued to give the largest number of votes to the Labor Alignment rather than to the parties whose platforms called for retention of territories. Whatever the opinions of the majority of Israelis concerning the territories, the issue was not the most salient issue in determining voting behavior, and Dayan's suspicion regarding the real meaning of these polls was well founded.

In retrospect it would appear that only in the case of Jerusalem, which both legally and emotionally became defined as part of the state of Israel, did the Six-Day War have an impact in transforming consciousness. Ironically, the effect of the war was more significant in throwing doubt on the legitimacy of Israel's right to the land it held prior to that war. The reason for this was that the war made the Palestinians' search for national identity an issue in the Israeli consciousness. Israelis had been aware of the problem of the refugees before, but the solution had been seen as lying in resettlement in some combination of Arab countries. Now, influenced by the peace movement, many Israelis redefined the problem as a national one; and since the claim of the Palestinians was to Palestine, a large part of which was occupied by the state of Israel, legitimation of the Palestinian claim was bound to cast at least some doubt on the Jewish claim.

The ideological conflict within Israel which threatened the government's cohesion occurred in the context of unfamiliar freedom to formulate policy created by the failure of the great powers to agree on an imposed solution for the region. Israel had been forced to retreat in 1956, and in the period immediately after the Six-Day War it looked as if such pressures might well be put once again upon the state. With the failure of the first round of the Jarring talks, the United States in the early part of 1969 embarked upon four-power talks at the urging of France, and two-power talks continued intermittently with the Soviet Union. But in neither of these formats did a consensus emerge, not because of disagreements concerning the necessity of a large-scale Israeli withdrawal, but because the United States supported Israel's insistence upon direct negotiations and a contractual peace, whereas the other powers simply backed the Arab position calling for a restoration of the June 1967 situation. The emergence of United States–Soviet détente also seemed to strengthen Israel's ability to impose her own will upon the territories, for it suggested that neither side would permit open warfare to break out in the Middle East to threaten East-West accommodation. The dismissal of Soviet advisers from Egypt in 1972 also was a favorable development from Israel's point of view, for it made her enemies seem less threatening. This also increased Israel's readiness to make concessions in relation to Egypt, but the readiness for concessions was concentrated there.

Before the October war the Nixon administration had turned its attention to the Middle East, and new pressures would undoubtedly have been placed upon Israel even in the absence of another war. Nonetheless, it is doubtful that the American government could have accomplished more than temporary accommodation with Egypt based on partial Israeli withdrawal, for which there was consensus in the Labor party. In respect to the Golan and the West Bank the Arabs wanted more, for less, than the Israeli government would have been prepared to give (or the United States to force her to give). This would have meant the perpetuation of the status quo in these areas, with continuing pressures for implementation of the Land of Israel Movement's ideology.

In summary, then, both the Land of Israel Movement and the peace movement, saw themselves as existing to provide ideological alternatives, alternate "symbolic universes" for decision makers, should their own policies prove incapable of realization. Both movements offered policies based upon traditional conceptions of Zionism applied to current realities, and saw themselves as addressing transcendent issues which should override party differences. There was no notion on the part of either movement of achieving power, for both movements saw themselves as intellectual in character, with the prime function of education: education of decision makers and the broader public for the creation of policy in terms of moral ideals. Commenting on the mani-

festo of the Land of Israel Movement, Zvi Shiloah said: "This document is of historic importance if we win—if history goes our way. We
gave new dimension to the conception of *shlemut haaretz* [the fullness
of the land]."[97] Menachem Dorman, confessing the organizational
weaknesses of the Movement, said "The Movement is not winning; its
ideas are winning."[98] And Efraim Ben-Haim asserted that in the end
the government would have to accept the Movement's ideas against its
own will, for it had no alternative.[99]

The peace movement saw itself as having additional functions. On
the one hand, as we have seen, it legitimated international constraints.
But some within the peace movement emphasized its expressive function. Gad Yatsiv, for example, leader of the peace list which ran for
election to the Knesset in 1969, spoke of its value as mental therapy:
"A reality in which the best political alternative left in the hands of
the Government is to send its sons to death is not a reality to which a
mentally healthy people can acquiesce. Anyone who does not understand this truth shows that he is unable to fathom the monstrous dimension of our life. This refusal to accept the present reality does not
necessarily have political consequences. This non-acceptance is not a
sign of defeatism, it is one of the healthy instincts of a life-loving social
organism. This type of protest is an important element in our capacity
to hold our own. This protest against the present reality is the real
'realism.' "[100] Others felt it was essential to express moral imperatives,
regardless of whether these could be translated into action. Joshua
Arieli said that, even though it might be necessary to hold the territories for a long period, there was an enormous difference between a
policy forced on Israel by circumstances and one chosen by her as
desirable.[101]

The government found itself forced, if it wished to avoid total inaction, to experiment with implementing the ideologies of both movements. It never gave credit to either one and continued successfully to
define both as irresponsible and extremist. But increasingly, government members found themselves forced to align themselves with one
or the other ideology; in this way these marginal movements cracked
the government's consensus, and the debate between the movements
became an internal government debate. The government moved, for
reasons that have been outlined, toward the Land of Israel Movement.
But that movement failed in its educational effort with consequences
that were to prove extremely significant. For, since no basic commitment to the territories as part of the state of Israel developed in the
consciousness of the majority, of either the government or the public,
once circumstances changed and pressures for territorial concessions
became severe, there was no universal violent sense of outrage—as

would have been the case if a consensus had developed concerning the legitimacy of Israel's hold upon the territories. A dramatic shift in policy away from the Land of Israel Movement and toward the peace movement was thus possible after the October war, precisely because the course upon which the country was embarked had been taken through lack of alternatives and not through internalization of its ideological basis by the majority. Nonetheless, within subgroups there had indeed been a change of consciousness, and this change meant growing internal strain as the government shifted its course.

6
The Resurgence of Ideology in Israel

Thus far we have been dealing with a process which is, presumably, ordinary enough, even if it tends to receive little emphasis in historical study: movements of intellectuals have defined ideological alternatives; and decision makers, under pressure of a combination of internal and external constraints, have moved reluctantly toward the adoption of one of these alternatives, without even grudging acknowledgment of the ideological debt. The peace movement in the United States, similarly might be considered as essentially an ideological movement providing alternative models of action and of orientation to the world for the government of a great power, which was subject to unfamiliar but serious constraints in its conduct of the Vietnam War. In such a situation there is no revolution, not even necessarily a change in decision makers; there is simply a change of policy, although such a change frequently is a fundamental one with far-reaching consequences for the value structure of the society.

But what is unusual in the case of Israel is that we witness a sharp and remarkable reversal: through the imposition of external constraints, the "normal" process is halted and decision makers embark immediately upon a process of implementing the programs of the movement that was, in terms of internal dynamics, *losing*. As a result, the impact of both movements promised to grow, rather than being confined to a role of providing ideological alternatives for decision makers. If the Land of Israel Movement's ideology had been implemented this provision of alternatives might indeed have been the entire function of these movements, for that ideology was being implemented so gradually that a consensus might have developed before the process was complete. The continued opposition of a small fringe peace movement would then have been of little significance. But the government's reversal of its ideological course under conditions of external pressures and the threat of war prevented the development of consensus; indeed, the resulting public disorientation threatened to destroy the traditional framework of Israeli politics and to produce a resurgence of ideology unknown since the pre-independence period. This ideological resurgence entailed the emergence of basic challenges to the legitimacy of the state's institutions, examined in relation to differing interpretations of Zionist goals.

138

The immediate impact of the Yom Kippur War was to reinforce—even for elements of the peace movement—the ideology of the Land of Israel Movement. In the early days of the war a group of intellectuals, including several who were prominently associated with the peace movement, published a letter in which they attributed Israel's ability to withstand the surprise attack to her control of the territories and emphasized that in any future peace settlement "the secure nature of the boundaries" was an imperative concern;[1] and Amnon Rubinstein, a journalist and law professor whose writings were in sympathy with the peace movement, wrote an article for the *New York Times* asserting that in Israel there were now "no more doves."[2] Such reactions lend credence to the assumption that, had the war ended with a speedy and decisive Israeli victory on the pattern of the 1967 war, the effect would have been to strengthen greatly the power of the Land of Israel Movement's ideology. Those who had urged the importance of the territories as buffer areas would have been seen as vindicated; the hawks within the government, especially Dayan as victorious Minister of Defense once again, would have been strengthened; and the government would probably have undertaken implementation of the Galili document in earnest, much more rapidly than it would have without the impact of the war. The great powers would have been reminded of the explosiveness of the Middle East, to be sure; but the United States would have had little leverage on a dramatically victorious Israel which might have continued willing, at best, to negotiate a partial withdrawal in Sinai.

But of course the war did not end that way. In Henry Kissinger's phrase, and partly of Kissinger's doing, Israel, tactically the winner, was strategically the loser.[3] The equivocal results of the war were such as to allow the government, as well as the movements that opposed its policy, to argue that the war proved the correctness of previous assumptions. One company commander at the front, asked the effect of the war on his men's political thinking, replied: "Well, I believe that everyone is more convinced now of what he thought before."[4] Government spokesmen argued that the war proved how right the government had been to reject territorial compromise without "true peace." For the Land of Israel Movement the war, by revealing anew the depth of Arab hostility, was striking proof that Israel needed the strategic depth of the post-1967 boundaries on a permanent basis; these boundaries had allowed Israel to survive even under conditions of surprise attack, government bungling, and inadequate preparation, and yet recover to penetrate within striking distance of Cairo and Damascus. But the peace movement argued that had its advice been heeded—had Israel declared its readiness to return the territories, recognized the national aspirations of the Palestinians, and accepted "arrangements" and stages toward peace in lieu of unobtainable full contractual peace—there would have been no war. For the peace movement the war was proof that the concept of "defensible borders" was worthless, for these had not prevented war.

For the government the culpable failure (*mechdal,* as it was called in Israel) at the outbreak of the war was a technical one. Intelligence reports had been wrongly evaluated, with the result that the reserves had not been called up until just hours before the war, too late to prevent the success of initial Arab assaults. But for both the Land of Israel Movement and the peace movement, the technical error was simply a reflection of a far more profound failure. For the peace movement the failure was the government's policy of "creeping annexation" which gave the Arabs no alternative but to seek the return of their territories by force. The Hebrew University's Jacob Talmon wrote:

We continued to declare our readiness, our demand for direct negotiations without prior conditions and at the same time the ruling party in Israel adopted the resolution, partly written doctrine, but its more operative part an oral doctrine, concerning settlement. . . . The unfortunate Galili document talked of a four year plan for settlement and acquisition of lands in the territories and Mr. Dayan prophesied concerning a port city in the approaches to Rafiah to include 350,000 inhabitants. Such transparent deception could only cause loathing in the wider world and deepen in the Arab world the recognition that indeed all hope for accommodation was over—the Arabs had nothing further to lose.[5]

The government, then, brought the war upon itself by its intransigence and arrogance, by its contempt for both the political rights and the military potential of the Arabs. The government misinterpreted intelligence reports because it misinterpreted the whole situation; it relied blindly on the protection given by territory, (partly, in the peace movement's view, because the government had accepted the Land of Israel Movement's ideology) and on the deterrence of military might, rather than on the need for the protection given by Arab acceptance of the state's legitimacy, following territorial relinquishment.

For the Land of Israel Movement, the government's underlying failure was in not having truly incorporated the territories into Israel. The Suez Canal was insufficiently defended because Dayan never really wanted to keep the East Bank of the Canal but continually sought ways to return it to Egypt; the equivocal nature of the government's commitment to the territories led to their equivocal defense. The technical *mechdal* was only the symptom of the moral collapse within the labor movement that provided Israel's leadership, which had become "a compromising cosmopolitan watered-down Brit Shalom, anti-national and anti-pioneering."[6] The loss of faith in the Zionist ideal of joining together people and land had led to the leadership's emphasis upon sectarian goals over national ones, and this in turn had produced the politicization of the military forces, whereby considerations of competence had been replaced by political criteria for promotion. Increasingly swayed by the peace movement's criticisms of Israel as the guilty partner in the conflict, the government had fallen prey to the concomitant perception that Israel had nothing to fear from the Arabs. The technical *mechdal* was rooted in the government's failure to perceive the legitimacy of its own title to the land of Israel. An article in *Zot Haaretz* pointed out that this basic problem had been understood with a poet's sensitivity by Uri Zvi Greenberg. Two days before the Yom Kippur War, at a time when Golda Meir in a New Year message to the nation talked of the "ever growing strength of the Israel Defense Forces and the increasing strength of our national enterprise," leading some of Israel's neighbors to realize "they have no wars to win,"[7] Greenberg published a poem on the impending loss of Jerusalem:

Anxiety in my bones today.
I come to you with the feeling of one again
Banished slowly and stealthily from the sacred landscapes;
Unredeemed landscapes of the enfeebled
Although still in the hands of the Fire Riders, sons of Joshua Ben Nun today;
And like the fickle, who do not know why they are that way,
So I, who differ from them in my view of the future
Cannot grasp with my reason
Why and wherefore this verdict of "lost tomorrow" can be possible
With Jewish signature upon the paper:
Back to the bottleneck.[8]

Even Jerusalem, the most sacred city of the Jewish people, will be lost, the poet senses, because those who hold it have lost their knowledge of why it is theirs and are prepared indeed to sign it away.

The war, while producing widespread but diffused dissatisfaction with the government, did not produce a wave of new converts to the existing movements. It did produce a wave of protest movements, composed largely of demobilized soldiers, but these were frankly anti-ideological, directed against the leadership rather than against its policies. Lacking tradition and any alternate ideology, these movements served as typical cases of collective behavior in which large numbers of individuals, confused, anxious, and disoriented by the failure of the institutional structures, went through the processes of milling and social contagion in search for new leadership and new norms.[9] Active protest groups searching for new norms were obvious targets for those with an ideology to provide; but the protest movements, not wanting to be captured by any existing ideology, sought issues on which almost all citizens could agree. Thus the protests broadened from attack on specific leaders to an attempt to reform the process by which leaders were selected and generally to enhance the "quality of life" in Israel. Those active in the protest movements were imbued with the hope that if Israel could produce better leaders—and they argued that potential leadership existed, although stifled and never brought forward because of the undemocratic methods by which the parties selected their representatives—these leaders might safely be left to themselves to find and follow better policies. The Land of Israel Movement sought to convince the protest movements' leaders that if they wanted change in any sphere, the only way to obtain it was by a change in government, which could only be brought about by the Likud. But the protest movements in practice found more in common, in the short run at least, with the peace movement. The two found common cause in the effort to bring down the leadership, especially Golda Meir and Moshe Dayan. To the peace movement these leaders represented the government's policy of annexation, while to the protest movements, they were those chiefly responsible for the wrong assessments of Arab intentions prior to the Yom Kippur attack. The Land of Israel Movement was deeply disappointed by the protest movements, which in its view were preoccupied with style rather than substance, with individuals rather than policies. Issues on which all could agree, said the Movement, were precisely those not central to the fate of the state.[10]

But despite the failure of the Yom Kippur War to provide new ideologies or even to produce any significant conversions to existing ideologies, the war had the impact of introducing constraints: powerful external ones in the form of united pressure from the great powers, and internal constraints which were produced by the enormous military losses, particularly in the crucial officer group, that made time for rebuilding the army essential and left a deep war-weariness in the population. The combined impact of these factors forced the government to make an abrupt shift in its policy. While eventually the leadership changed and individuals were brought to the fore who had greater sympathy to the ideology of the peace movement, initially the changes were carried out by the old leadership.

The swift change in direction by the existing leadership was possible because of the ambivalent attitude, noted earlier, toward the policies being carried out prior to the war. Most of the leadership had never adopted the ideology of the Land of Israel Movement but had been pushed toward adopting its programs. While the implementation of programs would eventually have necessitated adoption of the underlying justifications, the Yom Kippur War occurred while this process was still in a relatively early stage.[11] In fact, the government could look upon the outcome of the war as a victory for its own earlier policies. Not only did United Nations Security Council Resolution 338 call for immediate negotiations between the parties "under appropriate auspices aimed at establishing a just and durable peace in the Middle East," but the Arab states for the first time seemed to have accepted the idea of direct negotiations without prior conditions which the Israeli government had so long set as its goal.[12] Israeli leaders could argue that they had always said the Arabs would agree eventually to such negotiations, and their optimism had been vindicated.[13]

The change in course was obvious enough. What was called "disengagement" on the Egyptian and Syrian front was, in effect, the beginning of the implementation of the peace movement's policy of withdrawal by stages and violated the policy, adopted formally in the 1969 coalition agreement, that "the Army will not move from the 1967 cease-fire lines until contractual peace is achieved." The government scrapped the Galili document prior to the elections and substituted a fourteen-point program that put the search for peace as the main target of the state and made only the most perfunctory reference to settlement, which would be continued "in keeping with cabinet decisions giving priority to national security consideration." The accent was now on withdrawal, not settlement, and the government's "doves" spoke with a new confidence. Finance Minister Sapir stressed the need for Israel to be "much more flexible in offering concessions,"[14] and Abba Eban spoke of the illusions of the prewar period: "the illusion that a million Arabs would be kept under Israeli control forever . . . The illusion that Zionism forbade a sharing of national sovereignty between two nations in the former Palestine Mandate area; the illusion that Israel's historic legacy was exclusively a matter of geography and not also, and principally, a heritage of prophetic values of which the central value was peace. The fallacy that to see anything temporary in some of Israel's positions west of the Jordan was tantamount to alienation from Biblical culture."[15] Even Dayan, while warning against return to the "old shrunken and twisted borders if we do not wish to see this country doomed" spoke of readiness for "far reaching concessions."[16] The Ministry of Education, in anticipation of a settlement, sent out a circular to teachers concerning the need to prepare students for the shock of finding themselves in a state of sharply reduced size.[17]

Readiness to exchange territory for peace had been a long-standing element in official government policy, but now there was a growing acknowledgment by the government's leaders that peace in the sense that the government had long insisted was the absolute condition for territorial change ("shopping in Cairo," as Golda Meir put it) was not to be expected as the outcome of negotiations. Although during the war Dayan said that after this round he saw no point in any agreement that was not a real peace settlement,[18] once it was over he talked of the need for striving for an agreement with Egypt, "not necessarily a full-fledged peace treaty" and hoped to achieve after further withdrawals a "sort of permanent non-belligerency status."[19] Yitzhak Rabin, who was to become Prime Minister after both Dayan and Golda Meir were swept out of office by the protest movements[20] and the Agranat Commission's interim report on responsibility for the *mechdal*,[21] drew the distinction between a "political settlement" achieved through diplomacy and true peace, which could come only between peoples and was a slow process.[22] (This was of course what the peace movement had argued all along and the government had denied.) The value of negotiations was defined by Rabin: "After all we do want a settlement; if not full peace then at least a state of no-war."[23] Even the direct negotiations which had so long been a cardinal point of government policy were no longer seen as desirable. Negotiations were conducted with Secretary of State Kissinger, and Israel showed no eagerness to hasten to Geneva where direct negotiations were to be conducted under the guidance of both superpowers. Actually Israel was forced to abandon even the policy of withdrawal in exchange for "pieces of peace" from the Arab states, for the interim agreement in Sinai pressed upon Israel by the United States was essentially one in which Israel gave up territory, not for any return from the Egyptians, but for arms and economic aid from the United States.

Ironically, both the peace movement and the Land of Israel Movement advocated immediate return to the Geneva talks without interim settlements: thus Geneva, in a sense the vindication of the government's policy held so long in the face of bitter criticism, was seen by the government as a forum to be avoided as long as possible and was desired by *both* opposition movements. The peace movement argued that the step-by-step approach frittered away Israel's territorial bargaining power for minor Arab concessions, and that instead Israel should make a much larger and broader territorial offer in exchange for some kind of overall settlement. The Land of Israel Movement was convinced the Arabs would offer no overall settlement acceptable to Israel at Geneva and hoped for the deadlock they saw as inevitable in that forum—a deadlock which would mean that Israel relinquished no territory.[24]

To the Land of Israel Movement the course of events was one of unmitigated disaster. The parallel repeatedly drawn was to Munich, where the Czechs had been sold out by their supposed protectors and where even the overt issue was similar—the rights of a national grouping, in that case the Sudeten Germans, to self-determination. To the Land of Israel Movement, what was particularly infuriating was that this "Munich" was taking place with the connivance of the victim. *Zot Haaretz* pointed out that at Munich the Czechs did not stand applauding in the anteroom, nor were Czech leaders photographed, smiling, with Chamberlain, nor did they celebrate his efforts (as Israeli leaders did those of Kissinger) with cocktail parties.[25] As the Movement saw it, the United States was planning to reduce Soviet influence in the region and to ensure for itself a steady supply of oil, even if at high prices, by transforming Israel from a factor in the international global balance of power into an international welfare case, a protectorate incapable of self-defense that would become no more than a nuisance to her protector, continuing to poison relations with the Arab states and draining American resources. As Israel's defense needs grew in a shrunken area, the Movement warned, so would United States unwillingness to meet them. The government was deceiving the Israeli public, "calling retreat 'political momentum,' capitulation 'decent compromise' and collapse 'peace.' "[26] The Movement argued that the government should have tried to alert the American Jewish community to the disastrous course of American policy rather than neutralizing it by proclaiming satisfaction with United States policy.[27]

The peace movement was of course pleased with the direction the government had taken since the war, but anxiety continued. Rabin's government represented the long-awaited "generational transfer" from the founders to the sons and included more members clearly in sympathy with the peace movement's ideology (Dayan said he had never imagined such a government in his darkest dreams).[28] But within it were also some of the former hawks.[29] Rabin was an unknown quantity, but his quickly apparent antagonism to a new Palestinian state, indeed to any negotiations with the terrorists, alarmed the peace movement, within which there was growing consensus in the aftermath of the 1973 war that the creation of a Palestinian state on the West Bank and in Gaza was the most promising course of action.[30] In the view of the peace movement the new government failed, as the old had done, to come forward with its own detailed plan for peace.[31]

Although the war produced no significant increase in membership in the Land of Israel Movement and peace movements, and although the process of institutionalization continued as important sections of both movements merged into political parties, the impact of the ideologies of these movements deepened as their ideas threatened to break apart the framework of Israeli politics. The threat was a severe one, for the Israeli political system had proved among the most stable in the post-war western world, with a single party, democratically elected, retaining uninterrupted power.

In the first chapter we noted that Israeli politics, while retaining bitter ideological overtones for the rank and file, had moved toward consensus at the elite level. The period between the Six-Day War and the Yom Kippur War saw national-foreign policy issues gaining increased saliency when, for the first time, genuine choices for action were seen to lie before Israel. While tension developed within the ruling United Labor party as well as within its chief coalition partner, the National Religious party, successful accommodations continued to be reached, the last reflection of which prior to the 1973 war was the Galili document. These accommodations reflected the balance of opinion in the country rather than in the Labor party, for although Gahal was out of the government after 1970, Dayan and his Rafi following within the Labor party in effect served as spokesmen for the Gahal ideology and Dayan's position was so strong precisely because he represented a large body of opinion outside the Labor party. From Labor's point of view, the danger that Dayan and his following might leave the party was sufficiently serious that substantial accommodation to his views was seen as essential.

The war, which precipitated the government's ideological reversal and upset the previous pattern of accommodation, and its aftermath, which forced continual and unattractive choices upon the government, gave the national issue obvious transcendent importance. It appeared that the Labor Alignment, its internal differences so long papered over, might sooner or later split apart in a crisis forced by some decision on the national issue. Such a split, it seemed, would cut across the traditional divisions of Mapai, Achdut Haavoda, and Rafi, the activists moving into some form of alliance with Likud,[32] the others moving toward closer identification with the goals of the peace movement. Special-interest parties, notably the religious parties, which had traditionally avoided positions on both economic and foreign policies, could not escape this process of internal polarization and would themselves be subject to split.

But the signs of strain were not confined to the Labor and religious parties.[33] In the aftermath of the 1973 war, Likud, too, became divided on the same issues. Its component parties retained their separate identities; and the Liberal party, whose voters were primarily small businessmen and independent farmers, had never shared Herut's nationalist spirit. But even within Herut itself and within the other small parties that had joined Gahal to create the Likud there was dissension on these issues.[34] Thus, almost all of the parties could easily break asunder under the stress of coming to basic decisions on the national issue. For ultimately, although the issue of policy toward the Arabs and the territories could be called one of "foreign policy," it was a national issue—one which involved the definition of the state of Israel, the nature of its tasks as a nation, and the goals of its existence. Ironically, the anti-ideological protest groups, if they were successful in pushing electoral reforms, could presumably contribute to the process of polarization by reducing the number and the power of small parties.

These dangers were apparent to the Labor Alignment in the aftermath of the war, but it found no solution. In an effort to avoid the immediate threat of a split within Labor, the government moved for the first time to build a coalition on the very "size principle" previously antithetical to Israeli political practice. A "wall-to-wall" coalition could have been constructed on the pattern of the 1967 coalition, accepted as appropriate for situations of national emergency. Certainly Likud was anxious to participate; in its election platform, the party did not even ask for a mandate to govern, but rather for a mandate to participate in such a national emergency coalition. The National Religious party was anxious for such a coalition and even promised to put aside its controversial demands on the perennially troublesome "Who is a Jew?" issue if it were formed.[35] All polls showed the public wanted a coalition, and interestingly this was true of almost as high a percentage of voters for the Labor Alignment as of voters for the Likud.[36] But the Labor Alignment refused, and while its official position was that this would be a government of "national paralysis" because the Likud would prevent peace through territorial compromise, the essential consideration was that a national emergency coalition would destroy the heart of the Labor coalition and might split the Labor Alignment itself. Both Mapam and the Independent Liberals threatened to bolt if the national emergency government were formed, and they would presumably take with them members of the Labor Alignment most oriented toward the peace movement's ideology. Under these circumstances a government of national unity might in effect become a Gahal-dominated government. The Labor Alignment thus chose to save labor cohesion and when, after the downfall of Golda Meir's government, the National Religious party again made difficult demands,[37] the Alignment constructed a coalition with a majority of a single vote.[38] Later efforts by Prime Minister Rabin to widen the coalition through bringing back the National Religious party, which out of power was moving into informal alliance with Gahal,[39] encountered stiff opposition within his coalition; the new Citizens Rights Movement withdrew rather than remain in coalition with the National Religious party.[40]

But although the Labor Alignment had salvaged labor unity and retained hegemony, the continued dissension within Labor meant that it was unlikely to be able to follow the path of the peace movement, along which it had started, to the end of the road, and that it certainly could not do so on the basis of existing alignments. There was consensus in Israel on the desirability of negotiations, a consensus which was so strong that even the Likud, whose Herut leadership believed nothing good for Israel could possibly emerge, was forced to advocate entering into them. But there was no comparable consensus on the extent of the concessions Israel could offer.

What agreement there was centered on Egypt; and the policy upon which the Israeli government embarked, under pressure from, but also in cooperation with, Secretary of State Henry Kissinger, was essentially the policy advocated by Dayan prior to the Yom Kippur War of trying to split off Egypt from the other Arab states.[41] The various interim withdrawals advocated by Kissinger, including the strategic passes and the oil fields of Abu Rodeis, offered Egypt less territory than Dayan had sought to give Egypt prior to the Yom Kippur War when he had attempted to defuse the situation in relation to Israel's most formidable adversary and give Israel the opportunity of "realizing Zionism" in the rest of the territories. Rabin openly stated his belief that, even without peace territorial concessions to Egypt were justified because it was a cardinal Israeli interest to detach Egypt from the other Arab states and from the Soviet camp—so that in the best case, should Syria attack, Egypt would not join in, and in the worst, even if Egypt joined in, she might do so with less determination.[42]

The willingness, bordering on eagerness, to make territorial concessions in Sinai, could of course be interpreted as an application of realpolitik, and the policy was explained in those terms by Dayan. Once the chief Arab military power was taken out of the conflict, it was reasonable to argue, Israel's other neighbors would be in no position to make war by themselves. And yet the argument could as easily have been turned around: it might have been argued that the Sinai, with its vast empty spaces, served Israel as a vital buffer against her most serious enemy, while its known and potential resources made it essential to Israel's economy. The importance of the historical tie, or rather the lack of it in the case of Sinai, cannot be overlooked in explaining Israel's willingness to make concessions there. Despite the absence of population, the strategic value of the area, and its importance as Israel's only major source of oil, Sinai was by far the easiest territory to relinquish, for it had never been accepted as part of the Land of Israel. The nontraditional aspect of the Land of Israel Movement's ideology had been its insistence that Sinai must remain an integral part of the state, and even in 1975 the Likud had not come to share this perspective.[43]

Where "the liberated homeland" was concerned, there were basic disagreements in Israeli society. Both the Likud and the National Religious party opposed withdrawal from the West Bank. One of its leaders, Yitzhak Raphael, announced that while the National Religious party had approved Israel's acceptance of Security Council Resolution 242, the territorial concessions the National Religious party had in mind were confined to Egypt, and that the resolution had no significance, in the Party's eyes, in relation to Judea and Samaria.[44] Opposition to withdrawal on the West Bank was more intense than it was to withdrawal on the Golan, although on the Golan a number of Israeli settlements had been established; the land was empty of Arab population (Druse settlements there had announced they would ask to be relocated in Israel if the Golan were returned to Syria); and a Syrian presence would once again threaten the settlements of the northern Galilee which had been shelled regularly prior to the 1967 war. There was strong opposition to withdrawal on the Golan as well.[45] Nonetheless, the Likud's Ariel Sharon argued for the possibility of further territorial compromise in both Sinai and the Golan, but said there was no room for any territorial concessions whatever on the West Bank.[46]

In terms of realistic considerations the West Bank might have seemed most inviting for compromise. Heavily populated by Arabs, it constituted the core of the "demographic danger." Moreover, the West Bank could be restored to the rule of Israel's relatively moderate neighbor, Jordan—or at least so it appeared until the 1974 Rabat summit denied the legitimacy of Hussein's claim to the territory. The explanation for the fact that even before the Rabat summit the sharpest opposition to withdrawal focused on the West Bank could only lie in the ongoing power of the religious ideology described in Chapter 2. The West Bank was the most difficult area to relinquish because it was the core area of the promised land and of historic Israel.

As far as public opinion was concerned, there was surprisingly little change as the result of the Yom Kippur war. A series of polls conducted by Israel's Institute for Applied Social Research during the war and immediately following it showed that, although there was some rise during the war in the proportion of Israelis opposed to relinquishing territory, by the end of the war the figures were approximately what they had been before the war began.[47] Since the willingness to make concessions in Sinai thus continued to exist after the war as it had before October 1973, the government was not operating outside the framework of majority opinion in its search for an interim agreement with Egypt. While Rabin won overwhelming approval with his refusal to accept Sadat's conditions after Kissinger's March 1975 shuttle, two-thirds of the public thought the government should try to renew the talks and the majority thought this should be done through Secretary of State Kissinger.[48] On the other hand, a poll in November 1974 showed that three-quarters of the public wanted expansion of Jewish settlement on the West Bank and two-thirds agreed with the proposition that Israel should "declare immediately that Judea and Samaria are part of the State of Israel."[49]

There seems little doubt that, if peace were offered in exchange for territory, the majority of Israelis of all parties would have considered the exchange worth making, and the ruling Labor Alignment would not have experienced undue difficulty in taking the population with it the full length of the road advocated by the peace movement. This was indicated by a country-wide poll, commissioned by the Tel Aviv newspaper *Haaretz,* which found that almost 50 percent of the people said they were willing to return to the pre-1967 borders—with minor adjustments—in exchange for a final peace treaty.[50] But to the majority there seemed little prospect of a genuine peace; after the Yom Kippur War feelings remained substantially what they had been before the war, with roughly 80 percent pessimistic concerning the prospects for peace.[51] Indeed, polls taken following 1973 showed 83 percent of those interviewed expecting a new war "within a year or two."[52] The optimism concerning a change in Arab attitudes and the possibility of reaching a stable peace agreement reflected in United States government policy did not find an echo in Israeli public opinion.

What did seem probable was that if Israel retreated to the old borders, the burden of attack upon her might be shifted in the short term at least to the Palestinians, enshrined by international demand in a new Palestinian state under the leadership of the Palestinian Liberation Organization. The Palestinian problem had been redefined internationally from one of refugees to one of national self-determination. This formulation found expression in the October 1974 Rabat summit at which the Arab states, including Jordan, acknowledged Yassir Arafat as the "absolute" representative of the Palestinian people and the legitimate claimant to all territory on the West Bank relinquished by Israel; in the various forms of diplomatic recognition extended to the Palestine Liberation Organization even by nations maintaining relations with Israel; and in the United Nations forums.[53]

While the peace movement grew increasingly unified in placing its faith in a new Palestinian state as the solution to the Arab-Israel problem, the majority felt deeply threatened. Dayan said: "I am ready to shout and fight that no such Palestinian state come into being. . . . I regard it as the beginning of the destruction of the State of Israel."[54] Opponents feared a Palestinian state would become a lethal irredentist base against Israel (and possibly Jordan), while enjoying the full military and political backing of the Soviet Union and most of the other Arab states. Moreover, there was an implicit threat to Israeli sovereignty in a new Palestinian state which, as heir to the legitimacy of the original partition voted by the United Nations, might begin by arguing that Israel must return to the borders of the partition plan of 1947 which, it could be maintained, were the only legitimately recognized international borders.

For the government it meant that relinquishing territory on the West Bank became much more difficult. The solution a majority within the cabinet had contemplated after the Six-Day War was obvious enough: give Jordan a corridor into the West Bank at Jericho and then allow it to resume sovereignty over the areas heavily occupied by Arabs in two enclaves, one in Samaria, the other in Judea, while Israel retained control of the land along the Jordan and the Dead Sea. (See Map VIII.) But such a plan was obviously incapable of implementation if the task was not restoration of territory to a state viable even without it, but creation of a new state dependent wholly upon West Bank territory.

The prospects were extremely threatening. At Geneva, Israel faced unanimous agreement among the Arab states that there must be Israeli withdrawal to the lines existing prior to June 1967, and that Israel must relinquish sovereignty over the Old City of Jerusalem, symbolically central to Israel. It also appeared obvious that the demand for large-scale territorial withdrawal would have the backing of both superpowers. United States policy had never changed on this issue, although the Rogers Plan of December 1969, which formally enunciated the policy of only "insubstantial border changes," had been dropped from discussion after vigorous Israeli protests and the United States had embarked upon an approach emphasizing a partial agreement at the Canal. While Kissinger had not formally resuscitated the Rogers Plan, it was clear from his statements that he envisaged extensive Israeli retreat, to the point where Israel's ability to defend herself would come into serious question in the eyes of her leadership.[55]

Given Israeli fears of Arab intentions, any political settlement would necessarily rely heavily on demilitarized zones, United Nations forces, and great-power guarantees.[56] And yet these offered no genuine security. Professor Jochanan Bloch, a member of the Land of Israel Movement, published in *Zot Haaretz* in 1975 a vision of the future which articulated possibilities that must have occurred independently to members of the government.

But the worse our position becomes, the more we will be dependent upon the help of the United States. . . . A peace treaty we won't get; guarantees we'll get. Here there will be demilitarization; there will sit a U.N. force; here will be a corridor; there a mixed police force; here shared administration; there an enclave. Immigration will stop for such a state will not be able to attract Aliya. Emigration will resume and reach dimensions which have never been known. An economic crisis will reign in comparison to which the austerity regime prior to 1967 was a bed of roses. Defense expenditures will not decrease but grow in direct proportion to the worsening of our situation. And peace? It is clear that the Palestinian forces will increase their activity with the support of the Arab states, even if for the time being those states don't enter into war with us. Our defensive capability will be desperately handicapped in the choking collar of the "peace borders" and the international guard forces. And then we shall turn to our friendly protecting powers, and will ask for their help. And it isn't hard to guess what they will say.

They'll tell us that they are not willing to get involved in a world war. That we are not allowed to bring the world to war. The process of blackmail will begin. If the immigration should not have stopped by itself they'll demand that we stop it. And the guaranteeing powers will explain to us that it is evil for us to exist on this outdated Zionist principle that can drag us to war. They'll demand that we bring back the refugees and we will haggle whether a hundred thousand or two hundred thousand. In reality we will return to the Mandate period and in two or three years they will say in America that the "experiment of the Jewish state" has failed, and that one has to look for a reasonable solution to the problem of Israel. And why not a Palestinian state in which one will guarantee the lives of the Jews? What began with the silly slogan "territories for peace" is likely to end with the liquidation of the state, unless we can retrace our steps and escape from that nightmarish trap which we made with our own hands.[57]

Dayan put the problem more succinctly: "If we bow to all the withdrawal demands, then all we will have is a caricature of a state and what kind of security will we have then?"[58]

In other words, powerful as were the external constraints that operated toward pushing Israel into retreat to the old borders, all the external constraints did not operate the same way: continued Arab hostility served as a powerful constraint against doing so. And internal constraints, too, operated in both directions. The Israeli public was deeply fearful of the casualties another war, even a successful one, would entail, especially since another war held no prospect of resulting in peace, but only of postponing another confrontation. And Israelis worried that superpower pressures, at worst Soviet involvement, might rob them of the ability to inflict a decisive defeat even at the cost of heavy casualties.[59] On the other hand, there was the fear that retreats would only produce further pressures while reducing the state's ability to defend its citizenry. And, not to be minimized, there was the religio-historical attachment felt by a significant portion of the population for the provinces of Judea and Samaria, coupled now with the difficulty of finding any acceptable Arab leadership to which they could be relinquished. As Israel moved away from negotiations with Egypt, where comparatively little internal dissension was produced by territorial concessions, and toward Syria and most serious of all "the Palestinians," the risk grew that concessions on the scale demanded would result in an unacceptable degree of internal polarization.

For the major impact of the 1973 war upon public opinion was not in changing attitudes toward retention of territory or in altering perception of Arab attitudes toward Israel, but in reducing confidence in the government. Thus, while from 1967 to 1970 confidence in the government's handling of Israel's problems generally was in the range of 70 to 80 percent, after the Agranat Commission's investigation revealed the extent of the government's failures prior to the war, the confidence level fell substantially to hover in the neighborhood of 50 percent.[60] The waning level of confidence left the government with a smaller margin of ability to make unpopular decisions. Four out of five Israelis prior to the Yom Kippur War agreed with the statement that "Even if the United States placed great pressure upon Israel to return to the old borders, Israel should refuse to do so." After the war, as the prospect took on greater immediacy and as uncertainty concerning the country's ability to hold its own rose, the level of agreement declined to around 70 percent, still a substantial majority.[61] Dramatic territorial concessions made under external pressure could produce internal reactions that would bring down the government that made them.

But whatever the government's ultimate decisions (Arab impatience at the government's slowness in arriving at them might well take decisions out of the government's hands), the debate over questions touching central values must accelerate the process of polarization on ideological grounds and introduce, for the first time since the establishment of independence, challenges to the legitimacy of the state's basic institutions.

Even before any serious external pressures for retreat began, the onset of the process of polarization within the public was apparent.

Under sponsorship of Gush Emmunim[62] there were repeated attempts by a group of would-be settlers, largely from religious backgrounds, to settle in Samaria; until December 1975 they were evicted by army units. After the successful settlement of Hebron, there had been a number of settlement attempts which had been promptly terminated by the army, and in this sense the incidents in Samaria represented nothing new. However, there were a number of important differences in this instance: The settlement effort was a serious one, not simply a demonstration against government policy. The settlers, many of them from Kiryat Arba, had planned and organized the settlement core prior to the Yom Kippur War and had sought government approval of it then.[63] And, while previous efforts had involved a hand-ful of individuals unknown to a broader public, this time Rabbi Zvi Yehuda Kuk, the aged leader of the Merkaz Harav Yeshiva and son of Israel's famed chief rabbi of the early Mandate period, a man of great prestige for religious Israelis, himself joined the settlers, as did political leaders from the Likud and the National Religious party. And this time the settlement effort brought thousands of sympathizers into Samaria.

The settlement effort had serious implications. For one thing, it forced to the surface the divisions within the Labor Alignment on the future of Judea and Samaria. Dayan, while supporting the govern-ment on the issue of the exercise of authority against those who vio-lated the law, argued in the Knesset that the government under-mined its own national and security foundations by limiting settlement to the Jordan Valley.[64] David Koren, another Labor member, went so far as to question the legality of a government prohibition against Jews settling Samaria, on the view that they were asserting an inalien-able right.[65] The settlement efforts, and additional ones that promised to follow, also had the potential effect of exacerbating the conflict between religious and secular Jews which was always simmering beneath the surface and occasionally breaking it. This conflict had been held in check because of the concentration of the religious upon what everyone perceived as specifically religious issues and their will-ingness to conform in all other respects with Labor government policy. Should cleavage develop on what the public saw as other lines (to most of the religious the maintenance of Israeli control over the Holy Land *was* a religious issue), hostility toward the religious sector of the community could deepen. Conversely, the alienation of the religious from the institutions of the state could grow. (It was significant of the importance of specifically religious values, not only that the West Bank was the area arousing greatest emotion, but also that those who took the lead in directly confronting the government in violation of the law were not Likud members, whose ideology was a nationalist one, but Israeli orthodox Jews, who were motivated by a religious conception of Israel's tie to the land.)

And finally, the decision of the government to expel the settlers provided a basis for the Land of Israel Movement to question the legitimacy of the state as an institutional structure implementing Zionism. *Zot Haaretz* pointed out that those who threw off the central task of Zionism, the obligation to return the land of Israel to the Jewish people, forfeited the right to rule. Giving up the fatherland, wrote the Movement's Zvi Shiloah, was national treason. To remain in Samaria, Israelis must exhaust every struggle, "even those that remind us to our regret, of the struggles in the days of the Mandate."[66] Here was a not-so-veiled threat to attack the Israeli government as a new enforcer of the once-hated British Land Laws against Jewish settlement on the same grounds on which the British had once been attacked by the Jewish underground: failure to uphold the trust which gave it legitimate authority to govern. The perspective was reminiscent of that held by the Irish Republican Army, which saw the state's task to achieve both independence and territorial integrity as transcending rights of self-determination or democratic decision making, so that any government which failed to carry out this task was illegitimate. Ominously, a Committee for the Defense of Democracy was organized in response to the settlement efforts in Samaria by the peace movement and was backed by the political parties Moked, the Citizens Rights Movement, and Mapam. Its organizers promised, "We will take to the streets to defend the country against the right wing."[67] An article in the journal of the kibbutz movement of Mapam called for war against the "insane right" including "open eyed consideration of the use of force." According to its author, "This is the enemy. I prefer a just war of Jews against Jews than an unjust war of Jews against Arabs. . . . Everything depends on who wins the internal struggle."[68]

A potentially serious challenge to the state's institutions and authority was coming in an atmosphere of general demoralization. In the immediate aftermath of the war there was new interest in emigration (1974 saw 18,000 people leave Israel, the highest number since the War of Independence) and a new questioning by young Israelis of Israel's right to exist. Immigration into Israel from Western countries, which had soared after the Six-Day War, plummeted. Even from the Soviet Union, where "push" was combined with "pull" for the classic impetus to emigration, more than one-third of the emigrants chose countries other than Israel,[69] compared to a pre-1973 proportion of about 4 percent. While Israel's free press normally allows play for the widest range of opinions, it was surely significant that on Israel's first Independence Day after the war, an article appeared in *Davar*, the newspaper of the Labor party, arguing that too much emphasis had been placed upon Zionism and that Judaism could survive in the absence of the state; on the same day, a chapter from a novel appeared in *Haaretz*, Israel's major independent newspaper, describing events following the destruction of the state. Israelis no longer had the sense they had formerly had that they directed their own destinies. The proportion of Israelis who accepted the statement that Israel was so dependent upon the United States that it could not be independent in its resolutions rose to 64 percent after the war, a striking change in perception compared to the pre-war period.[70] Despite the continuing threat of war, a wave of strikes in essential services broke out as Israel struggled with an inflation rate that was the highest in the Western world. The peace movement may have served the function of easing what might otherwise have been a more overwhelming sense of powerlessness and alienation, for by legitimating external constraints it presented them as an Israeli alternative, a set of morally and politically desirable goals.

Also important was a growing demoralization within American Jewry, Israel's most important reservoir of support outside the state. Israeli leaders referred with concern to the pessimism concerning Israel's prospects that they found among American Jewish audiences and sought to counteract this attitude by optimistic statements.[71] American Jewry was curiously silent as political pressures were brought by the United States on Israel, a silence partially explained by the Israeli government's discouragement of independent political action by American Jewry.[72] The level of financial support continued high, considering the problems of recession in the United States; but it was possible that as Israel's problems became more acute, a significant segment of American Jewry might distance itself emotionally and psychologically from Israel and seek renewed vitality for Judaism in dispora institutions instead.

If withdrawals continued, demoralization within Israel could be expected to grow worse. Arend Lijphart has described the intense emotional reaction of the Netherlands to giving up West New Guinea and how the ultimately unsuccessful resistance left the country internally divided, frustrated, and humiliated.[73] If this was the impact of giving up a colony that Lijphart demonstrates was wholly without economic or strategic value to the Netherlands, the impact of "decolonization" in the case of Israel, where the territory involved is central to the religio-national mythos and in alien hands constitutes a strategic danger of the first order, could be expected to be much greater. That this should happen in the aftermath of a costly war that was defined publicly as having ended in an Israeli *victory* must make it even harder for the public to accept the aftermath, which would have been much more readily understood if it had followed military defeat.

That ideological politics will replace consensual politics in Israel appears inevitable. Fragmentation along ideological lines had decreased because of what one writer called "growing consensus among most of the parties as to the nature of the state."[74] That consensus was now vanishing rapidly. While ideological disputes would center initially upon the national issue, with its potential for splitting almost all parties in time of crisis, it was probable that renewed ideological energy would spill over into other areas, including religious and economic issues, which were in any case easy to entangle with the national issue. Ironically, as Israelis had less sense of their power to shape events, they might, as in the pre-state period, find in ideological struggles an outlet for the frustration of their capacity for action.

What, then, are the prospects for the fulfillment of the ideology of either of the opposing movements that have been described? What, of greater concern to the world, are the prospects for peace if either movement's programs are implemented? This question assumes particular force in relation to the programs of the peace movement, since it is in effect this movement's conceptions which the United States administration seeks to implement on the assumption that satisfaction of Arabs demands for the return of territory lost in 1967 and satisfaction of Palestinian Arab desire for self-determination will produce, in turn, Arab acceptance of the legitimacy of Israel's existence in the old borders. The unpalatable answer must be that the chances of obtaining a settlement of the Arab-Israel conflict on this basis are virtually nonexistent.

For the Arab-Israeli conflict is not over where a given boundary line should be drawn; it is over the existence of the state of Israel, which the Arabs have defined since the inception of the state as a threat to their national survival. This Arab attitude has proved incomprehensible to most Western diplomats and social scientists, who have in consequence discounted it and redefined the conflict in terms familiar to themselves as a symmetrical conflict, fed by mutual misunderstandings and fears, over concrete and resolvable issues. It is seen as a particularly stubborn problem to be sure, but one, for all that, subject to techniques of conflict resolution provided that the proper formula can be found. Yet there are Western students of Arab society who have attempted to explain and studies that document the Arab perception of Israel. The most extensive analysis of Arab attitudes toward Israel has been made in a series of volumes by Yehoshafat Harkabi, a former chief of Israeli intelligence. Documented in these volumes is the profound and multifaceted nature of Arab hostility to Israel, which is perceived as a demonic force, as well as the extreme goals that develop from such hostility—politicide and genocide.[75] Notable among American students of the problem is

Gil Carl AlRoy whose *Behind the Middle East Conflict: The Real Impasse between Arab and Jew* explores both the basis of Arab hostility and the reasons for the misconceptions concerning it prevalent among the diplomats and journalists who have shaped both policy and public opinion.[76]

Among students of the problem there is agreement concerning the reasons for the distortions in Arab perception regarding Israel. Israel's existence symbolizes to the Arabs the comparative failure of Arab-Moslem as compared to Western-Christian civilization in the modern period.[77] That the Jews, who suffered so deeply under that civilization, should become its symbol to the Arabs is ironic, but it is an irony that only exacerbates Arab anger and frustration, for it appears to them that even a small and rejected remnant of Western civilization, a group moreover that was despised within Islam,[78] has been able to humiliate the entire Arab world. As AlRoy points out, given the absence of separation between religion and politics in Islam, so that the truth of Islam is vindicated by success in this world, the "humiliation of the power of Islam in its heartland, in Palestine, is thus felt as a cosmic disorder, not just rhetoric; in the Muslim context the ordeal is personal: disorientation, feeling of insufficiency and depravity, a state of utter disgrace. . . . Overcoming the state of the Jews means restoring Islam to its Truth; the end of Israel would be the vindication of Islam."[79] Moreover, Israel's existence is a religious offense not merely in the broad sense of demonstrating Islam's impotence, but in the more technical sense of violating specific Islamic precepts which decree that land once Islamic must never be relinquished. While Islam has relinquished land in the past, notably in Europe, without undue theological problem, the situation is different when that land is located in the center of the Arab world.

When such Arab attitudes have been grasped at all by Western statesmen, they have been misunderstood: thus Secretary of State Kissinger believed that by producing a stalemate at the end of the Yom Kippur War he would allow the Arabs to restore the honor they had lost through repeated defeats by Israel, which in turn would allow them to accept Israel. But in the Arab view the Yom Kippur War merely marked the beginning of the restoration of Arab honor, to be fully restored only when the Arab world could prove that it did not and need not tolerate a non-Arab nation in the heart of the Middle East.[80] Perception of Israel as a threat to Arab existence did not change, a fact quite clearly brought out when to the discomfiture of Israeli leaders, in the midst of intensive negotiations through Kissinger for an interim agreement, Sadat made a speech calling Israel "a dagger in Egypt's side and in the heart of the Arab nation."[81]

Should Israel return to the old borders she would greatly increase her vulnerability. On the other hand, the Arab states must see their power immensely enhanced through the new effectiveness of their oil resources, and recognize that Europe has been neutralized now that its fear of an oil boycott makes it unwilling to oppose the Arabs forcefully on any issue, presumably including the issue of Israel's survival. While Arab oil revenues are concentrated in states peripheral to the major combatants, these will undoubtedly be invested in substantial part in Western armaments, which will be available to Israel's immediate neighbors. Under these circumstances the survival of a sovereign Israel could be expected to be an even greater irritant, a proof of Arab impotence at the apparent height of Arab power, and the temptation to make one more, this time in Arab perception surely successful, attempt to eliminate Israel would probably prove irresistible.[82] It becomes highly questionable if the Soviet Union, presuming it wished to, could restrain the Arab states.

While the Israeli government has never acknowledged that the conflict is incapable of resolution through Israel's territorial concessions, there has been no escaping the persistence of Arab attempts, since the establishment of the state, to eliminate it. This means that even unreserved United States pressure cannot be expected to persuade Israel to allow the full program of the peace movement to be implemented, including establishment of a new Palestinian state. In bowing to United States demands for an interim accord in Sinai, Israel leaders have elected to postpone confrontation with their powerful—and only —patron. Nonetheless, another war that ended unsuccessfully or even equivocally, in combination with great power pressures, might push Israel into a position where she believed she had no choice but to submit. If this happened, the effect could only be to give new life to the ideology of the radical wing of the peace movement. For once the ideology of the moderate wing was tested and the peace that the peace movement believed must then come failed to result, those convinced that only by winning Arab acceptance could Israel survive would be pushed toward advocating further concessions, including the limitation of Israeli sovereignty. The radical wing, it will be remembered, proposed abandoning the central law of the state, the Law of Return, and ending the tie of the state of Israel to the Jewish people, the basis of Zionist ideology. That this would fit in with at least initial Arab demands was suggested by an Egyptian declaration in December 1974 that a condition for peace was that Israel's population be frozen at its current level and immigration be prohibited for fifty years.[83]

The United States, if it emerged, as it must in any settlement involving Israel's retreat to the old borders, as the chief guarantor of the agreement, might well find itself underwriting further Arab demands. In place of "stages toward peace," the United States might find itself pressing for stages in the elimination of Israeli sovereignty, especially if Arab demands were formulated in piecemeal fashion. Demands for reduction or elimination of immigration, or for the admission of a certain number of Arab refugees could be treated as reasonable Arab requests that did not violate agreements as to borders. The United States would be tempted to give in to Arab demands for the same reasons that it now seeks Israeli retreat; to prevent the eruption of another war, with its danger of great power confrontation (presumably all the greater if the United States had formally committed itself to preserving Israel's territorial integrity, whether through a security treaty or in some other way); to reduce Soviet influence in the area and substitute American influence; and to ensure the continued flow of oil. An Israel geographically highly vulnerable, isolated internationally, internally riven as it must be following large-scale withdrawals, and utterly dependent upon the United States, would find it difficult to withstand such demands.

On the other hand, the prospects for fulfillment of the ideology of the Land of Israel Movement at this writing look bleaker than they in fact may be. A new war might end in a decisive Israeli victory. Barring direct Soviet intervention, this outcome is not merely possible, but predictable, for the military balance of forces in the region remains favorable to Israel. Within Israel there is enormous reluctance to go to war once again, which contributes to a willingness on the part of the majority to make concessions past the point where a sizable minority within Israel feels there is justification. Nonetheless, should Israel be pushed to the point where her leaders perceive survival immediately threatened, her full military force will be unleashed with what may well prove enormous effectiveness.

Thus far Arab-Israeli wars have produced great power pressures, exerted quickly after the 1956 war, more tardily after the 1967 war, to restore the status quo ante. Yet a new war might occur in a changed constellation of international forces and might itself help to produce shifts within the Middle Eastern power balance.[84] There has been major structural change in the Middle East with the Arab exercise of their oil weapon through boycott and subsequent dramatic price increases. Thus far this change has worked to the benefit of the Arabs, whose wealth and political strength have simultaneously been enormously increased. The West has reacted with efforts to recycle petrodollars and to secure Arab political objectives. The price increases have been accepted, albeit reluctantly, as a legitimate exercise of sovereignty and force has been rejected as an unacceptable way of securing change.

Yet there is no assurance that the definition of the situation by Western statesmen and publics will not alter, resulting in a new approach to the Arab world, one for once not inimical to Israel's interests. Thus far Israel has been viewed by many influential elements in the West as a political liability, interfering with a normal process of good relations with the Arab states, numerically and strategically important, and the reliable source of the fuel upon which Western industrial society depends. But now the Arab states have moved into what can easily be redefined as an adversary position. If Western living standards are eroded and the political stability of Western societies are threatened by economic crisis and dislocation, a redefinition is likely to occur, and the demands of the oil producers interpreted as unilateral decrees that the wealth and productivity of the western world be transferred to a handful of states, many of them with tiny populations, all of which will be seen as lacking the moral right to siphon off the West's wealth. The voices thus far raised to say these things are few[85] (most economists are still optimistic about the possibility of coping satisfactorily with the situation), but the chorus and volume will grow if those who have spoken are correct, and fundamental systemic change has occurred, which cannot be handled within the international monetary system. Force may then no longer be viewed as inappropriate to the stimulus; the Arab-Israel conflict may come to seem an opportunity rather than a disaster, offering excuse, much as the Israeli attack in Sinai in 1956 offered excuse for the Franco-British invasion, for taking over of selected Arab oil fields. Logically there would seem considerable benefit to the West in using Israel, with its military superiority, as a means of keeping the Arabs in check. There is of course no certainty that redefinition of Arab behavior as justifying military intervention will occur in the West,[86] or that if it does it will occur in time to be useful to Israel, but the point is that the situation in the Middle East has changed in important ways that may only in the short term be disadvantageous to Israel.

In the event of a successful war, Israel will also be ideologically better prepared to benefit from its results than it was in 1967. Prior to that war the ideology of the Land of Israel Movement was unavailable to the Israeli government, which had accepted the legitimacy of the 1949 borders and had reiterated constantly in the period of emergency prior to the war that it had no claim to territory. Taken aback by the war and its surprisingly successful results, the government was unable abruptly to reverse ideological course; it found itself using territories as potential bargaining cards and accepting Security Council Resolution 242, which was seen as promising peace for territory. In a future war the ideology would be available; indeed, a future war might well be conducted by a government composed of a coalition of parties unified by acceptance of the ideology. Suitably adapted to whatever borders resulted from a new war, the ideology of the Land of Israel Movement might yet be implemented.

In such circumstances peace could also not be expected to result, but it must be remembered that whatever happens in the Middle East—even if Israel is destroyed—peace cannot be expected to ensue. As Elie Kedourie has pointed out, disorder is endemic to the region,[87] and inter-Arab conflicts will fill any lull in the Arab-Israel struggle or replace it altogether should that struggle end. Israel, oddly enough, has in a sense been a force for stability in the region, her presence acting as a restraint upon the Arab states in their disputes with each other. By appearing to the Arabs as the most serious threat requiring cooperation to eliminate, Israel has served to counter the centrifugal forces in the Arab world. Should Israel, for a time at least, seem impossible to defeat, inter-Arab conflicts could be expected to erupt with greater force, which in turn would make the unity necessary for a successful war against Israel more difficult to achieve.

Inter-Arab conflict paradoxically is fueled by the genuine longing for unity that pervades the Arab world. It is a longing that is in permanent tension with the particularity of the Arab states, whose boundaries, although for the most part accidental, the product of European twentieth-century imperial division of spheres of influence, have assumed meaning, and have acted as effective barriers to unification efforts. The urge to unity itself becomes a force for division and conflict as different states seek to assume leadership in the drive for its achievement. Inter-Arab conflicts have the same capacity to involve the superpowers as the Arab-Israel conflict, for the stakes remain control of the region's crucial oil resources.

In sum, peace in the Middle East is a mirage for the foreseeable future, and the net result of United States efforts to achieve it will be to put Israel in a more disadvantageous position when she fights the next war. Israel's sovereignty will presumably be exercised over borders considerably beyond those contemplated in any currently considered "peace settlement"—or not be exercised at all. In a Middle East characterized by wholly incompatible aspirations, there is simply no way of satisfying, or even partially satisfying, the desires of all those in the region.

Students of Israeli political life have paid little attention to the Land of Israel Movement and the peace movement, and when these movements have attracted notice, they have usually been dismissed as unimportant. For example, in his massive study, *The Foreign Policy System of Israel,* Michael Brecher writes:

Associational interest groups have had virtually no influence on decisions, although the Land of Israel Movement has been an intangible constraint on Israeli decision makers' freedom of action since the 1967 war concerning the terms of a peace settlement. And while Israeli academics and commentators have become increasingly vocal in criticism of Israel's policy towards her Arab neighbors, their impact on decisions has not been evident.[88]

According to this typical assessment, the impact of the Land of Israel Movement has been marginal, and that of the peace movement non-existent.

On the contrary. Whatever the outcome of negotiations and of battles—and the outlook is for both—the Land of Israel Movement and the peace movement will have made a decisive mark upon Israel's political future. In shaping traditional ideologies to fit the circumstances of post-1967 Israel, they framed the issues and enunciated the alternatives that will guide—and divide—Israel's policy makers in the foreseeable future.

Appendix 1. Manifesto of the Land of Israel Movement, August 1967

Zahal's [Israel Defence Force's] victory in the Six-Day War placed the people and the state within a new and fateful period. The whole of Eretz Yisrael is now in the hands of the Jewish people, and just as we are not allowed to give up the *State of Israel*, so we are ordered to keep what we received there from *Eretz Yisrael*.

We are bound to be loyal to the entirety of our country—for the sake of the people's past as well as its future, and no government in Israel is entitled to give up this entirety, which represents the inherent and inalienable right of our people from the beginnings of its history.

Our present boundaries are a guarantee of security and peace and open up unprecedented vistas of national material and spiritual consolidation. Within these boundaries, equality and freedom, the fundamental tenets of the State of Israel, shall be the share of all citizens without discrimination.

The two prime endeavours on which our future existence depends are immigration and settlement. Only by means of great influx of new immigrants from all parts of the Diaspora can we hope to build up and establish the Land of Israel as a unified national entity. Let us regard the tasks and responsibilities of this hour as a challenge to us all, and as a call to a new awakening of endeavour on behalf of the people of Israel and its land.

The undersigned hereby dedicate themselves to the fulfillment of these tasks and responsibilities, and will do all within their power to bring about their active implementation by the people as a whole.

S. Y. Agnon
Prof. Yonatan Aharoni
Natan Alterman
Dr. Moshe Ater
Dr. Aharon Ben-Ami
Oved Ben-Ami
Haim Ben-Asher
Efraim Ben-Haim
Aluf [Brigadier General]
   Eliahu Ben-Hur
Yehoshua Ben-Zion
Rachel Yanait Ben-Zvi
Dr. Shmuel Braverman
Yehuda Burla
Hillel Dan
Rav Aluf [Major General]
   Yaakov Dori
Dr. Yehuda Don

Menachem Dorman
Prof. Yehuda Elitzur
Dr. Israel Eldad
Dr. Gedalya Elkoshi
Uzzi Feinerman
Prof. Harold Fisch
Sgan-Aluf [Lieutenant Colonel]
   Yehuda Pri-Har
Uri Zvi Greenberg
Zerubavel Gilad
Haim Guri
Rabbi Dr. Zvi Harcavi
Dr. Aryeh Harel
Isser Harel
Aharon Hareuveny
Haim Hazaz
Dr. Reuven Hecht
Abraham Ikar

Prof. Eri Jabotinsky	Eliezer Shefer
Michael Kabiri	Zvi Shiloah
Abraham Kariv	Israel Sheinbaum
Rivka Katzenelson	Gershon Shoffman
David Koren	Moshe Tabenkin
Eliezer Livneh	Yoseph Tabenkin
Shalom Lurie	Aluf [Brigadier General]
Benny Marshak	Dan Tolkowski
Moshe Moskowitz	Sgan Aluf [Lieutenant Colonel]
Rabbi Zvi Neriah	Yehoshua Verbin
Yaakov Orland	Dr. Zev Vilnay
Ariel Renan	Dr. Abraham Weinshal
Rabbi Dr. Levi Y. Rabinowitz	Aluf [Brigadier General]
Yoseph Yoel Rivlin	Abraham Yaffe
Prof. Dov Sadan	Reuben Yaffe
Dr. Haim Symons	Dr. Haim Yachil
Dr. Avner Shaki	Alexander Zarchin
Yitzhak Shalev	Yitzhak Zuckerman (Antek)
Prof. Abraham Shalit	Ziviah Zuckerman (Lubetkin)
Moshe Shamir	Aluf [Brigadier General]
Yariv Shapira	Meir Zorea
Dr. Tamar Shay	

Shmuel Yoseph Agnon: born Galicia 1888; to Israel 1907; writer, winner Bialik and Israel Prizes, among others; first Israeli Nobel Prize winner for literature; died 1970.

Prof. Yonatan Aharoni: born 1919; to Israel 1933; head, Institute of Archaeology, Tel Aviv University, and chairman, Dept. of Archaeology and Ancient Near Eastern Studies.

Natan Alterman: born Warsaw, Poland 1910; to Israel 1925; Hebrew poet, playwright, novelist, publicist, translator, winner Israel Prize 1968; died 1970.

Dr. Moshe Ater: economist, economic editor *Jerusalem Post.*

Dr. Aharon Ben-Ami: member Palmach, later Irgun, sociologist, taught universities United States, presently at Haifa University.

Oved Ben-Ami: born Petakh Tikva 1905; co-founder *Doar Hayom,* first Jerusalem daily, and daily *Maariv*; a founder of Netanya of which he was mayor up to 1969; industrialist.

Haim Ben-Asher: member of first Knesset for Mapai.

Efraim Ben Haim: born Holland; emissary Jewish agency to organize aliya, one-time ambassador to Central African Republic and Chad, member Achdut Haavoda and kibbutz Bet Oren.

Aluf Eliahu Ben-Hur: officer of Haganah, brigadier general Israeli army, engineer, director of Koor industries after retirement from army, then of Yeda Research and Development Corporation of Weizmann Institute; 1969 organized national volunteer guard duty to assist in protection of exposed settlements.

Yehoshua Ben Zion: born Israel, early childhood U.S.; member Irgun, captain Israel army; prior to its collapse (and his prison conviction) director of the Israel British Bank.

Rachel Yanait Ben-Zvi: born Malin, Russia; founders girls' agricultural school in East Jerusalem, cofounder Histadrut 1920; cofounder Pioneer Women 1928; widow of Yitzhak Ben-Zvi, second President, state of Israel.

Dr. Shmuel Braverman: born Rumania 1934; to Israel 1952; professor of chemistry, Bar Ilan University.

Yehuda Burla: born Jerusalem 1886; one-time head of Arab department of Histadrut, teacher, novelist, and short story writer, winner Bialik and numerous other prizes, died 1969.

Hillel Dan: born Lithuania 1900; to Israel 1920; member of secretariat Kibbutz Ein Harod; member executive Histadrut and Prime Minister's economic council, director Solel Bonei; died January 1969.

Rav Aluf Yaakov Dori: born Odessa, Russia, 1899; joined Jewish Legion 1918; engineer, chief Haganah staff; Chief of Staff Israel Army 1948-9; President of Technion to 1965; died 1973.

Dr. Yehuda Don: born Hungary 1930; to Israel 1947; chairman, department of economics, Bar Ilan University.

Menachem Dorman: born Berlin 1909; to Israel 1931; member Kibbutz Givat Brenner, literary and political essayist and translator, editor of writings of Natan Alterman.

Prof. Yehuda Elitzur: born Hungary 1915; to Israel 1929; one-time Director, Institute of Biblical Research; member Public Broadcasting Commission; professor of Bible, Bar Ilan University.

Dr. Israel Eldad: born Lvov, Poland 1910; to Israel 1940; leader Fighters for Freedom of Israel (Lechi); editor *Chronicles of Israel, Sulam;* author, editor, translator of Nietzsche into Hebrew.

Dr. Gedalya Elkoshi: born Poland 1910; to Israel 1932; professor Modern Hebrew literature, Tel Aviv University.

Uzzi Feinerman: born Israel 1933; secretary Moshav Movement; member of Knesset for Maarach; died 1975.

Prof. Harold Fisch: born 1925 Birmingham, England; to Israel 1957; one-time rector Bar Ilan University; professor English literature Bar Ilan.

Sgan Aluf Yehuda Pri-Har: lieutenant colonel Israeli army; director, Soldier's Welfare Organization.

Uri Zvi Greenberg: born Galicia, Poland 1898; to Israel 1924; member first Knesset for Herut, poet, winner numerous prizes for his poetry.

Zerubavel Gilad: member Kibbutz Ein Harod, poet.

Haim Guri: born Tel Aviv, 1923; member Palmach, 1941-9; board of editors *Lamerchav,* essayist and poet.

Rabbi Dr. Zvi Harcavi: born Russia 1908; leader Zionist underground in Soviet Union during 1920s, Chaplain of Israel Army, War of Liberation, founder and director Maalei High School, Jerusalem; director Central Rabbinical Library of Israel 1953-58; author numerous books and articles.

Dr. Aryeh Harel: born Kiev, Ukraine 1911; to Israel 1937; associate professor Tel Aviv University Medical School, director Ichilov Hospital, Tel Aviv.

Isser Harel: born Russia 1912; to Israel 1930; lieutenant colonel Israeli army, founder and first head of Israel Intelligence (Shin Bet); captured Eichmann in Argentina; member of Knesset for State List.

Aharon Hareuveny: born 1886 in Ukraine; novelist, translator Voltaire, winner Bialik Prize 1969 for his *Jerusalem Trilogy;* brother of Yitzhak Ben Zvi, second President of Israel; died 1971.

Haim Hazaz: born Russia 1898; to Israel 1931; novelist; winner numerous prizes including Bialik, Israel, Ussishkin Prizes; died 1973.

Dr. Reuven Hecht: born Antwerp 1909; to Israel 1936-39; leading figure Irgun, active illegal immigration in Mandate period; founder Dagon Silos; chairman of the Board, Shikmona Publishers.

Abraham Ikar: leader of Haganah.

Professor Eri Jabotinsky: born Odessa, Russia, 1910; to Israel 1919; son of Vladimir Jabotinsky, founder of Zionist Revisionist Organization; leader Betar Movement in Palestine in late 1930s, mathematician, lecturer at Technion, member of Knesset for Herut 1949–51; died 1969.

Michael Kabiri, engineer.

Abraham Kariv, born 1900 Slobodka, Lithuania; to Israel 1934; literary editor *Davar* and biweekly *Moznaim;* translator of classical Russian literature into Hebrew; poet and essayist, literary critic, winner of Bialik Prize.

Rivka Katzenelson: daughter Berl Katzenelson; former editor *Devar Hapoelet* ("Word of the woman worker").

David Koren: member kibbutz Gesher Haziv, member Knesset for Maarach (Rafi faction).

Eliezer Livneh: born Lodz, Poland 1902; to Israel 1920; cofounder and editor *Maarakhot* 1939–42; editor *Eshnav* (illegal Haganah weekly) 1942–47, cofounder, editor *Hador* 1949; member of Knesset for Mapai; author, editor, politician; died 1975.

Shalom Lurie: member kibbutz Merchavia.

Benny Marshak: born Kiev, Ukraine 1907; to Israel late 1930s; member Achdut Haavoda; Palmach leader instrumental in developing its ideology; member Kibbutz Givat Hashlosha; died 1975.

Moshe Moskowitz: born Bratislava, Czechoslovakia 1925; to Israel 1935; a founding member of Kibbutz Massuot Yitzhak; leader in religious kibbutz movement; chairman, Regional Council Shafir, Regional Center Gush Etzion.

Rabbi Zvi Neriah: B'nai Akiva leader; head of Yeshiva Kfar Haroeh, member of Knesset for National Religious party.

Yaacov Orland: born 1914 Ukraine; to Israel 1921; founder first Jewish military theatrical group, leading actor and playwright; poet, essayist, translator of Wilde, Shaw, Byron into Hebrew.

Ariel Renan: member Kibbutz Hamadia; official in Mapai sponsored kibbutz movement (Ihud Hakvutzot Vehakibbutzim); one of the leaders in Mapai party conflict in the early 1950s (the "youth" faction).

Rabbi Dr. Levi Yitzhak Rabinowitz: born Edinburgh, Scotland 1906; rabbi various congregations London; chief rabbi Transvaal and Orange Free State; councilman for Jerusalem (Gahal); deputy editor in chief, Encyclopedia Judaica; expert on Biblical flora.

Yoseph Yoel Rivlin: born Jerusalem 1889; involved in battle for Hebrew in pre-World War I Palestine for use in Jewish schools; ran Damascus Jewish School for Girls; professor Arabic studies Hebrew University, translator Koran into Hebrew; author various scholarly and political articles and books; died 1971.

Prof. Dov Sadan: born Galicia, Poland 1902; to Israel 1925; participated in founding various kibbutzim; editor literary supplement of *Davar*; editor *Hegeh* for German speakers; editor publishing house Am Oved; professor of Yiddish language and literature Hebrew University; member Knesset 1965–68 for Labor Alignment; winner Israel Prize.

Dr. Haim (Clive) Symons: born England 1942; to Israel 1966, lecturer chemistry at Bar Ilan University to 1969.

Dr. Avner Shaki: professor of law, Tel Aviv University, member of Knesset for National Religious Party, assistant Minister of Education; ran unsuccessfully on own list for Knesset elections of 1973.

Yitzhak Shalev: writer and poet.

Prof. Abraham Shalit: born Galicia, Poland 1898; professor of Jewish history, Hebrew University; winner Israel Prize 1960; retired 1966.

Moshe Shamir: born Israel 1921; founder *Bamachaneh* (weekly); author, playwright; winner numerous prizes including Brenner, Bialik, Ussishkin.

Yariv Shapira: archaeologist.

Eliezer Shefer: member, National Religious Party.

Zvi Shiloah: born Galicia 1911; to Israel 1931; acting editor *Hador* (daily) 1949–54; head Information Department of Israel Institute of Productivity 1954– ; editor *Hamifal;* member Central Committee Labor Party; editor *Zot Haaretz.*

Israel Sheinbaum: founder of youth movement of Kibbutz Hameuchad; one-time director Mapai Information Services; member kibbutz Glil-Yam.

Gershon Shoffman: born 1880 Mohilev, Russia; to Israel 1938; writer of Hebrew novellas; died 1974.

Moshe Tabenkin: born 1917 Israel; member of kibbutz Ein Harod (Hameuchad); son of Yitzhak Tabenkin; poet.

Joseph Tabenkin: born Israel; member kibbutz Ein Harod (Hameuchad); youngest general War of Liberation, commander Harel brigade; son of Yitzhak Tabenkin; engineer.

Aluf Dan Tolkowski: born Tel Aviv 1921; British Royal Air Force; commander Israeli Air Force 1958; managing director Discount Bank Investment Corp. Ltd.; industrial manager Clal industries.

Aluf Mishne [Colonel] Yehoshua Verbin; born Omsk, Siberia 1910; to Israel 1913; officer Haganah; officer Israeli Army War of Independence; served as military governor frontier zones; after 1967 deputy governor of Jerusalem and West Bank.

Dr. Zeev Vilnay: born Haifa 1900; geographer-ethnographer. Foremost historian of places in Palestine; author atlases and guidebooks.

Dr. Abraham Weinshal: born 1895 Caucasus; lawyer and founding member of Revisionist Party and chairman of its Central Committee; died 1968.

Aluf Avraham Yaffe: born Israel 1913; commander Ninth Brigade in march to Sharm el Sheikh (Sinai Campaign); commander officer's training school 1957; northern commander 1962–65; chairman Nature Reserve Authority; member of Knesset for Likud.

Reuven Yaffe: farmer, Nahalal.

Dr. Haim Yachil: born Czechoslovakia 1905; to Israel 1929; ambassador to Sweden, Norway, and Iceland 1955–59; Director General Ministry for Foreign Affairs 1960–64; died 1975.

Alexander Zarchin: born Ukraine 1897; engineer, inventor, notably desalinization of sea water (Zarchin freezing process).

Yitzhak Zuckerman (Antek):

Ziviah Zuckerman (Lubetkin): husband and wife, among organizers of rebellion against the Nazis in the Warsaw ghetto; members of Kibbutz Lohamei Hagetaot.

Aluf Meir Zorea: born Rumania 1923; second in command southern front Sinai campaign of 1956; Brigadier general northern command; head Training Section General Headquarters.

Appendix 2. For Peace and Security—Against Annexation

(Statement adopted at a meeting of the Tel Aviv Area Council for Peace and Security—Against Annexation on July 1, 1968)

The Six-Day War was a defensive action waged for our very existence. Therefore, following this war that has been forced upon us in order to repel aggression and to maintain our existence as a nation and as a state, the Government of Israel declared that it was not our purpose to conquer new territories. The stated aim of Israel's governmental policy is, therefore, peace within secure and agreed-upon borders. Accordingly, no territory should be evacuated without a peace agreement ensuring our security.

We view with concern every act of commission or omission, as well as every statement running counter to these principles.

We consider the creation of *faits accomplis* to be very dangerous—whether the facts be established with the prior agreement of the government, or with its *post factum* endorsement. We also consider statements by ministers deviating from these lines of policy to be a source of grave peril. Chauvinistic pronouncements and annexationist propaganda—accompanied, *inter alia,* by pseudo religious rationalizations—falsify the Jewish people's spiritual tradition, as well as the democratic and humanitarian image of our state.

In our endeavor to attain security and peace we call upon the public at large to support the following demands:

1. The Government should once more unambiguously declare that Israel is not seeking territorial aggrandisement, but that it continues to adhere, now as in the past, to the principle that occupied areas should be evacuated following a peace treaty based on secure and agreed-upon borders, as expressed in the statement made by Israel's representative at the United Nations in connection with our acceptance of the Security Council resolution of November 22, 1967.

2. The government should take immediate action to put an end to Jewish civilian settlement in the areas in question aimed at creating new facts in the occupied areas. The government should also refrain from expropriating lands for this purpose.

3. The government should make public a plan for the rehabilitation of the Arab refugees. This plan should be part and parcel of a peace settlement and immediate steps should be taken for its preliminary implementation. Any action likely to increase the number of refugees should be avoided.

4. The government should allow the population of the occupied territories to be a factor in, and party to, the general effort to attain peace.

Whatever the difficulties and obstacles heaped up by the Arab states and their supporters throughout the world, *Israel should not relax her political*

171

initiative in order to achieve peace, nor should anything be done in order to impede a peace settlement.

Appendix 3. A Proposal for a Just and Lasting Peace between Israel and the Arab Countries

Statement of the Movement for Federation published in the July-August 1967 issue of *New Outlook,* vol. 10, no. 6, p. 57.

In the desire to have the war of June 1967 appear in history as the last of the wars between Israel and her neighbors, the undersigned feel it necessary to resolve the problem of the relations of the peoples of this country by a political solution that will be fundamental and lasting.

It is Israel's aim to make peace with all the Arab countries or with any Arab country prepared to do so, on fair conditions securing the basic interests and rights of both sides; a peace that will assure Israel's security, a fundamental solution of the refugee problem, and satisfy the national aspirations of the Palestinian Arabs. This aim can only be achieved in an atmosphere of mutual respect without any feelings of victors and vanquished.

As a basis for a logical and just solution we make the following suggestion:

1. That a Palestine Federation be established, to include the territories of the State of Israel, the Gaza Strip and the Western Bank, and whose capital will be Greater Jerusalem.*

2. The federation will be composed of the State of Israel and an Arab state which will satisfy the desire of the Palestinian Arab people for a national and political identity.

3. The Palestine Federation will be open to membership by Jordan in a separate unit or in union with the Palestinian Arab state.

4. The fundamental statute of the federation will assure the security of its two components by a system of effective mutual guarantees which will prevent the danger of any one being exploited by any foreign element to the detriment of the other.

5. Within the framework of the federation and with the help of an international consortium, the refugee problem will be solved fundamentally and inclusively, by the economic and social as well as national rehabilitation of the refugees.

6. The scope of the federation's jurisdiction and activities in economics, trade, transportation, communications, education, culture, etc., will be determined in course of time in the dynamic process of growing mutual trust and with the cooperation of all the components of the federation.

* One of the signatories, Dr. Haim Darin-Drabkin, wishes to express his reservations concerning this clause and clause 3; he believes that an attempt at federation with Jordan (East and West Bank) should have preference; only if that proves impossible should a federation with the West Bank alone be broached.

7. The Palestine Federation will welcome the adherence of other neighboring states.

8. The Palestine Federation will strive for the neutralization of the region so that it cease serving as the battlefield of the great powers. A joint political framework for the peoples of the region will make possible the proper expression of all ethnic, religious and cultural particularities.

Assurance of a stable peace in the region is primarily the concern of the peoples inhabiting it, who must overcome the legacy of hatred and hostility in order to secure their own futures while guarding the just rights and interests of the two sides.

World public opinion, peace-seeking persons everywhere, desiring the good of the two sides, can contribute their share in this historic moment by exerting all their influence in order to bring the two sides to direct negotiations and a stable peace for all the peoples of the region.

The dispute between the Arab countries and Israel, which began as a conflict between the Jewish national movement and the Arab national movement, will be terminated with the attainment of peace between them by the establishment of a federation. This new situation will make it possible for the first time to divert the tremendous military budgets to peaceful development and will mark the beginning of a new era—an era of well-being, economic prosperity and cultural flowering for the whole region.

The peoples of this country and the peoples of the region face a common future and destiny.

> Victor Cygielman
> Dr. Haim Darin-Drabkin
> Ya'akov Farhi
> Natan Yalin-Mor

Victor Cygielman: born Poland; journalist, foreign correspondent for Radio Luxemburg and *Nouvel Observateur;* member, editorial council of *New Outlook.*

Dr. Haim Darin-Drabkin: born 1908 Warsaw; to Israel 1934; economist, Scientific Director of the International Research Center of Cooperative Rural Communities; Chairman, Editorial Council of *New Outlook.*

Ya'akov Farhi: born Bulgaria, member Kibbutz Hatzor; public relations man, journalist for *Al Hamishmar.*

Natan Yalin-Mor: born Grodno, White Russia 1913; to Israel 1941; editor of paper of Irgun in Poland; member Central Committee of Revisionist Party in Poland; leader of Fighters for the Freedom of Israel (Lechi); arrested following assassination of Bernadotte and sentenced to eight years (granted amnesty 1949); in prison elected to Knesset on Lechi list (Lochamim); served 1949–51; 1958 active with Uri Avnery in Semitic Action Movement calling for federation with Arabs; engineer; writer for *Haaretz.*

Notes

CHAPTER 1

1. For a report of this process see Clarke A. Chambers, *Seedtime of Reform 1918–33* (Minneapolis: University of Minnesota Press, 1963).

2. Floyd Hunter pioneered the reputational method in his study of Atlanta, *Community Power Structure* (Chapel Hill: University of North Carolina Press, 1953). The positional approach, which assumes that those who head institutional structures control them, is associated with the work of C. Wright Mills, especially *The Power Elite* (New York: Oxford University Press, 1956).

3. See Yuval Elizur and Eliahu Salpeter, *Who Rules Israel?* (New York: Harper & Row, 1973). A few individuals associated with the Land of Israel Movement and peace movement are included, but it is because they are well-known industrialists, writers, actors, etc. The major figures of the Land of Israel Movement and peace movement are not in the book, and the association with the movement is not mentioned for the peripheral figures who are in the book.

4. Ben Halpern, *The Idea of the Jewish State* (Cambridge: Harvard University Press, 1961), p. 247.

5. See Neil J. Smelser, *Theory of Collective Behavior* (New York: The Free Press, 1962), pp. 325, 338–39. While Smelser points out that strain is most likely to be the product of an unsuccessful war, here strain was produced by a successful war because of the problem of both external constraints (international pressures) and internal constraints (the "demographic problem") that created the problem of what to do with victory.

6. Interview, Menachem Dorman, February 10, 1970.

7. Haolam Hazeh was unusual in that a magazine (of the same name) served as the basis for a political party. The name was changed in 1973 to Meri, the Israeli Radical party, reflecting the accretion of some splinters from radical groups; it failed to win any seats in Israel's Knesset.

8. Interview, Uri Avnery, March 29, 1970. Avnery had even found a name for the proposed federation: Brit Yerushalayim (the Jerusalem Federation); he proposed making Jerusalem capital of both Israel and the new federated state.

9. Michael Brecher, *The Foreign Policy System of Israel* (New Haven: Yale University Press, 1972), p. 174.

10. Land of Israel Movement member Moshe Shamir was most explicit about the bargaining position this stance gave Israel; to the government, of course, it did not seem as if Israel could bargain on the basis of territories she did not currently control.

11. See for example Shabtai Teveth, *Moshe Dayan* (London: Weidenfeld and Nicolson, 1972), p. 341.

12. The roots of the problem go back to the beginning of the century. Questions have been raised concerning the applicability of the doctrines of class struggle which were carried from industrial or developed agrarian European societies to the swamps and deserts of Palestine, where industry and farming alike had to

be developed, so to speak, from scratch. Whatever the applicability of the doctrines, many of the settlers brought them and sought to create in Palestine a new society in conformity with them. The Poalei Zion, the Palestinian branch of which was founded in 1906, advanced an ideology of class struggle for a Jewish proletariat that did not yet exist. While the rival Hapoel Hazair argued that doctrines of international socialism were incongruous with the situation in Palestine, the necessity of countering the arguments of the Poalei Zion gave it too a strong ideological cast. Walter Laqueur points out that, bearing in mind that after five years the two groupings had no more than five hundred members between them, "the solemn speeches and writings about the historical mission of the working class and the necessity of the class struggle make strange reading" (*A History of Zionism* [New York: Holt, Rinehart and Winston, 1972], p. 282).

13. Alan Arian, *Ideological Change in Israel* (Cleveland: The Press of Case Western Reserve University, 1968), p. 172–73. Nadav Safran similarly points to the religious fervor with which ideological conflict was conducted by Zionist, and later Israeli, parties, in *The United States and Israel* (Cambridge: Harvard University Press, 1963), p. 113.

14. Ronald Mark Sirkin, "Coalition, Conflict and Compromise. The Party Politics of Israel" (Ph.D. dissertation, Pennsylvania State University, 1971), pp. 363–64.

15. Ibid., p. 25.

16. The very closeness of beliefs contributed to such dogmatism for, as Arian observes, fear of competition from the adjacent party tended "to cause political communication to be passionate and the message to be rigid." *Ideological Change in Israel*, p. 173.

17. The hotly debated questions concerned the extent to which the economy should be planned and state-controlled or operate through free enterprise, the degree to which Jewish tradition and religious laws should shape the laws of the state, the form a constitution for the state should take, the virtues of the existing party list system versus a representational constituency system on the pattern of the United States, and others. The problems that bothered the numerous parties were essentially those of self-definition in relation to parties most similar in their attitudes toward these problems: Mapai was concerned about how its ideas differentiated it from the other socialist labor parties—Mapam, Achdut Haavoda, and, after its formation, Rafi; the National Religious party was ideologically preoccupied with its differences from the more extreme religious Aguda party.

18. See Samuel Katz, *Days of Fire* (London: W. H. Allen, 1968), pp. 239–50. In the Hebrew version (This section was not translated for inclusion in the English version), Katz has an interesting explanation for the special hostility of the Hameuchad movement (of which the Palmach was the military force) to the Irgun, despite the fact that in basic attitudes they were very similar. He argues that the Irgun did what the Palmach and its ideological leadership would have liked to do but were restrained from doing by adherence to the doctrine of national discipline, which required that decisions of the Jewish Agency be respected, regardless of whether one agreed or disagreed with them. (See the Hebrew text, *Yom Haesh* [Tel Aviv: Karni Publishers, 1966], pp. 415–16).

19. Interview, January 22, 1970.

20. Uri Zvi Greenberg, *Sefer Hakitrug Vehaemunah* [Book of chastisement and faith], (Jerusalem: Sdan Publishers, 1938), p. 164.

21. Interview, Samuel Katz, November 24, 1969.

22. Interview, Israel Eldad, March 5, 1970.

23. Gad Yatsiv, "Al Mah Havikuach?" ["What is the debate about?"] *Sikui* (Jerusalem: Movement for Peace and Security, June 1970), p. 46.

24. Halpern, *Idea of the Jewish State*, pp. 22–25.

25. *International Encyclopedia of the Social Sciences* (1968), vol. 14, s.v. "Social Institutions."

CHAPTER 2

1. Martin Buber, *Israel and Palestine: The History of an Idea* (London: East & West Library, 1952), p. 49.

2. On the Uganda proposal see Robert G. Weisbord, *African Zion: The Attempt to Establish a Jewish Colony in the East African Protectorate 1903–5* (Philadelphia: Jewish Publication Society, 1968). Awareness of the importance of religio-historical ties came from individuals who were themselves committed secularists. Thus Ber Borochov, for example, who was primarily concerned with embarking the Jewish people upon the class struggle, asserted that only Palestine offered "objective" conditions suitable for Jewish immigration in the sense of being semi-agricultural, thinly populated, and fitted for the immigration of the petty bourgeoisie. While Borochov asserted, "Our Palestinism is not a matter of principle, because it has nothing to do with old traditions," he was in fact recognizing that for the Jews only Palestine could be attractive as a national center. See Ber Borochov, *Nationalism and the Class Struggle* (New York: Poalei Zion of America, 1937), pp. 38–39, 203. For an analysis of emotional and cultural factors interacting with the religious tie in the rejection of Uganda see Moshe Ben Yoseph, *Haayarah* [The townlet] (Tel Aviv: Aleph Publishers, 1968), pp. 39–45.

3. From the inception of Zionism the term "state" had to be avoided in public statements, but this did not mean that Zionist leaders failed to have this goal firmly in mind. At the first Zionist Congress in 1897, the Basel program asserted that the aim of Zionism was to create for the Jewish people a homeland (*"Heimstatte"*) in Palestine in order to avoid offending the Turkish Sultan who then ruled over Palestine. But when someone complained to Herzl that the language was obscure, Herzl replied "No need to worry. The people will read it as the Jewish state anyway" (Amos Elon, *Herzl* [New York: Holt, Rinehart and Winston, 1975], p. 242). Similarly, in his memoirs Herzl's close associate Max Bodenheimer emphasizes the essentially tactical nature of the dispute between those who emphasized colonization efforts and those like Herzl who disapproved of them without first obtaining a charter under "public law": the aim for all was a Jewish state (*Prelude to Israel* [New York: Thomas Yoseloff, 1963], pp. 93, 103, 111). With the Balfour Declaration of 1917 and in the decades following, the problem of avoiding statement of the goal of statehood remained, because of the British, Arab sensitivities, and the sensitivities of non-Zionist Jews opposed to statehood but ready to encourage settlement by Jews in Palestine as long as the goal of statehood was not affirmed. Nonetheless, for the vast majority of Zionists the disagreement continued to be simply tactical, the question concerning when and under what conditions the common goal was to be pursued.

4. There are dissenters. Bar-Deroma in a massive study, *Wezeh Gevul Haares* [And these are the boundaries of the land] published in 1958 (Jerusalem: B.E.R. Publishers), has argued that Numbers merely offers a detailed description of the border of Abraham's promise, even though neither the northern (the river Euphrates) nor the southern (the River of Egypt) border is mentioned. In Bar-Deroma's view it is inconceivable on religious and psychological grounds that the

borders could be different, for it is repeated in the Bible a number of times that the promise to the patriarchs will be kept, and a second competing promise could not be presented without explanation of the difference. Since there is no such explanation, there can be no difference between the two promises. Bar-Deroma thus interprets the borders of Numbers as extending farther than any previous student has done.

5. The eastern border of the promise is clearly specified as the Jordan river; yet in the actual conquest the eastern side of the Jordan, now the country of Jordan, was divided among the tribes of Reuben, Gad, and Menasseh. Moreover, in the promise terrible enemies are defined, who, in fact, became friendly peoples. Conversely, Edom is treated as a brother, when actually this people became a serious enemy. For a summary of the difficulties with this perspective see Yehezkel Kaufmann, *Toldot Haemunah Hayisraelit* [The History of Israelite Religion] (Jerusalem: Bialik Institute, 1960), vol. 1, book 1, pp. 190–94, 196. Kaufmann argues that for a while during the period of the Judges, the failure to carry out the entire plan of conquest bothered the leadership (When some of the tribes settled in Transjordan, the Israelites lacked the manpower to settle the northern portion of the territory supposed to be conquered under the plan), but that eventually the whole plan was abandoned (vol. 2, book 1, p. 379).

6. H. F. Tozer, *A Hisory of Ancient Geography* (London: Hafner Publishing Co., 1964), maps facing pp. 71, 75.

7. Kaufmann, *History of Israelite Religion*, vol. 1, book 1, p. 190.

8. Actually, there were rebellions against Rome and later against Byzantium even after 135 A.D. Then followed a period of relative tranquillity between defeated Jews and Romans lasting until the third century. In 351 A.D. a Jewish uprising was defeated by Gallus, the governor appointed by Constantine; in 556 the Jews rose against Justinian; and in 611 they helped the Persian invaders. After the destruction of the Second Temple, areas of Jewish settlement were mainly in the north or northeast (Galilee, the Golan, the Hauran, and Gilead) or in the far south (northern Negev). On the extent of settlement in the Biblical period see Yohanan Aharoni, *The Land of the Bible: A Historical Geography,* trans. A. F. Rainey (London: Burns and Oates, 1966); on the Second Temple period see Yehoshua M. Grintz, *Perakim Betoldot Bayit Sheni* [Chapters in the history of the second temple times] (Jerusalem: Y. Marcus Publishers, 1969), pp. 9–40; on settlement in the period after the destruction see Michael Ish-Shalom, *Mas'ei Notzrim Leeretz Yisrael* [Christian travels in the holy land] (Tel Aviv: Am Oved and Dvir Co., 1965), pp. 51–205 and Israel Schepansky, *Eretz Yisrael Besafrut Hatshuvot* [Eretz Israel in the responsa literature], 2 vols. (Jerusalem: Mosad Harav Kuk, 1968); and for the period from 135 A.D. to 1920 treated in one volume see Mordechai Gichon, *Atlas Carta Letoldot Eretz Yisrael Mibetar Vead Tel-Chai* [Carta's atlas of Palestine from Beththter to Tel Hai] (Jerusalem: Carta, 1969).

9. See "Gevulot Haaretz" [The borders of the land], *Encyclopedia Talmudit,* vol. 2, pp. 209–14 and Pinchas Neaman, "Geographical Problems in the Law of the Sabbatical Year," (in Hebrew) (Master's thesis, Tel Aviv University, 1968).

10. The Arab national movement, far from being an expression of Moslem religious attitudes, interestingly enough, was largely the work of Greek Orthodox. George Antonius, Rafiq Rizq Sallum, Issa al Issa, Ya'aqub Faraj, Khalil Sakakini, George Hanna, Khalil Iskandar Qubrusi were all Greek Orthodox; there were also some Maronite Catholics—such as Amin al-Rayhani, Marun Abbud, and Faris al-Shidiaq—but Muslims were marginal in it. It could not be otherwise because the Arab national movement at its inception was anti-Turk, and Turkey was the seat of the Caliphate and Sultanate. For that reason the Arab national movement

was greeted with hostility by Moslems in India and had a hard time even after World War I explaining its anti-Turkish stand to Indian Moslems. It was the marginality of Christian minorities which made them look to nationalism or pan-Arabism as a means of establishing a more central identity in the Islamic world. Russia realized this and sought to foster Arab nationalism among Greek Orthodox lay people in the Middle East in the hope that this would be an anti-Ottoman force. While there is of course an Islamic "nationalism" or pan-Islamism, it is not the same as pan-Arabism, and early Arab nationalism had to work against specifically religious Islamic attitudes, for the central symbol of religious "nationalism" was the Ottoman Empire. See Elie Kedourie, *The Chatham House Version and Other Middle Eastern Studies* (New York: Praeger, 1970), pp. 317–50; and Yaacov Shimoni, *Medinot Arav Beyamenu* [The Arab states: their contemporary history and politics] (Tel Aviv: Am Oved Publishers, 1965), pp. 22–26, 39–42.

11. These homilies, among others, are cited in "Gevulot Haaretz," *Talmudic Encyclopedia*, vol. 2, pp. 223–25.

12. Samuel Hillel Isaacs, *The True Boundaries of the Holy Land* (Chicago: privately printed, 1917). The promise of Numbers gives as the southern border "the Brook of Egypt" and, while some interpreters have identified this as the Nile, the majority (Isaacs among them) have identified it as Wadi El Arish. For a summary of the debate on this point, see "Gevulot Haaretz" *Talmudic Encyclopedia*, vol. 2, p. 206.

13. H. F. Frishchwasser-Ra'anan, *The Frontiers of a Nation: A Reexamination of the Forces Which Created the Palestine Mandate and Determined its Territorial Shape* (London: Batchworth Press, 1955), pp. 85–86.

14. Ibid., pp. 86–92.

15. Eliezer Livneh describes the important role taken by Aharon Aaronson in determining the Zionist map in *Aharon Aharanson: Haish Uzmano* [Aaron Aaronson: The Man and his Time] (Jerusalem: Mosad Bialik, 1969). An interesting divergent perspective on desirable boundaries was presented by Jacob de Haas, Executive Secretary of the Zionist Organization in the United States, who advocated a wide extension of territory to the south so that Palestine might include the whole of the Gulf of Aqaba and thus become a factor in the Indian Ocean. To draw the country down to the uninhabited area of the deserts, he argued, and forgo much of the northern territory, would limit the possibility of quarrels with the Syrians, the Arabs, and the French. See Frischwasser-Ra'anan, *Frontiers of a Nation*, pp. 102–3.

16. Frischwasser-Ra'anan, *Frontiers of a Nation*, p. 141.

17. Aaron S. Klieman, *Foundations of British Policy in the Arab World: The Cairo Conference of 1921* (Baltimore: The Johns Hopkins Press, 1970), p. 39. See also David Lloyd George, *Memoirs of the Peace Conference*, vol. 2 (New Haven: Yale University Press, 1939), pp. 721–773.

18. Frischwasser-Ra'anan, *Frontiers of a Nation*, p. 100.

19. A leitmotif of developing British policy toward the disintegrating Ottoman empire in the face of the emergence of rival claims of British allies was the securing of land routes from the Mediterranean to the Persian Gulf. See for example K.W.B. Middleton, *Britain and Russia: An Historical Essay* (New York: Kennikat Press, 1947), pp. 70–75; Y. M. Goblet, *The Twilight of Treaties*, trans. W. Bradley Wells (Port Washington, N.Y.: Kennikat Press, 1970), pp. 69–102; Yaacov Shimoni, *The Arab States*, pp. 18, 19–31, 36–39; M. A. Fitzsimons, *Empire by Treaty: Britain and the Middle East in the Twentieth Century* (Indiana: University of Notre Dame Press, 1964), pp. 4–92.

20. See Frischwasser-Ra'anan, *Frontiers of a Nation*, pp. 36–85, and P. Elman,

"The Peninsula of Sinai," mimeographed (Jerusalem: Ministry of Justice, February 1971), pp. 25–41.

21. Frischwasser-Ra'anan, *Frontiers of a Nation*, p. 146.

22. Chaim Weizmann, *Trial and Error* (New York: Harper & Bros., 1949), p. 291.

23. Klieman, *Foundations of British Policy*, p. 231.

24. Ibid., p. 233.

25. Elkana Margalit, *Hashomer Hazair: Meadat Neurim Lemarxism Mahabchani, 1913-36* [Hashomer Hazair: from youth community to revolutionary Marxism, 1913–36] (Tel Aviv: Hakibbutz Hameuchad Publishing House, 1971), p. 161.

26. Joseph B. Schechtman, "Soviet Russia, Zionism, and Israel," in *Russian Jewry 1917–67*, ed. Jacob Frumkin, Gregor Aronson, et al. (New York: Thomas Yoseloff, 1969), p. 422. See also Guido G. Goldman, *Zionism under Soviet Rule, 1917–28* (New York: Herzl Press, 1960), pp. 73–89.

27. Joseph B. Schechtman, *Rebel and Statesman: The Vladimir Jabotinsky Story*, 2 vols. (New York: Thomas Yoseloff Inc., 1956), vol. 2, p. 281.

28. Ibid., vol. 2, pp. 320–21.

29. *New Judaea* (London), August-September 1937, p. 214.

30. Ibid., p. 220.

31. Ibid., p. 216.

32. Ibid., p. 222. Wise was not representative of American Reform Judaism, most of whose representatives viewed Zionism with alarm.

33. Ibid., p. 216.

34. Ibid., pp. 220–24.

35. By 1948, with the establishment of the state, Lechi's position became modified from its original extreme statement. At this time Lechi literature emphasized the varying borders of the Land of Israel in Jewish history and argued that within the borders of the promise a Hebrew nation would endeavor to expand its territory, but only in desert areas, and not at the cost of foreign peoples. Nonetheless the wider vision was not abandoned. In 1948 Israel Scheib (Eldad), with Natan Friedman (Yalin-Mor) and Isernitzsky, commanders of Lechi after the death of its founder Abraham Stern, treated the state of Israel as a bridgehead to *malchut Yisrael*, ("the sovereignty of Israel"). See Miriam Getter, "Haideologia Shel Lechi" [The ideology of Lechi] (Master's thesis, Tel Aviv University, 1967), pp. 56–98.

36. *Jewish Outlook* (New York: Mizrachi Organization of America), 1947, p. 1.

37. *Jewish Herald* (Johannesburg), December 24, 1947.

38. *Palestine: A Study of Jewish, Arab and British Policies*, 2 vols. (New Haven, Conn.: Published for the Esco Foundation for Palestine, Yale University Press), 1947, vol. 2, pp. 1104–5.

39. Buber, *Israel and Palestine*, p. xiii.

40. Margalit, *Hashomer Hazair*, pp. 166–68.

41. *Palestine: Jewish, Arab and British Policies*, vol. 1, p. 580.

42. Ibid., vol. 2, pp. 1161–62.

43. Ibid.

44. Martin Buber, "The Bi-National Approach to Zionism," in *Towards Union in Palestine: Essays on Zionism and Jewish-Arab Cooperation*, ed. Buber (Jerusalem: Ihud Association, 1947), p. 7.

45. Judah Magnes, "A Solution Through Force?," in *Towards Union in Palestine*, p. 20.

46. *Palestine: A Bi-National State* (New York: Ihud Association of Palestine, August 1946), p. 13.

47. *New Judaea,* December 1946–January 1947, p. 42.

48. Within the peace movement, as well as in Mapam, there was considerable talk of confederation as a solution. Prior to the Yom Kippur War, Mapam and a majority within the peace movement talked of confederation with Jordan, others of confederation with a Palestinian entity to be created by Israel in cooperation with the Arabs of the West Bank and Gaza.

49. See Emanuel Rackman, *Israel's Emerging Constitution 1948–51* (New York: Columbia University Press, 1955), pp. 146–48.

50. In a minor way, the Sinai War of 1956 produced a new sense of direction among those who carried on the emphasis upon agreement with the Arabs as the primary target. In the year following a journal was established, *New Outlook,* which sought to promote Arab-Jewish reconciliation through opening channels of communication with Arabs, Europeans, and indeed all those concerned with the problem of the region; it was published, presumably with the aim of easing that communication, in English.

51. Shabtai Teveth, *Moshe Dayan,* p. 342.

52. See for example Jochanan Bloch, "Selbstbehauptung: Zionistische Aufsatze," *Evangelische Zeitstimmen,* vol. 61/62 (Hamburg, 1972), p. 65.

53. According to Amos Perlmutter, "The mobilization of ideas is the process by which various elements of an ideology are catalyzed, energized and unified into an operational entity. Such a process leads to the modification of old ideological structures and to the development of new ways to stimulate preferences and expectations" (*Anatomy of Political Institutionalization: The Case of Israel and Some Comparative Analyses* [Occasional Papers in International Affairs No. 25, August 1970, Harvard University Center for International Affairs], p. 8).

54. Security Council Resolution 242 was adopted in November 1967 but not accepted by Israel until May 1968. Even then, the mode of acceptance was ambiguous. On May 1, 1968 Israel's Ambassador to the United Nations, Joseph Tekoah, announced Israel's acceptance at the U.N.; but a storm then developed in the government because the cabinet itself had not authorized the statement, Foreign Minister Abba Eban apparently having instructed Tekoah with permission from Prime Minister Eshkol. The crisis was ended when the cabinet resolved that it noted all the statements of the Foreign Ministry between certain dates—thus including Tekoah's statement and thus in effect consenting to the adoption of 242. Dayan repeatedly stated that he thought acceptance of the resolution was a serious mistake.

CHAPTER 3

1. The place of origin of the soldier is given variously in different versions of the story. Harold Fisch, then rector of Bar Ilan University, gave the place of origin as Haifa in an interview with the author, January 20, 1970.

2. There has been considerable interest recently in movements that are viewed as "expressive," in which the motivation of members is seen as expression of a grievance unrelated to the movement's stated goals. The ultimate explanatory variable continues to be class; but the movements, rather than being seen as an expression of class interest, are seen as an expression of "status discontent" with goals that may not in fact serve class interests. See for example Richard Hofstadter, "The Pseudo-Conservative Revolt," in *The New American Right,* ed. Daniel Bell

(New York: Criterion Books, 1955), pp. 33–35 and Joseph R. Gusfield, *Symbolic Crusade: Status Politics and the American Temperance Movement* (Urbana: University of Illinois Press, 1963). For an analysis in similar terms, this time explaining movement participation through a failure to be "normatively" integrated with the society (that is, to share its values) see Frank Parkin, *Middle Class Radicalism* (New York: Praeger, 1968).

3. The exception was Eliezer Livneh, who apparently experienced a classical conversion and indeed used religious terms, describing the Six-Day War as, for him, a "rebirth" and "reconversion." The turning point, he said, came when he stood in Bethlehem, in the hills of Judah. Suddenly it was clear to him that this was more a part of him than Tel Aviv. "I felt that if I had a choice of what to give up, Mount Hebron or Tel Aviv, I should give up Tel Aviv" (Typed minutes of meeting held at Bet Sokolov, Tel Aviv, August 10, 1967). Livneh was unusual in that his journey away from the ruling Mapai party in the years prior to the Six-Day War had been toward Mapam to the left; he had become increasingly critical of the government for failing to do enough toward rapprochement with the Arabs. The Six-Day War thus served in Livneh's case, not to solidify an emerging viewpoint, but to produce a complete reversal of perspective which necessitated the classical kind of conversion he indeed describes.

4. Hans Toch, *The Social Psychology of Social Movements* (Indianapolis: Bobbs-Merrill, 1965).

5. Interview, February 10, 1970.

6. Moshe Shamir, *Chayai im Yishmael* [My life with Ishmael] (Tel Aviv: Maariv Books, 1969), pp. 26–29. While Shamir reports in his book that he was never a rebel within the Hashomer Hazair, the experience of others who came to the Land of Israel Movement from the Hashomer Hazair suggests that converts may be most easily drawn from those in a movement who have been ideologically troublesome or have had specific tasks which tended to sharpen their perception of the conflict between ideology and reality. Abraham Yaffe, a general in Israel's army prior to joining the Movement, told the author, "I was always an outcast in the Hashomer Hazair." Another recruit to the Land of Israel Movement from Mapam was Amnon Lin, although in his case a period of affiliation with Mapai intervened. Lin was director of the Arab Department of the Haifa Labor Committee, and he found his ideological indoctrination increasingly at variance with his perception of the reality of developments within the Arab countries.

7. Zvi Shiloah, *Eretz Gedola Leam Gadol* [A great country for a great people: the tale of a believer] (Tel Aviv: Ot Paz Publishers, 1970), pp. 128, 172. According to Shiloah's testimony, he had developed a geo-political conception of the Israel that was-to-be years before the establishment of the state, for which the boundaries of Palestine were only a beginning. Shiloah, for example, reports crossing the Suez Canal during World War II as a soldier in the British Army's Jewish Brigade and turning to his soldier friend with the words, "We have just left Israel." His friend replied that they had left it yesterday. "No," said Shiloah, "the Asiatic side of the Canal is in Israel" (p. 41).

8. Interview, January 29, 1970.

9. Interview, January 29, 1970.

10. It should be noted, however, that while marginality may be treated as a contributing factor to conversion in some cases, the entire weight of explanation cannot be attached to it, and that in some cases the notion does not seem applicable at all. Haim Yachil of Mapai, for example, had been director general of the Foreign Ministry and was head of the Broadcasting Authority when he became

active in the Movement. Mordecai Surkiss was a member of the Knesset for the United Labor party and had formerly been mayor of the town of Kfar Saba. Obviously, anyone not Prime Minister may have a position less central than the one he believes he deserves, but to call individuals like Yachil and Surkiss marginal is to stretch the term so far that it ceases to be helpful.

11. Interview, February 10, 1970.

12. Interview, Moshe Tabenkin, February 19, 1970.

13. There was, nonetheless, an important sense in which "conversion" was required for members of the Kibbutz Hameuchad coming to the Movement, namely conversion to the view that it was possible or desirable to work with non-socialist or anti-socialist groups in a common effort. In the pre-state period the Kibbutz Hameuchad had been a particularly bitter foe of the underground movements, despite the fact that its ideology, at least in respect to the border issue and the need for a militarily activist policy, was very similar. Reluctance to associate with the political heirs of the underground movements continued within the Hameuchad, with the result that few members joined the Land of Israel Movement. Moshe Tabenkin reported that many of those who were most in sympathy with the ideology in the Hameuchad opposed his participation in the Movement: "One reason is their attitude of disdain and hostility to the right. They talk, and we do. It makes no sense that they should reap the political capital from our sacrifices. . . . Both rationally and emotionally Achdut Haavoda objects to my joining the Movement" (Interview, Moshe Tabenkin, February 19, 1970).

14. Interview, December 25, 1969.

15. Interview, March 1, 1970.

16. Interview, March 5, 1970.

17. The Canaanites are an interesting example of what Anthony Wallace has termed movements "which profess to *revive* a traditional culture now fallen into desuetude." They profess to revive a golden age of regional harmony prior to the existence of Jew and Arab. The intellectual underpinning for the view is two-fold. On the one hand, it depended upon acceptance of the historical analysis of Protestant German Biblical higher criticism which saw the Israelite tribes as having merged with the inhabitants of the land of Canaan to produce the synthesis that was Hebrew culture. (Recent scholarship asserts that such a synthesis never in fact occurred.) On the other hand, it involved acceptance of the nineteenth-century German romantic view of nationalism described so well by Eli Kedourie. In this perspective the only basis for statehood was nationality, and the fundamental cement for nationality was language. Thus, not only was it crucial for the Canaanites that in a remote period the peoples of the region had a common language, but it became essential for the recreation of the Canaanite nation that all the people of Canaan once again speak Hebrew. As a start the Arabs living in Israel were to study with Jewish students in integrated Hebrew schools as a precondition for creating a single nation with a single language. "Mi Atem Hakenaanim?" ([Who Are you, the Canaanites?] *Aleph* [Tel Aviv, Summer 1970], p. 5). See also Baruch Kurzweil, "The Young Hebrews," *Jewish Spectator*, Sept. 1953, pp. 21–25.

18. Interview, Aharon Amir, January 28, 1970.

19. The manifesto was published in the Israeli newspaper *Haaretz* (Tel Aviv), September 22, 1967, p. 12. See Appendix I.

20. While this reasoning sounds odd now, it must be remembered that Shamir reacted in the immediate aftermath of Israel's victory, in which he was not alone (Dayan waited for a phone call from Hussein) in feeling that dramatic changes in Arab attitudes must result.

21. Interview, Aharon Amir, January 28, 1970.
22. Interview, January 20, 1970.
23. Interview, Aharon Amir, January 28, 1970. It is not without irony that one of the first activities of the anti-Jewish Canaanites was an effort on behalf of the would-be settlers (all religious) of the Ezion block and the circulation of propaganda for the establishment of yeshivot (religious schools) in Hebron.
24. Interview, Moshe Tabenkin, February 19, 1970.
25. Interview, Israel Eldad, March 5, 1970.
26. Interview, April 16, 1970.
27. The settlement of Hebron was carried out by religious Jews who had studied at the Yeshiva Merkaz Harav. According to Rabbi Levinger, they had talked even then of the eventual settlement of Hebron. After the Six-Day War, Levinger and others who were to form the group, thought at first, not of Hebron, but of Kfar Ezion. Kfar Ezion decided not to accept families in the initial period, and Hebron became the next logical target for settlement.
28. Eldad asserted that the decision to run had been a last-minute one. One reason the decision was taken so late was that those within the Movement who were eager to take a stand in the elections were not sure until a short time before the elections that Dayan might not break away from the labor list and run on an independent list. (Similar uncertainty about Dayan's intentions developed before the elections—and the war—of 1973.) While there was distrust of Dayan in the Movement, most members would have supported him; Dayan's chances for achieving power would at least have been reasonable, since at that time he was the single individual in whom the majority of Israelis had the greatest confidence regarding matters of security.
29. Mordecai Surkiss, who defied party discipline on several votes, was voted out of his local committee of the labor party in Kfar Saba, an action which paved the way for his transfer to a place far down on the list of the Maarach for the 1973 elections. (He was not reelected.) Similar punishment was meted out to Amnon Lin (who had been a member of the Sixth Knesset) and Efraim Ben-Haim, both of whom were removed from their respective labor party local committees. Lin, however, subsequently changed parties and was elected to the Knesset for the Likud in 1973.
30. Interview, January 30, 1970.
31. Interview, January 26, 1970.
32. Interview, January 22, 1970.
33. Movement member Samuel Katz wrote a book documenting the length and persistence of Jewish settlement after the Bar Kochba Revolt and arguing against any validity for the Palestinian claim to the country (*Battleground: Fact and Fantasy in Palestine* [New York: Bantam, 1973], see especially chapts. 4 and 6).
34. *Palestine Royal Commission: Minutes of Evidence Heard at Public Sessions* (London: His Majesty's Stationery Office, 1937), p. 371.
35. Interview, February 19, 1970.
36. Harold Fisch, "Hirhurim al Hazechut Hahistorit" [Reflections on historical rights], *Zot Haaretz*, February 5, 1971, p. 3.
37. Interview, February 4, 1970. Eldad reported that prior to the war Shiloah had sought to persuade him of the mistaken character of his own historical-religious conception of Israel's border. "Shiloah would come to my house trying to persuade me to put Kuwait into the borders of Erez Israel. He said to me, 'Be realistic. Why put Damascus in? One needs some realism. But to go to Kuwait makes sense—there is just desert and oil'" (Interview, March 5, 1970).

38. Elisha Efrat, "Geographia mul Idiologia" [Geography vs. ideology], *Zot Haaretz,* May 8, 1970, p. 5.

39. Israel Eldad, "Geographia Veidiologia" [Geography and ideology], *Zot Haaretz,* June 5, 1970, p. 4–5.

40. Israel Eldad, "Al Chet Shechatanu Leeretz Yisrael Velanu" [On the sin we have sinned—against the land of Israel and ourselves] *Zot Haaretz,* Sept. (n.d.) 1969, p. 4.

41. Interview, February 19, 1970.

42. The most outspoken critics of the Movement within the Israeli cabinet were Foreign Minister Abba Eban and Finance Minister Pinchas Sapir.

43. Eldad, "Al Chet Shechatanu Leeretz Yisrael Velanu," *Zot Haaretz,* September (n.d.) 1969, pp. 4–5.

44. Israel Eldad "Ze Hagadol Katon Yihieh" [Why is the land still divided?], *Zot Haaretz,* August 1, 1969, pp. 4–5. Eldad had reached these formulations long before the war of 1967, and *Sulam,* the journal published by his ideological circle at that period, is full of them. For example, an article in that journal in 1957 (vol. 9, no. 4) asserts that this little state (Israel), which for believers is the doorstep to *Malchut Yisrael Hagdola* ("the kingdom of a great Israel"), serves the apostates as a sufficiently large arena for the release of the drives and qualities that have fed on the soil of party life and hypocritical socialism.

45. Lewis Killian has distinguished between the explicit and implicit goals of a movement, the implicit goals being those ends of which the participants may be aware only tacitly, or indeed of which they may be quite ignorant. (Lewis M. Killian, "Social Movements," in *Handbook of Modern Sociology,* ed. Robert E. L. Faris [Skokie, Ill.: Rand McNally, 1964], pp. 435–36). Although only the Canaanites could sincerely welcome the prospect of an enormous increase in the Arab population, the removal of part or all of that population from the state of Israel was not an explicit goal of the Movement. Some admitted privately to the view that a large Arab minority could not be absorbed and so their emigration should be encouraged (Eldad asserted this publicly as part of the election campaign for his unsuccessful Land of Israel party); others professed liking, even love, for the Arabs, and expressed the hope the two communities could live amicably together within Israel; some believed integration would have to be accomplished gradually; still others felt it would be highly desirable if the Arabs would leave but that, since it was not practicable, there was no point in considering this as an alternative.

46. Interview, February 10, 1970. Within the next decades, according to the Movement, a huge aliya of Jews—from the Soviet Union, the United States, South America, and Europe, especially France—would pour into Israel, for, according to its analysis, Jewish communities almost everywhere were experiencing pressure and would experience more.

47. Interview, February 3, 1970. Efraim Ben-Haim asserted that it was the government, against its own will, which had ensured that the territories would be kept when it had annexed Jerusalem: "When Jerusalem was united, the die was cast. . . . I don't see how those smart people in the Knesset would vote for the unification of Jerusalem when they were against Eretz Yisrael Hashlema. That isn't rational. . . . The Arabs can make concessions on villages here and there, but Jerusalem is central" (Interview, January 22, 1970).

48. Samuel Katz, "Yisrael, Hasovietim Vehataalah" [Israel, the Soviets, and the canal: a letter to the president of the United States], *Zot Haaretz,* March 7, 1969, p. 2.

49. While the countermovement, as we shall see, considered Israel as essentially a helpless object once international forces became truly mobilized, the Land of Israel Movement believed that Israel's power of will could itself become a decisive international force. After the invasion of Czechoslovakia, Haim Yachil asserted in an editorial in *Zot Haaretz* (August 30, 1968, p. 1) that Israel now stood guard over the whole free world.

50. Norman Cohn traces the origin of millenial conceptions to Jewish religious literature of the period of the destruction of the Second Temple, when despair at oppression led to fantasies concerning the total triumph God would bestow upon his Elect in the fullness of time. Actually, however, such conceptions in Judaism are much older and were not a product of dissatisfaction with an unhappy present. For the sources of the idea and a view of how deeply embedded these conceptions are in Judaism see Yehuda Ibn Shmuel, *Midreshei Geula* [Midrashim of redemption] (Tel Aviv: Mossad Bialik, 1944), pp. 15–55. For an example of the vast literature reflecting this perspective, in this case presenting the point of view of a believer who sees the unification of the land following the 1967 war and surrounding events as part of God's plan for man's redemption see Yehuda Amital, *Hamaalot Himaamakim* [The stairs from the deep] (Jerusalem: Agudat Yeshivat Har Ezion, 1974). For Norman Cohn's analysis of the Jewish origin of millenialism see *The Pursuit of the Millenium* (London: Temple Smith, 1957), pp. 13–20.

51. Interview, February 19, 1970. In Tabenkin's view, "Zionism is not only ownership of the land by the Jewish people, but is revolutionary in its structure."

52. According to Zvi Shiloah: "Israel is now what the United States was in 1776. . . . Israel will be the United States of the Near East" (Interview, February 4, 1970). See also Zvi Shiloah, "Yisrael Vemered Hakurdim" [Israel and the Kurdish uprising], *Zot Haaretz*, March 21, 1969, pp. 2, 6; Joseph Dorial, "Istrategia Shel Taamul mul Mediniut Shel Yozmah" [Strategy of retaliation vs. the policy of initiative], *Zot Haaretz*, September 1969, pp. 3, 6; and Eri Jabotinsky, "Yisrael, Levanon, Vehamaronim" [Israel, Lebanon, and the Maronites], *Zot Haaretz*, May 30, 1969, p. 8.

53. S. B. Bet Zvi, "Hatenuah Einenah Yecholah Lirchotz Benikayon Kapeha" [The movement cannot wash its hands in purity], *Zot Haaretz*, May 30, 1969, p. 2.

54. Ibid., p. 2. The author of this scenario did not insist this was the necessary course of events. Arab leaders seeking to sign a peace treaty might be murdered, inhibiting the unfolding of the sequence of events described. He argued, however, that it was a reasonable prediction because of the serious flaws in a Jewish state that was rooted in Zionism but conducted in non-Zionist ways.

55. Eric Hoffer, *The True Believer* (New York: Harper & Row, 1951), p. 86.

56. Interview, March 5, 1970.

57. See, for example, Haim Yachil, "Hateshuva Leneum Rogers" [The answer to Rogers' speech], *Zot Haaretz*, December 19, 1969, p. 3.

58. *Jerusalem Post*, June 6, 1969, pp. 3–4. The Movement in turn ridiculed Eban, calling him Abba *Teven* ("strawhead") and begging Abba ("father" in Hebrew) to make them orphans.

59. The pamphlet was called *Sakanah, Ushemah Abba Even* [Menace—and its name is Abba Eban] and the author was Professor Jochanan Bloch, director of the Beersheba branch of the Land of Israel Movement.

CHAPTER 4

1. [Editorial], "Are We Going Over the Threshold?," *New Outlook*, vol. 10, no. 5 (June 1967), p. 3.

2. Amnon Kapeliuk, "Peace by Stages," *New Outlook,* vol. 11, no. 3 (March–April 1968), p. 38.

3. Natan Yalin-Mor, "We Need a Declaration of Policy," *New Outlook,* vol. 11, no. 3 (March–April 1968), p. 30.

4. Elkana Margalit, *Hashomer Hazair,* p. 98.

5. Avraham Ben-Shalom, *Deep Furrows* (New York: Hashomer Hazair Organization, 1937), p. 92.

6. Ibid., p. 24.

7. Ibid., p. 88.

8. Ibid., p. 25.

9. Ibid., p. 301.

10. Margalit, *Hashomer Hazair,* pp. 167–68, 196.

11. Ibid., pp. 204–6.

12. Ben-Shalom, *Deep Furrows,* p. 291.

13. Ibid., p. 296.

14. Dan Sachs, "Mapam Joins the Alignment," *New Outlook,* vol. 12, no. 1 (January 1969), p. 39.

15. Horace M. Kallen, *Utopians at Bay* (New York: Theodor Herzl Foundation, 1958), p. 124.

16. Martin Buber, *Israel and Palestine,* p. xiii.

17. Joshua Arieli, "Drift or Mastery," *New Outlook,* vol. 12, no. 7 (October 1969), p. 15. There were many professors in the Land of Israel Movement as well, although they were not perceived as prominent in that movement. They tended, moreover, to be concentrated in different areas: those active in the Land of Israel Movement for the most part were geographers, archaeologists (both fields concerned with "land" in a very specific way), natural scientists, and engineers. In the peace movement professors of social science and literature were more heavily represented. Interestingly, law professors were well represented in both movements.

18. Interview, Pinchas Rosenbluth, May 20, 1970.

19. Furthermore, these men were extremely unhappy with the alleged religious revival that had accompanied the Six-Day War. They found it spurious, less a religious awakening than a "dangerous mixture of religious mysticism and chauvinistic nationalism." Interview, Pinchas Rosenbluth, May 20, 1970.

20. Ibid.

21. This position was put sharply by Menachem Hacohen, a religious member of the Knesset who is a member of the ruling United Labor party. He distinguished between a Jewish state and a state of Jews, the latter meaning simply a state in which Jews live. Israel, in his view, was a secular state with secular laws—a state of Jews—and thus there was no religious value at all to the state. Whether this secular state ruled or did not rule over the holy Land of Israel was not a religious issue and, said Hacohen, the failure to distinguish between the religious and the political issue was in itself sinful—a case of forbidden "impure mixture." For Hacohen's views see his interview with *Haaretz* (Tel Aviv), January 25, 1974.

22. See Moshe Unna, "Hamaarachah Hapolitit" [The political struggle], and Pinchas Rosenbluth, "Zehirut Behaarachah [Caution in evaluation], *Amudim,* July–August 1967, pp. 328–31, 343–47; and Moshe Unna, "Daat Torah Vehachraah Medinit" [Torah knowledge and political decision], *Amudim,* October 1967, pp. 16–29.

23. Avnery, in the Hebrew version of his book *Milchemet Hayom Hashvii* [War of the seventh day] (The chapter is omitted in the English *Israel without Zionists*), describes his initial sympathy with Ratosh's analysis of the emergence of a

Hebrew identity, but says he did not join the Canaanites because he found Ratosh lacking in any political conception. (Tel Aviv: Daf Chadash, 1969, pp. 170–75). Kenan said he had joined the Canaanites for a brief period in 1949. (Interview, August 11, 1970).

24. Robert Merton makes the notion of "non-belonging" central, stating that reference group theory aims "to systematize the determinants and consequences of those processes of evaluation and self-appraisal in which the individual takes the values or standards of other individuals and groups as a . . . frame of reference." (Robert K. Merton and Alice Kitt Rossi, "Contributions to the Theory of Reference Group Behavior," in *Readings in Reference Group Theory and Research,* ed. Herbert H. Hyman and Eleanor Singer [New York: The Free Press, 1968], p. 35). In the same book Muzapher Sherif, on the other hand, treats reference groups as "those groups to which the individual relates himself as a part or to which he aspires to relate himself psychologically": in other words, they may or may not be groups to which the individual belongs (Introduction, p. 24). According to Tamotsu Shibutani, reference groups need not exist at all as "real groups" "Reference Groups as Perspectives" in Ibid., pp. 105–7).

25. There are parallels in the belief of the Dutch that their retention of West New Guinea (West Irian) was in the strategic interest of the Western alliance and that they should therefore have received full support from the West in their dispute with Indonesia over control of the island. But such support was not forthcoming. Australia was the only country evincing strong feelings about the strategic importance of the territory, but even this was never translated into effective support for the Dutch (Arend Lijphart, *The Trauma of Decolonization: The Dutch and West New Guinea* [New Haven: Yale University Press, 1966], pp. 62–65). Arnold Wolfers distinguishes between "possession goals" and "milieu goals" of foreign policy, the first being directed at enhancement or preservation of the things to which the nation attaches value, the second directed toward shaping conditions beyond national boundaries. To the Land of Israel Movement a strong Israel, and to the Dutch a territory that had proved strategically important in World War II, should have been milieu goals of Western countries. However, Western countries did not define them as such, but rather seem to have had as their milieu goals satisfying former colonies of their good will toward the possession goals of these colonies. See Arnold Wolfers, *Discord and Collaboration: Essays in International Politics* (Baltimore: Johns Hopkins University Press, 1962), pp. 73–77.

26. Eliezer Livneh, *Yisrael Umashber Hatzvilisatzia Hamaaravit* [Israel and the crisis of western civilization] (Tel Aviv: Schocken Publishing House, 1972), pp. 131–49, 189–238.

27. Reprinted in *New Outlook,* vol. 11, no. 4 (May 1968), p. 47.

28. Interview, August 11, 1970.

29. Livneh, *Yisrael Umashber Hatzvilisatzia Hamaaravit,* p. 89.

30. *Jerusalem Post Weekly,* March 19, 1974, p. 3.

31. Interview, Jacob Riftin, June 3, 1970.

32. Interview, Uri Avnery, March 29, 1970.

33. Interview, Ernest Simon, May 7, 1970.

34. Arieli, "Drift or Mastery," p. 16.

35. Gabriel Stein, "The Refugee Problem," *New Outlook,* vol. 11, no. 6 (July–August 1968), p. 13.

36. Jacob L. Talmon, "History as Fixation and Guide," *To Make War or Make Peace: Symposium on the Middle East* (Tel Aviv: *New Outlook,* 1969), p. 50.

37. Interview, May 20, 1970.

38. Interview, August 12, 1970.

39. Amnon Kapeliuk, "Peace by Stages," *New Outlook,* vol. 11, no. 3 (March–April 1968), p. 40.

40. Haim Darin-Drabkin, "Peace by Federation," *New Outlook,* vol. 10, no. 6 (July–August 1967), p. 37.

41. Shmuel Bari, "Let's Not Make Bi-Nationalism an Escape," *New Outlook,* vol. 12, no. 9 (November–December 1969), p. 37.

42. Interview, June 26, 1970.

43. Peretz Merchav, "Bi-Nationalism and Confederation," *New Outlook,* vol. 11, no. 5 (June 1968), p. 47.

44. See Shlomo Avineri, "The Palestinians and Israel," *Commentary,* vol. 49, no. 6 (June 1970), p. 42 and the replies to the article in the September 1970 issue.

45. H. Shlomo, "The Case for Palestinian Self-Determination," *New Outlook,* vol. 11, no. 6 (July–August 1968), p. 41.

46. For a bi-national proposal see Zalman Chen, "A Bi-National Solution," *New Outlook,* vol. 11, no. 5 (June 1968), pp. 36–42; for one of the proposals for a Jewish state confederated with Jordan see Merhav, "Bi-Nationalism and Confederation," pp. 43–48, 63; for the proposal that the territories be transformed through a vigorous economic program see Zvi Bisk, "Needed: A Stated Policy," *New Outlook,* vol. 11, no. 9 (November–December 1968), pp. 37–41; for the proposal that political rights of the Palestinians be recognized to be implemented at some future time see Shimon Shamir, "The Palestinian Challenge," *New Outlook,* vol. 12, no. 3 (March–April 1969), pp. 12–19; for an argument in favor of giving up the territories for a statement "in principle" by the Arabs see Ran Cohen, "The Security of Israel and Her Borders," (in Hebrew) Siach, November 1969, pp. 15–18.

47. See for example Haim Darin-Drabkin, "Palestinians, Jordan, and Israel," *New Outlook,* vol. 11, no. 9 (November–December 1968), pp. 17–19; Attalah Mansour, "Solving the Refugee Problem," *New Outlook,* vol. 12, no. 9 (November–December 1969), pp. 44–49; Shmuel Bari, "Refugee Problem in the Knesset," *New Outlook,* vol. 11, no. 7 (September 1968), pp. 6–8; Aryeh Simon, "We Can't Do without Justice," ibid., p. 44.

48. Most members of the peace movement explicitly rejected this view. Peretz Merhav wrote, for example, "The idea of 'de-Zionization,' even when proposed in good faith, is a utopian one because it asks of a state which was established in order to find a legal, territorial, national, social and economic solution for the Jewish problem (what we call Zionism), that it cut itself off from its sources and from its very reason to exist in order the more easily to be accepted by the Arabs: that is advice, malicious or innocent, for national suicide or treason for the sake of physical existence." See "Is De-Zionization the Answer," *New Outlook,* vol. 12, no. 2 (February 1969), p. 30. The professor quoted, who wishes to remain anonymous, was seeking to ease Arab fears that Jewish immigration meant inevitable expansion by Israel. An interesting reference to this problem is in Shabtai Teveth's *The Cursed Blessing* (New York: Random House, 1970), p. 300–301. Speaking of the relationship between an Israeli agricultural officer and the Arab officials who worked with him, Teveth writes: "Whenever the newscaster announced the arrival of new immigrants to Lydda or Haifa, their faces paled. Once, while Eytan was chatting with Yasin about a plot of land belonging to his family near Kfar Yona in Israel, he inquired from him whether he would prefer compensation for

the land or to wait for a peace settlement, whereupon Yasin replied, 'Look, Eytan, you don't want to return the land. On the contrary, you are bringing in increased numbers of people all the time.' . . . Information on new immigration appeared to be confirmation of Israel's intention to rob the Arabs of their lands and also served the Arabs as an excuse for their defeat."

49. The first is the view of a fellow member of the peace movement, Amos Kenan, who said that Avnery posed as an anti-Zionist but would wind up, on different excuses, after abolishing the Law of Return, admitting chiefly Jews (Interview, August 11, 1970). The second was the view of the Land of Israel Movement, and of many in the peace movement, who called him a Canaanite.

50. Interview, June 3, 1970.

51. Interview, August 11, 1970.

52. Interview, May 7, 1970.

53. Nahum Goldmann, "The Future of Israel," *Foreign Affairs,* vol. 48, no. 3 (April 1970), pp. 443–459. After the 1973 war Goldmann said: "Without the acceptance of the Jewish state by the Arab world this state has no future or ability to exist" (From an interview with Goldmann by the Israeli newspaper *Yediot Achronoth,* quoted by Zvi Shiloah in *Zot Haaretz,* February 14, 1975, p. 8).

54. A major effort at unity was made prior to the elections of 1969 when a "peace front" was proposed, to include Uri Avnery's Haolam Hazeh party, Moshe Sneh's Maki party, various groups within the peace movement, and it was hoped, dissident elements in Mapam (close to one-third of whose members had voted against joining the Labor Alignment). The front foundered promptly on Avnery's perception of it as a direct threat to his own power. As he saw it, to the public it would appear that the peace front consisted simply of the Communists, Haolam Hazeh, and "some people." He would lose a lot of votes because of the association with the Communists, and the "some people" would lend no support of consequence. When the front collapsed, a "peace list" was nonetheless established, consisting of the "some people" to whom Avnery referred, which then competed for the same votes as Haolam Hazeh and Maki. To Avnery the peace list seemed designed as an attack on himself and Sneh. Moreover, Avnery viewed Jacob Riftin of Brit Hasmol as out to destroy Maki because of hostility to Sneh dating from the period when both had been members of Mapam, and Sneh had left to join the Communists while Riftin remained. He viewed Yalin-Mor as out to damage him, because of the frustration of his desire to run in second place on the proposed peace front. Be this as it may, Avnery and Sneh, each with a constituency to preserve, had an agreement not to attack each other; but the peace list, necessarily seeking part of the constituency of both, attacked both Haolam Hazeh and Maki, and was attacked in turn by them. Avnery noted that the consequent disarray in the peace movement weakened its credibility and enabled opponents to say mockingly, "They want peace with the Arabs and can't make peace among themselves." In 1973 the attempt to achieve unity proved unworkable once again, although this time both Haolam Hazeh and Maki transformed themselves to include some segments of the peace movement. This did not help Haolam Hazeh, which failed in 1973 to obtain any seats in the Knesset.

55. Luther Gerlach and Virginia Hine in *People, Power, Change* (Indianapolis: Bobbs-Merrill, 1970) have analyzed the positive functions of disunity for a movement in promoting its growth, preventing effective suppression, and facilitating desired personal and social changes (pp. 63–65).

56. The Israel Communist party (Maki) split on the issue of acceptance of the basic tenets of Zionism. Moshe Sneh kept the name and in effect became the

leader of the Jewish communists, while the other group called itself the New Communists (Rakah) and became the institutional outlet for Arab nationalists to express their opposition to the state.

57. Interview, May 20, 1970.

58. These issues never produced widespread public indignation on the scale of the Goldmann affair. The circumstances surrounding the settlement of Hebron have been described in the previous chapter, and here the selection specifically of Hebron was important. The strength of the Jewish claim to the city was sufficient in the public view to counterbalance hypothetical future impediments to peace with the Arabs, who at that time were showing no desire to reach agreement with Israel. The crackdown on terrorism in Gaza followed a series of murders, including that of several members of an Israeli family driving through the city, and was in fact approved by most Israelis; and the displacement of nomadic Bedouin in Sinai, who henceforth had to graze their cattle elsewhere, was not seen as of vital concern. Interestingly, on the issue of Ikrit and Bir'am, which involved the efforts of Maronite Christian villagers to return to their villages on the Lebanese border, from which they had been displaced for military reasons in Israel's War of Independence, the peace movement was joined—not in demonstrations and sit-ins but in sentiment—by the Land of Israel Movement. The villages had remained within Israel and affirmed their loyalty to the state. For the peace movement this was another issue of injustice to the Arabs; for the Land of Israel Movement it was a case of the Israeli government, which seems to have been opposed to the return chiefly on the grounds that it would set a precedent for restoration of "Arab rights" to lands long evacuated, knowing no distinction between friends and enemies.

59. Simha Flapan, "Viewpoint," *New Outlook,* vol. 14, no. 7 (December 1971), p. 4.

60. Joshua Arieli, "The Fate of Israeli Democracy will be Decided in the Territories" (in Hebrew), *Symposium on the Problems of Peace and Security,* pp. 4–5.

61. For example, this was the view of Uri Davis of the War Resister's League in Israel, as presented in a speech given to the Hillel Society, the City College, December 15, 1970, New York City.

62. Arieli, "The Fate of Israeli Democracy," pp. 8–9.

63. Ran Cohen, "The Security of Israel and Her Borders" (in Hebrew), *Siach,* November 1969, p. 16.

64. Amos Elon, "Poets as Conquerors," *Haaretz,* Nov. 1, 1967.

65. Ibid.

CHAPTER 5

1. It is interesting to consider in this connection Kurt Lewin's "field theory." Lewin argues that social events depend upon the social field as a whole rather than on a few selected items. One of the fundamental characteristics of the social field is the relative position of the entities which are part of it. What happens within the field depends upon the distribution of social forces through it, a quasi-stationary state, for example, corresponding to equally strong opposing forces. See Kurt Lewin, *Field Theory in Social Science: Selected Theoretical Papers* (New York: Harper & Row, 1964), pp. 150, 192, 200–204. Looking upon the interrelationships of the Land of Israel Movement, the peace movement, and the government in terms of a dynamic field, it becomes apparent that the field changes dramatically when the initial confrontation of government vs. the Land of

Israel Movement is complicated by the appearance of the peace movement attacking the government from the opposite direction. The government moved from its position at the opposite end of the field from the Land of Israel Movement to dead center, and the peace movement took the place opposite the Land of Israel Movement.

2. The reason for the government's failure to lend such tacit support must be a matter for conjecture, but presumably it had to do with the traditional conception of "national discipline" in Israel and with the belief held by many in the cabinet that the Movement was a threat to the character of the state. Dissent in Israel was supposed to stop "at the water's edge" to avoid fostering the impression that there were major internal disagreements which could be exploited for the benefit of foreign powers pursuing their own policies in respect to the Arab-Israeli conflict. This tradition of national discipline in foreign policy presumably interfered with a perspective that could view the Movement as a useful tool in respect to foreign powers in forwarding the government's own policy. And if the Movement might increase the government's possibilities of maneuvering in relation to foreign powers, a strong Movement might also drastically cut down the government's internal maneuverability. It would be a heavy price to pay for a slightly better deal from the United States as a result of its appreciation of the government's difficulties with the Movement, if the government then had to face a public aroused by that same Movement to oppose return of any territory.

3. *Maariv* (Tel Aviv), August 13, 1972.

4. Gahal tabled a vote of non-confidence in the government on the basis of the interview and the ministers of the National Religious party took exception to her "unauthorized map-making." *Jerusalem Post*, March 15, 1971.

5. Actually, the oral doctrine seems to have been written down. Shimon Peres, in the midst of the angry debate in the closing hours of the Labor party's convention of August 1969, pointed out that the so-called oral interpretation of the future borders had been formulated in writing by the platform committee and formed an integral fourth part of the party platform, in addition to the three written sections dealing with security, foreign policy, and policy in the territories. *Jerusalem Post*, August 6, 1969.

6. *Jerusalem Post*, May 6, 1970.

7. *New York Times*, June 12, 1967.

8. For a detailed description see David Ben-Gurion, *My Talks with Arab Leaders*, trans. Aryeh Rubinstein and Misha Louvish (New York: The Third Press, 1973). There were repeated reports in Israel of meetings with Arab leaders after 1967: in 1974, for example, Eban reported there had been two meetings with Hussein in 1967 (*Jerusalem Post Weekly*, December 10, 1974).

9. See *Jerusalem Post*, February 6, 1970, *Maariv*, August 13, 1972, and Naftali Feder, "Mapam Views Labor Platform as Radical Shift in its Direction," *New Outlook*, vol. 16, no. 9 and vol. 17, no. 1 (December 1973–January 1974). A minority in Mapam wanted to go even farther. As early as 1970 a minority proposal won thirteen of twenty-five votes within the Mapam Political Committee which called for withdrawal back to the June 4, 1967 lines "plus some adjustments" (*Jerusalem Post*, February 6, 1970).

10. Interview with Arie Eliav, *New Outlook*, vol. 15, no. 8 (October 1972), p. 21.

11. Arie Lova Eliav, *Land of the Hart: Israelis, Arabs, the Territories, and a Vision of the Future* (Philadelphia: Jewish Publication Society of America, 1974), pp. 134, 144, 147–48, 150.

12. Reprinted from *Davar* in *New Outlook,* vol. 16, no. 2 (February 1973), p. 47.

13. Arie Eliav, "Summary of Proposed Platform for the Israeli Labor Movement: July 1973," reprinted in *New Outlook,* vol. 16, no. 7 (September 1973), pp. 51–52.

14. *Jerusalem Post,* September 4, 1973.

15. Eban held informal evenings at home for writers, artists, and other intellectuals, many of them involved in the peace movement, and in his speeches courted intellectuals and academics, calling upon them to take a greater role in national policy making. *Jewish Chronicle of Pittsburgh,* August 23, 1973.

16. *Jerusalem Post Magazine,* April 24, 1970.

17. *New York Times,* August 9, 1973.

18. *Jerusalem Post,* October 27, 1972.

19. Speech by Abba Eban to General Assembly of the United Nations, September 30, 1971, in Zionist Archives files, New York City.

20. Yigal Allon, *Masach Shel Chol: Yisrael Vearav ben Milchama Veshalom* [A curtain of sand: Israel and the Arabs between war and peace] (Tel Aviv: Kibbutz Hameuchad, 1959), pp. 81–82.

21. Shabtai Teveth, *Moshe Dayan,* p. 335.

22. Yigal Allon, "Chinuch Lehumaniut Beitot Milchama" [Education for humanism in time of war], *Mibbifnim,* vol. 32, no. 1-2 (April 1970), p. 14.

23. Yigal Allon, "Istrategia Shel Shalom" [Strategy for peace], *Mibbifnim,* vol. 35, no. 4 (December 1973), p. 438.

24. Speech by Dayan, August 3, 1967, printed in *Mappa Hadasha: Yechasim Acherim* [A new map: other relationships] (Tel Aviv: Maariv Books and Shikmona Publishers, 1969), p. 173.

25. *Jerusalem Post Weekly,* December 7, 1970.

26. For example, in a speech given before students at the Technion on November 8, 1967 and printed in *Mappa Hadasha,* pp. 46–47; a speech to the Command School on August 1, 1968, also in *Mappa Hadasha,* p. 29, and a speech to a Labor Party Convention reported in *The New York Times,* April 6, 1971. The Land of Israel Movement argued that keeping the territories would bring peace because the Arabs would not dare to attack Israel in the new borders.

27. Speech given at Beersheba, November 6, 1968. See *Mappa Hadasha,* p. 152.

28. Interview, *New York Times Magazine,* June 8, 1968. A year after this Dayan observed he saw no point in allowing Syrian law to apply in the Golan where there were no Syrian citizens, judges, or lawyers. *Jerusalem Post,* August 15, 1969.

29. *New York Times,* March 6, 1969.

30. *Jerusalem Post,* August 5, 1969.

31. *Jerusalem Post,* August 15, 1969.

32. January 15, 1969 in *Mappa Hadasha,* pp. 32–33.

33. *South African Jewish Times,* August 29, 1969.

34. *New York Times,* April 6, 1971.

35. *Jerusalem Post,* May 10, 1970.

36. *New York Times,* August 20, 1971.

37. *Davar* (Tel Aviv), October 18, 1972.

38. Ibid.

39. *Jerusalem Post,* March 30, 1973.

40. *Jewish Chronicle of Pittsburgh,* August 23, 1973.

41. *Jewish World* (Boston), September 13, 1973.

42. Shabtai Teveth, *Moshe Dayan*, pp. 348, 350–51.

43. *Jewish Observer and Middle East Review*, April 25, 1969.

44. *Maariv*, August 16, 1973.

45. Teveth, *Moshe Dayan*, p. 333.

46. Ibid.

47. *Jerusalem Post*, September 24, 1973.

48. January 15, 1969 in *Mappa Hadasha*, p. 32.

49. *Jerusalem Post*, September 24, 1973.

50. *Hazofe* (Tel Aviv), February 28, 1969.

51. *Hazofe*, March 2, 1973.

52. *New York Times*, April 6, 1971.

53. Quoted in Mordechai Nahumi, "Meir and Galili: The Political Pivot," *New Outlook*, vol. 16, no. 2 (February 1973), p. 20.

54. *Jerusalem Post*, November 24, 1968.

55. Dayan responded to this charge on April 29, 1969. See *Mappa Hadasha*, p. 155.

56. *Jerusalem Post*, December 1, 1968.

57. So much so that, a day later, Sapir said that his speech was distorted and that he had not meant to say he had no sentiments for Hebron; he had been referring to Nablus and Jenin. *The Jerusalem Post*, December 2, 1968.

58. *Jerusalem Post*, November 24, 1968.

59. March 5, 1969 in *Mappa Hadasha*, p. 164.

60. Ibid., p. 163.

61. *Jerusalem Post*, August 6, 1969.

62. *New York Times*, August 20, 1971.

63. *Jerusalem Post*, October 27, 1962.

64. Nahumi, "Meir and Galili," pp. 22–23.

65. *New York Times*, November 10, 1972.

66. *Jerusalem Post*, November 10, 1972.

67. Discussed in *Zot Haaretz*, September 3, 1971, p. 1.

68. *Jewish Chronicle of Pittsburgh*, August 23, 1973.

69. *Maariv*, August 8, 1973.

70. *Davar*, April 28, 1972.

71. Mordechai Nahumi, "Israel as an Occupying Power," *New Outlook*, vol. 15, no. 5 (June 1972), p. 17.

72. *Maariv*, August 8, 1973.

73. For a discussion of Ben-Gurion's letter to Ezer Weizman and two interviews he gave see Haim Yachil, "Ben-Gurion Ushealot Hagevulot" [Ben-Gurion and the question of boundaries], *Zot Haaretz*, August 25, 1972, p. 2. Also personal communication to author from Ben-Gurion, July 1973.

74. *Jerusalem Post*, March 4, 1972.

75. *Jerusalem Post*, August 15, 1969.

76. This suggestion was first advanced by Egypt's Mahmoud Riad in Washington on September 25, 1969. The suggestion was taken up by Golda Meir, and then Riad's statement was denied by the Egyptian press. *American Jewish Yearbook* (New York: American Jewish Committee, 1970), p. 494.

77. Walter Laqueur in *Confrontation: The Middle East and World Politics* (New York: Bantam Books, 1974) argues that a response would have been made and cites as periods when Israeli concessions would have drawn a response August 1970 and 1972 (pp. 34–37, 254). It has become something in the nature of a favorite sport for students of the Middle East to point to alleged "lost opportunities" for the Israeli government.

78. For a list of the settlements see *New Outlook*, vol. 16, no. 2 (February 1973), pp. 58–59. On the other hand comparatively few people were involved: Eliezer Livneh of the Land of Israel Movement complained that fewer than 6,000 persons had been settled on the other side of the "Green Line."

79. *Jerusalem Post*, September 3, 1973.

80. Yamit brought a major battle, not only between Sapir and Dayan, but also between former Chief of Staff Haim Bar Lev (then Minister of Commerce and Industry) and Dayan. In fact, Dayan said in a labor party meeting that he did not see how he could run in the same party list as Bar Lev after the accusations that Bar Lev had made against him. *Maariv*, August 3, 1973.

81. Simha Flapan, "Storm Over Gaza," *New Outlook*, vol. 15, no. 3 (March–April 1972), p. 19.

82. Interview, Zvi Shiloah, August 1973.

83. Abraham Shapira, ed., *The Seventh Day: Soldiers Talk about the Six-Day War* (New York: Scribner Publishers, 1970), p. 173.

84. [Editorial], *Zot Haaretz*, April 18, 1972, p. 1.

85. "Haim Hazaz," *Zot Haaretz*, March 30, 1973, pp. 1, 8.

86. February 6, 1968 in *Mappa Hadasha*, p. 177.

87. Ibid., p. 176. Compare Dayan's speech with the following poem by Natan Alterman, quoted frequently in *Zot Haaretz* (including March 14, 1975):

Then said Satan: This besieged one
How shall I overcome him?
He has courage and ability
He has weapons and imagination

And he said: I shall not take his strength
Nor muzzle nor bridle him
Nor soften nor weaken his hands
Only one thing I'll do: I shall dull his brain
And he will forget that he is in the right

Thus spoke the devil
And it was as if the heavens paled
When they saw him arise
To carry out his plot.

88. December 12, 1967 in *Mappa Hadasha*, p. 174.

89. February 6, 1968 in Ibid., p. 178.

90. Interview with Dayan, *New York Times Magazine*, June 8, 1968.

91. December 12, 1967 in *Mappa Hadasha*, p. 174.

92. November 6, 1968 in Ibid., p. 153.

93. The first two polls gave only two choices, keeping or not keeping the territory, whereas the later polls presented more choices. If the presumption is made that those who later say they wish to return "some" of the territories would have given as their choices "keeping the territories" when presented with a simple dichotomy, then the proportion of those unwilling to return territory remained stable. See Abel Jacob, "Trends in Israeli Public Opinion on Issues Related to the Arab-Israeli Conflict 1967–72," *The Jewish Journal of Sociology*, vol. 16, no. 2 (December 1974), pp. 193–95. The poll data provide no explanation for the relative degrees of attachment shown to different territories, but it is possible to hypothesize concerning the reasons. Three factors would appear to be involved: the previous experience with the territory under Arab rule, the size of the territory, and salience of the territory in terms of traditional ideology. The Golan

Heights produced the greatest unanimity, presumably because of Israel's experience of years of shelling in times of "peace," while the Gaza Strip and Sharm el Sheikh were also identifiably sources of pre-1967 problems, the first as a base for fedayeen and the second as a precipitating cause of the 1967 war when Nasser used it to blockade Israel's port of Eilat. The West Bank, while potentially the most threatening of all since it bordered Israel's most populous areas, had not been a primary source of difficulties. But size was also important in shaping attitudes: as Table 1 indicates, the sharpest drop in the proportion opposed to returning territory was in the March–April 1971 poll for the West Bank and Sinai, when for the first time the question was posed in such a way as to offer the respondents the chance to say they wished to return part rather than keep all or return all of the territories. Presumably both territories were large enough to persuade a substantial number of Israelis that they offered scope for territorial compromise. However, the willingness to compromise was stronger in Sinai than in the West Bank; it was found in the March–April 1971 poll that 68 percent of those interviewed were ready to return all or part of Sinai, while only 44 percent were ready to return all or part of the West Bank (only 5 per cent all of it). The far greater importance of Judea and Samaria in Jewish history and religion presumably offers part of the explanation for the discrepancy.

94. Abel Jacob finds it "hopeful" that those with better than a high school education were less likely to advocate a more aggressive policy toward the Arab states. He argues that "since the continuation of the conflict over the past two generations was reinforced by the accretion of perceptions based on suspicion, fear, bad memories and/or low self esteem, education, proven to be a strong moderating force in the past, may show the way out of the tunnel." To this writer there appears little ground for Jacobs' conclusion. It reflects the familiar assumption that the Arab-Israeli conflict is a mutual one, so that a lowering of Israeli perception of threat and Israeli unilateral actions would produce change in the situation. There is no evidence that Arab attitudes toward the conflict become more moderate with increasing education, and, indeed, what evidence there is points to quite the reverse. (Yochanan Peres in a study of Israeli Arabs found that students were more than twice as likely as their parents to deny that Israel had a right to exist. See "Modernization and Nationalism in the Identity of the Israeli Arab" in *Attitudes toward Jewish Statehood in the Arab World,* ed. Gil Carl AlRoy, American Academic Association for Peace in the Middle East, 1971, p. 162.) There is also reason to question the assumption that, even within Israel, education must act as a spur to "moderation." The 1974 elections in all the major universities found an overwhelming preponderance of votes going to student organizations affiliated with Likud and the National Religious Party, both of which of course advocated maximal retention of territory. (In Tel Aviv the proportion was 85 percent, in Bar Ilan 100 per cent, at the Hebrew University 58 percent, at Haifa University 75 percent. Source: Letter from Dubi Bergman, Chairman, Tel Aviv University National Union of Israel Students, June 23, 1975). It must be remembered that the majority of Israeli students are young adults, who come to college after completing two to three years of military service.

95. See note 7 of table 1 .

96. See for example Louis Guttman's letter in the *Jerusalem Post* dated June 5, 1970, in which he presents poll data from 1967 on and reports general support of the government as settled within the range of 70 to 80 percent, as measured by the Continuing Survey of the Israel Institute of Applied Social Research.

97. Interview, Zvi Shiloah, February 4, 1970.

98. Interview, Menachem Dorman, February 10, 1970.

99. Interview, Efraim Ben-Haim, January 22, 1970.

100. Amnon Rubinstein, "And Now in Israel a Fluttering of Doves," *New York Times Magazine,* July 26, 1970, pp. 47–48.

101. Joshua Arieli, "The Fate of Israeli Democracy will be Decided in the Territories" (In Hebrew) *Symposium on the Problems of Peace and Security* (Tel Aviv: Movement for Peace and Security, 1969), p. 4.

CHAPTER 6

1. *Jerusalem Post,* October 12, 1973. Signatories included, in addition to professors not closely identified with the peace movement, Shlomo Avineri, Saul Friedlander, Joshua Prawer, Gabriel Stein, and Jacob Talmon.

2. Amnon Rubinstein, "The Israelis: No More Doves," *New York Times Magazine,* October 21, 1973. Rubinstein argued that the doves were in fact more furious than the hard-liners.

3. The phrase was reportedly used by Kissinger in a meeting with Harvard professors on December 6, 1973, one of whom subsequently circulated a memo on what Kissinger said there (*New York Times,* March 25, 1974). The Israeli government seems to have been slow to realize the consequences of acceptance of the cease-fire. The cabinet voted unanimously to accept the cease-fire proposed by Secretary of State Kissinger but had not had any prior knowledge that this was being decided upon in his meetings with Soviet leaders in Moscow. One Israeli commentator noted that the end of the war took Israeli leaders as much by surprise as its beginning (*Jerusalem Post,* October 23, 1973). Nonetheless, although the cease-fire was to turn incipient victory into defeat, there is no evidence that the decision was taken against the will of the government. Both Golda Meir and Moshe Dayan, prior to the Moscow decision, were speaking of the possibility of a cease-fire in place, apparently in the belief that Israeli positions deep in Syria and on the West Bank of the Canal were sufficient counterweight to Egyptian presence on the East Bank (*Jerusalem Post,* October 17 and October 21, 1973). Shimon Peres, a member of the cabinet, asked why Israel accepted the cease-fire, replied: "The reason for the cease-fire was because it was offered to us. We did not want war, so there was no reason to oppose the cease-fire" (*Jerusalem Post,* October 30, 1973). It was only after the war was resumed and Israel had succeeded in cutting off the Egyptian Third Army that the Israeli government acknowledged coercion. Challenged for permitting supplies to go through to the Egyptians, Dayan said in the Knesset that it was done "because we had no choice —or more precisely because the alternatives to our permitting the food convoy were worse to the best of our judgment" (*Jerusalem Post Weekly Overseas Edition,* November 6, 1973). The nature of the pressure exerted upon Israel was only divulged a year later (*New York Times,* December 20 and 21, 1974) by Dayan: Kissinger had threatened that the United States would supply the trapped Egyptian armies herself if Israel refused to allow convoys through. Whatever the reasons for the United States threats—and they were presumably dictated by a fear of Soviet intervention, a desire to improve the United States position among the Arabs, and an attempt by Kissinger to create the conditions under which his model of conflict-solving could be brought to bear (when both sides are in an untenable position), by successfully posing the threats Kissinger contributed to inflicting the strategic defeat he described. With the Egyptian military position on the east bank of the canal thus artificially preserved, the Israeli government

became aware that while the Egyptian position on the East Bank had political significance, its own position on the West Bank was without comparable value.

4. *Jerusalem Post Weekly Overseas Edition,* November 13, 1973.

5. *Haaretz,* December 7, 1973.

6. S. Shalom, "Lihiot o lo Lihiot" [To be or not to be], *Zot Haaretz,* April 17, 1974, p. 3.

7. *Jerusalem Post Weekly Overseas Edition,* September 25, 1973.

8. The poem, originally published in *Maariv,* September 26, 1973, was reprinted in part in *Zot Haaretz* in an article by Rivka Kazenelson, "Hameshorer Bechutzot Avelim" [The poet in the streets of mourning], December 21, 1973, p. 4.

9. These processes have been described by a number of students of collective behavior. Perhaps the most influential formulation has been that of Herbert Blumer, "Outline of Collective Behavior" reprinted in *Readings in Collective Behavior,* ed. Robert R. Evans (Chicago: Rand McNally & Co., 1969), pp. 68–71.

10. Zvi Shiloah, "Hamitlavshim al Hatmimim" [Hoodwinking the innocents], *Zot Haaretz,* April 5, 1974, p. 8. This is not to say that the Land of Israel Movement supported the old leadership: members were particularly bitter against Dayan because of his pragmatic adaptation to the post-war situation, his optimistic statements concerning the possibility of a lasting agreement with Egypt and support of disengagement. *Zot Haaretz* prophesied, before the protest movements arose: "He will navigate himself into a miserable position in Israel as he navigated Israel to a miserable position in the region" (Zvi Shiloah, "Gam Lo Dayan" [Not even Dayan], January 25, 1974, p. 8). Israel Eldad devoted an article to describing the essential failure of Dayan's moral vision and leadership: "Dayan Bechulshato" [Dayan in his weakness], *Zot Haaretz,* November 23, 1973, p. 2.

11. Also in terms of the values of the Labor government, dedicated to socialism, equality, democracy, and national self-determination (What was Zionism if not a movement of self-determination for a long-oppressed people?), there was much that was deeply repugnant in a policy that would involve domination over a hostile conquered population, while the alternative, equal rights for the conquered, promised the end of the Zionist dream of a specifically Jewish state. Thus, deeply held values were not outraged by the change of course forced on the government; rather, hopes were aroused that perhaps the long-awaited negotiations could produce peace through territorial compromise.

12. There was much that was spurious in this definition of Arab intentions, for the Arabs appear to have seen "direct negotiations" as not really involving compromise with the Israelis but rather as the imposition by the great powers of the Arab will on Israel. When the Geneva Conference was convened briefly on December 21, 1973 no Arab state was willing even to be seated next to Israel. (*Jerusalem Post Weekly Overseas Edition,* December 25, 1973.)

13. Abba Eban saw in the Geneva talks "the fulfillment of political targets which we did not reach after the Six-Day War," and an article in the Labor Alignment's journal *Ot* (December 6, 1973) complained that, although many in Israel saw the Geneva talks as a victory for Israeli political doctrine greater than any military victory, the impression was created that Israel went to the Conference with great reluctance.

14. *Jerusalem Post,* December 7, 1973.

15. Ibid., November 28, 1973.

16. For the warning see *Jerusalem Post,* November 25, 1973; for the willingness to make concessions, see the issue of November 11, 1973.

17. The circular brought a sharp protest from the Likud and, after first denying

its existence (*Jerusalem Post*, November 26, 1973), the Education Ministry Executive reprimanded the social education unit for circulating it to teachers. (*Jerusalem Post Weekly Overseas Edition*, November 27, 1973).

18. *Jerusalem Post Weekly Overseas Edition*, October 23, 1973.

19. Ibid., February 26, 1974.

20. The protest against Dayan was begun in February 1974 by Captain Motti Ashkenazi, who had commanded one of the fortifications of the ill-fated Bar-Lev line along the Canal and who at first picketed alone outside the Prime Minister's office.

21. The Agranat Commission did not blame Dayan in either the interim report or the final report; nonetheless, the interim report of April 1974 had enormous impact because it made clear that disastrous errors had been committed by those responsible for Israel's defense. This report strengthened the new protest movements; and while the Agranat Commission did not specifically blame Dayan, the public did. He had been Minister of Defense at the time of the war; he was a former commander of Israel's armed forces; and it was in him above all others that the public had put its trust in defense matters. The widespread feeling in the wake of the Agranat Commission disclosures was that Dayan had betrayed his trust.

22. *Jerusalem Post Weekly Overseas Edition*, January 15, 1974.

23. *Jerusalem Post*, July 26, 1974.

24. The government's view of the Geneva Conference was similar to that of the Land of Israel Movement. Rabin said: "Resumption of the Geneva Conference in its general (multilateral) form would mean that the parties were preparing for the war option." (*Jerusalem Post Weekly Overseas Edition*, December 3, 1974).

25. See for example Samuel Katz, "Halahatut—Vehamechir" [The jugglery—and its price], *Zot Haaretz*, January 25, 1974. There has been surprisingly little question in the United States press at the spectacle of Israeli leaders vying with Arab leaders in praise of the American Secretary of State. An exception is an article in *National Review*, June 21, 1974, by John Bowling. One can only speculate as to the reasons for the Israeli leadership's behavior toward Kissinger. An obvious consideration was Israel's almost total dependence upon the United States for supplies, for problems would have been caused by simultaneous pleading for military aid and attack upon the administration which provided it. But equally important, the United States policy was one of Arab-Israeli peace negotiations; to attack United States policy might be equivalent to stating the government's conviction that the negotiations could not succeed (and the fallacy of its own long-stated policy). Samuel Katz argued that the government was waiting to oppose United States policy until such time as demands were made that the government felt were impossible to meet. Katz argued that, far from being in a better position to oppose United States policy at that point, the government would find opposition wholly unrealistic.

26. Y. Iti, "Himur Mesukan Beyoter" [A most dangerous gamble], *Zot Haaretz*, June 25, 1974, p. 4.

27. In desperation the Movement participated in a direct signature appeal to Senator Henry Jackson, long known for his sympathy to Israel, to stop Kissinger from bringing a third destruction upon the state of Israel. The telegram read "Kissinger delivers Mid-East to Soviets as result brings Third Destruction on Jewish State. Desperately pray your help to stop Kissinger before it is too late." It was signed by Citizens for the Prevention of Political Catastrophe (*Zot Haaretz*, January 25, 1974).

28. *Jerusalem Post*, May 31, 1974. The cabinet included Avraham Ofer, who

with Arie Eliav had been one of the most outspoken critics of the government from the perspective of the peace movement.

29. Shimon Peres, a Dayan follower in Rafi, became Minister of Defense; and Yisrael Galili, architect of the ill-fated Galili document, remained as Minister without Portfolio.

30. Some members of the peace movement were also uneasy at the government's stress upon its ability to bring peace, and were concerned that ultimately there might be widespread disenchantment with the new leadership when the meaning of "peace" became apparent. See for example an article by Shlomo Avineri in *Maariv*, January 18, 1974. Avineri argued that the Arabs could not be expected to give up the goal of Israel's destruction, but that once territory had been returned the goal would have less salience and Egypt especially would be less willing to make the sacrifices necessary for war.

31. The public articulation of such a plan had been a consistent demand of the peace movement after 1967. The Rabin government seemed content to follow the path laid down by Golda Meir, who said after the Yom Kippur War that Israel would be prepared to argue for her vital security needs when the time came. Asked in an interview to specify the essential points that Israel could not abandon, Mrs. Meir had said, "We shall decide when we come to it. The new government will make its decision when it goes to the Geneva Conference. The government has made such decisions in the past: thus, when the Rogers Plan came up we said 'no' " (*Jerusalem Post Weekly Overseas Edition*, December 11, 1974). The peace movement circulated a petition for a "Peace Initiative Now" urging the government to take the initiative to formulate a realistic peace plan. The Land of Israel Movement derided the peace movement's emphasis upon Israeli declarations of intent, pointing out that when, in the pre-state period, the Revisionists had issued declarations of intent in relation to Jewish statehood, the "doves" within Zionism had treated declarations as an empty exercise. (Jacob Shavit, "Hamishvaah Hasimetrit shel Yozmat Hashalom" [The symmetric equation of the peace initiative], *Zot Haaretz*, January 11, 1974, p. 6.)

32. Within the Labor party, Achdut Haavoda immediately after the Yom Kippur War showed signs of ideological tension. Its core, the Hameuchad movement, as heir to the nationalism of Yitzhak Tabenkin, continued to have members imbued with his ideology; many others had moved to a dovish position and found common ground with Mapam, with which Achdut Haavoda had once formed a united party. In Hameuchad meetings only weeks after the end of the war, the ideological division manifested itself in attacks by the dovish wing on Hameuchad cabinet minister Yisrael Galili (*Haaretz*, January 13 and 18, 1974). The tensions in the Rafi wing of the Labor Alignment became extremely obvious when several members, including Dayan, in October 1974 went so far as to sign a Likud petition calling for the retention of Israeli rule over Judea and Samaria. (The others were Mordecai Ben-Porat, Matilda Gez, and David Koren, of whom only the last was not a member of the Rafi faction.) And within the Knesset, party leaders were disturbed as a dovish caucus called "The Free Platform," which came into being to focus opposition to formation of a national unity government, was matched by an activist caucus named after Yitzhak Tabenkin.

33. Within the National Religious party, those identifying with the ideology of the Land of Israel Movement were the 40 percent of the central committee which voted against joining the government in October 1974. Although they failed to prevent the coalition, they did succeed in pushing through a resolution which said: "The National Religious Party in the Cabinet and the Knesset will adhere to

their convention's decisions and their national-religious principles and will vote against territorial concessons in the Land of Israel, our ancestral heritage." Since the Labor party's policy was built upon the principle of territorial concessions in return for peace agreements, the contradiction obviously was potentially explosive. The Agudat Yisrael-Poalei Agudat Yisrael party came out with a platform in 1973 that advocated making peace with Arab states on the basis "of God's promise to His People, strategic necessity, political expediency and international law." The contradictions inherent in this platform could presumably also eventually serve to divide the membership (David M. Zohar, *Political Parties in Israel: The Evolution of Israeli Democracy* [New York: Praeger Publishers, 1974], p. 180).

34. Within Herut, Benjamin Halevi (a Land of Israel Movement member) departed from party orthodoxy to sign a petition with Arie Eliav advocating a National Unity government on the basis of territorial compromise with the Arabs. Ariel Sharon said bitterly that the government might yet find sufficient votes to return Judea and Samaria to the Arabs through votes from his own Likud Party (*Jerusalem Post Weekly Overseas Edition*, August 6, 1974). The small Free Center Party within Likud formally split into two, as Shmuel Tamir, its leader, asserted the need for territorial compromise with the Arabs (*Jerusalem Post Weekly Overseas Edition*, February 4, 1975).

35. *Haaretz*, January 4, 1974.

36. *Jerusalem Post Weekly Overseas Edition*, August 27, 1974. 78 percent of Likud voters supported the formation of a National Unity government, as did 70 percent of Labor Alignment voters.

37. The National Religious party sought to ensure that only individuals converted by Orthodox, as against Conservative or Reform rabbis, would be recognized by the state as Jews.

38. This was done through bringing into the coalition, in place of the National Religious party, the New Citizens Rights Movement led by Shulamit Aloni, which in the major surprise of the post-war elections had won three seats in the Knesset. The new party was critical of the Labor establishment, dovish on foreign policy, and opposed to religious control in issues of personal status; and it included Israel's major advocate of women's liberation, American-raised Marcia Friedman.

39. The Labor Alignment was anxious to get the National Religious party back for a number of reasons. It was uncomfortable with the extent to which it was dependent upon parties identified with the peace movement, since this identification gave ammunition to the Likud and Land of Israel Movement. *Zot Haaretz* noted that this was the first time in the history of the state that non-Zionists assured a government for Israel and anti-Zionists (the four Knesset members representing Rakah, the Soviet Communist-Arab nationalist party), did not vote against it (Zvi Shiloah, "Lo Lefi Klalei Hamischak" [Not according to the rules of the game], June 14, 1974, p. 8). Also, while the National Religious party was in sympathy with Likud on the national issue, any parties that might leave the coalition in protest at the entry of the religious would be unable to work together with Likud as an opposition with a united policy. The final impetus from Rabin's point of view was the wave of settlement efforts by religious Jews of Gush Emmunim. The best way to cope with the problems which these settlement efforts caused was to make the National Religious party take responsibility for the government's actions in response to the settlers.

40. This was the case although Rabin ultimately won National Religious party consent to enter the government on the terms originally offered and at the time refused by the National Religious party. For the majority in the party which still

saw it as primarily a special interest party, it was deemed highly undesirable to remain outside the government, since the special interests it won in exchange for its support of the Labor party in the government threatened to be lost if the quid pro quo was over, and then the whole purpose of the party's existence could be thrown into question.

41. The policy was not simply the product of Kissinger's pressure upon the Israeli government, for it was similar to the policy the government had unsuccessfully tried to implement before the war. However, Kissinger wanted more from Israel in return for less from Egypt than the Israeli government in the absence of pressure would have been likely to accept.

42. *Jerusalem Post Weekly Overseas Edition,* December 10, 1974.

43. There was little notice in Israel when the first Jewish settlement in the territories taken after 1967 was eliminated. Shalhevet, an embryo settlement at the Abu Rodeis oil fields in Sinai composed of families of workers in the fields who had decided to remain there permanently, was evacuated at the beginning of the war and the families were not permitted to return. The Herut convention (Since the parties retained their independence within Likud they still had their own conventions) in January 1975 staved off a demand by the youth division that Sinai be mentioned specifically in legislation Herut planned to propose proclaiming Israel's sovereignty over "all the liberated homeland." The argument within Herut was interesting not merely in that it revealed the awareness that the phrase did not imply Sinai, but also in that it showed the party's unwillingness to change the definition to include Sinai within it (*Jerusalem Post Weekly Overseas Edition,* January 14, 1975).

44. *Jerusalem Post Weekly Overseas Edition,* December 25, 1974.

45. After initial neglect of that area, the National Religious party also affirmed its religious significance. While the government at first promised that no territory taken in 1967 would be returned to Syria, the weakening of that position soon became obvious. The Council of Golan settlements sponsored the creation of a new "settlement" called Keshet in the ruins of Kuneitra. But active protests and demonstrations were confined on the whole to those directly affected—settlers in the Golan, the Jordan Valley, and Hebron who were in danger of losing their homes in case of Israeli withdrawal. None of the Golan settlements was dismantled as a result of the Golan disengagement, and the public in the boundaries of 1949 did not feel threatened. After negotiating the disengagement agreement with Syria, however, Dayan said he believed it should be viewed, not as a stage toward a subsequent agreement, but as an end in itself, one that entailed no further steps (*The Jerusalem Post,* May 26, 1974).

46. Speech to Zionist Revisionists of America, New York City, October 13, 1974.

47. *Jerusalem Post Weekly Overseas Edition,* November 6, 1973.

48. "Social Problem Indicators for the Month of March 1975," mimeographed (Israel Institute of Applied Social Research), p. 3.

49. "Public Reactions to Various Issues Following the Appearance of Yassar Arafat at the U.N. Assembly," mimeographed (Israel Institute of Applied Social Research), p. 2.

50. *Haaretz,* June 27, 1975. The poll is misleading because it suggests that half the public wishes to return the territories. Actually the question is an "ideal" one, which poses a choice that most respondents may not perceive as existing in the real world. *Haaretz* does not report that there was any accompanying question asking, "Do you believe that the Arabs are ready to make a final peace if Israel

returns the territories?" Since *Haaretz* commissioned the poll one presumes the newspaper would report fully the results, but one question without the other gives a tendentious result.

51. "Public Reactions Following the Appearance of Yassar Arafat," p. 2.

52. Ibid., p. 9.

53. Thus, not only was Arafat invited to represent the Palestinians at the U.N. debate before the General Assembly, but the Palestine Liberation Organization was given special status (and Israel excluded from regional groupings) in UNESCO and other United Nations organizations. While the United States supported Israel in asserting that Israel could not be expected to negotiate with a grouping that failed to recognize her sovereignty, this left open the door to a change in United States policy once some formula was found whereby the P.L.O. could be interpreted as giving such recognition. Israeli efforts to find an alternate "moderate" leadership for the Palestinians on the West Bank met with no success.

54. *Jerusalem Post Weekly Overseas Edition,* December 11, 1974.

55. In Peking Kissinger had said: "If the peace conference succeeds, there will be a very serious problem especially for Israel, of how its security can be assured under conditions when the final borders will certainly be different from the cease-fire lines and when withdrawals are involved as Security Council Resolution 242 provides. At this point the question of guarantees will arise and we have to ask then the question of what sort of guarantees—unilateral, several countries and so forth" (*New York Times,* November 13, 1973). Golda Meir reacted to the speech by saying she was "not at all pleased" and Israel "would have to clear the matter up." (*Jerusalem Post,* November 14, 1973). At a meeting of Harvard professors on December 6, 1973, according to a memorandum issued by one of them (*New York Times,* March 25, 1974), Kissinger said: "Israel must recognize that it cannot afford to stall during the negotiations. It cannot hold out in hopes of something changing in its favor. The Arabs won more than they yet realize."

56. Israel had already relied upon and found wanting United Nations forces prior to 1967 when they were withdrawn from Sinai at Nasser's request. The example of Cyprus was likely to point up the lesson that U.N. forces, even if they remained, were of no avail. Demilitarized zones could be useful as a warning of impending attack when they were remilitarized, but even this would not be the case if they were remilitarized gradually; and the international climate gave little promise of supporting Israeli preventive attack simply on the ground of Arab violation of demilitarization clauses. That left international guarantees. Only a United States guarantee would have any meaning for Israel, and given the non-interventionist climate in the United States, even this might lack credibility.

57. Jochanan Bloch, "Eidut Mesayaat" [Supporting evidence], *Zot Haaretz,* Jan. 3, 1975, p. 4. Bloch had originally written the article, he notes in the introduction, under the title "The Trap" in August 1970 after the cease-fire with Egypt along the Canal; but it had been rejected by several newspapers as being too demoralizing for the public.

58. *Jerusalem Post Weekly Overseas Edition,* November 27, 1973.

59. Rabin, for example, said that the Israel-Arab dispute could not be decided on the battlefield because the world would not let that happen, but that people in Israel were not sufficiently aware of this reality. *Jerusalem Post Weekly Overseas Edition,* January 28, 1975.

60. "Social Problem Indicators for the Month of April 1975," mimeographed (Israel Institute of Applied Social Research), p. 3.

61. For prewar attitudes see Abel Jacob, "Trends in Israeli Public Opinion 1967–72," and for post war attitudes see "Social Problem Indicators for April 1975," p. 3.

62. The background of the settlement effort was described in detail in *Maariv,* June 14, 1974. Gush Emmunim ("group of those who keep faith") began after the 1973 elections as a pressure group within the National Religious party to prevent it from joining the government, but the settlement effort that it sponsored had older roots. Talk of settling in Shechem had begun immediately in Kiryat Arba, but progress toward implementation had been slow because the settlers recognized that public consciousness concerning a tie to Shechem was much weaker than in relation to Hebron.

63. The group had sought permission from the government and military authorities but had been put off. During the Yom Kippur War a delegation of women from the proposed settlement core suggested to the Prime Minister that the settlement be started immediately to raise public morale. Mrs. Meir, needless to say, refused. It was not until the following June that the first actual settlement effort in defiance of the law was made.

64. *Jerusalem Post Weekly Overseas Edition,* August 6, 1974.

65. Disagreements within the Labor party were described by Zvi Shiloah in "Habgidah, Hechan He?" [Treason, where is it?], *Zot Haaretz,* August 9, 1974, p. 8.

66. Ibid.

67. *Jerusalem Post Weekly Overseas Edition,* July 30, 1974.

68. *Yediot Achronoth* (Tel Aviv), June 8, 1975.

69. *Jerusalem Post Weekly Overseas Edition,* December 10, 1974.

70. *Maariv,* January 18, 1974.

71. See for example the speech by Israel's ambassador to the U.S., Simcha Dinitz, assailing the "despair and desperation" among friends of Israel in the United States. *Jewish Week,* December 21, 1974.

72. This well-known phenomenon drew public complaint from radio commentator Judah Shapiro, WEVD Jewish news, March 10, 1975. American Jewry was also inhibited from criticism by the fact that Kissinger was himself Jewish.

73. Arend Lijphart, *The Trauma of Decolonization,* pp. 125–291.

74. Ronald Mark Sirkin, "Coalition, Conflict, and Compromise," p. 27.

75. See Yehoshafat Harkabi, *Arab Attitudes to Israel* (Jerusalem: Israel Universities Press, 1972); *Ben Yisrael Learav* [Between Israel and the Arabs] (Tel Aviv: Maarachot Publications, 1968); *Keitzad Husberah Haemda Haaravit Neged Yisrael Bezava Hamizri* [The indoctrination Against Israel in UAR armed forces] (Tel Aviv: Maarachot Publications, 1967); and *Palestinians and Israel* (New York: John Wiley and Sons; Jerusalem: Israel Universities Press, 1974).

76. See especially Chapters 1, 4, 5, 6 and 7. (New York: G. P. Putnam's Sons, 1975)

77. See for example, Gil Carl AlRoy, *Behind the Middle East Conflict,* pp. 159–75; Gil Carl AlRoy, ed., *Attitudes Toward Jewish Statehood in the Arab World* (New York: American Association for Peace in the Middle East, 1971), pp. 1–69; Aharon Ben Ami, "Can the Problem of the Palestinians Be Separated from the Israel-Arab Conflict?" (Jerusalem: Israel Academic Committee on the Middle East, 1975); Elie Kedourie, *The Chatham House Version and Other Middle-Eastern Studies* (New York: Praeger Publishers, 1970), esp. pp. 317–42; Hans E. Tütsch, *Facets of Arab Nationalism* (Detroit: Wayne State University Press,

1965); Moshe Sharon, "Shalom Yisraeli Veshalom Aravi" [Israeli peace and Arab peace] *Maariv,* December 28, 1973.

78. See Bernard Lewis, "The Pro-Islamic Jews" *Judaism,* vol. 17, no. 4, Fall 1968, pp. 391–404, for a discussion of the myth of the golden age of equal rights in Islam as one invented by Jews in nineteenth-century Europe as a reproach to Christians—and taken up by Muslims in our own time as a reproach to Jews.

79. AlRoy, *Behind the Middle East Conflict,* pp. 162–63.

80. Ben Ami, "Can the Problem of the Palestinians Be Separated from the Israel-Arab Conflict?" p. 13.

81. *Jerusalem Post Weekly Overseas Edition,* July 29, 1975.

82. Kissinger's personal effort to achieve peace in the Middle East through the exchange of "territory" for "legitimacy" is puzzling because in terms of his own theoretical perspectives, he could be expected to find it improbable that diplomacy could be exerted constructively in a situation like that which obtains in the Middle East. In *A World Restored,* Kissinger argues that diplomacy, "the art of restraining the exercise of power," cannot function where the basic order is not accepted as legitimate. He argues that, in the absence of agreement on what is a reasonable demand, diplomatic conferences "are occupied with sterile repetitions of basic positions and accusations of bad faith, or allegations of 'unreasonableness' and 'subversion.' " (This is a perfect forecast of any possible Geneva Conference.) Kissinger further observes that defenders of the status quo are reluctant to take "revolutionary" demands seriously, and tend to treat the revolutionary power "as if it really accepted the existing legitimacy but overstated its case for bargaining purposes; as if it were motivated by specific grievances to be assuaged by limited concessions. . . . 'Appeasement,' where it is not a device to gain time, is the result of an inability to come to grips with a policy of unlimited objectives." (This would appear an excellent description of American attitudes toward the conflict.) See *A World Restored: Metternich, Castlereagh, and the Problems of Peace 1812–22* (Boston: Houghton, Mifflin, Sentry Edition, n.d.) pp. 2–3. Yet it does not appear that Kissinger sees himself in a Machiavellian role "selling out" Israel; rather he has described himself as a "savior" of the country (*Jerusalem Post Weekly Overseas Edition,* August 12, 1975). In office, Kissinger seems to act on the principle that diplomacy can transform the policy of unlimited objectives of the Arab states into one of limited objectives, a notion he explicitly rejects in his writing.

83. *Jerusalem Post Weekly Overseas Edition,* December 17, 1974. While this suggestion was treated as "absurd" by Israeli spokesmen, one could expect such demands to be repeated—and to be taken more seriously—once Israel had returned to the former borders.

84. Aharon Ben Ami, in "Chalukat Yarden Ulevanon" [The partition of Jordan and Lebanon] (*Zot Haaretz,* September 6, 1974), suggested that the Arabs might embark upon a series of wars with limited targets and that in the course of this Syria (which traditionally claimed all of Palestine as southern Syria) might expand at the expense of the "artificial states" of Jordan and Lebanon, making it possible for Israel to divide these territories with Syria and reach an accommodation with her. To this writer a more probable constellation might see Iran bidding for control of part of the oil-producing territories of the Persian Gulf, and Iran would serve as a more realistic negotiating partner for Israel.

85. On the legitimacy of using force to obtain Arab oil see Robert W. Tucker, "Oil: The Issue of American Intervention," *Commentary,* vol. 59, no. 1, January 1975; (author anonymous) "Seizing Arab Oil," *Harper's,* vol. 250, no. 1498,

206 Notes to Pages 161–63

March 1975; Anthony Harrigan, "Oil: A Military Solution," *The Alternative,* March 1975; and Edward Friedland, Paul Seabury, and Aaron Wildavsky, *The Great Détente Disaster: Oil and the Decline of American Foreign Policy* (New York: Basic Books, 1975).

86. The authors of *The Great Détente Disaster* speak of the alternative possibility that the United States might embark upon a policy of what they call "isopopulism," seeking self-sufficiency and withdrawing from world politics, relying for safety upon its nuclear umbrella. (p. 169, 201–3)

87. Elie Kedourie, *The Chatham House Version and Other Middle-Eastern Studies* (New York: Praeger Publishers, 1970), p. 1.

88. Michael Brecher, *The Foreign Policy System of Israel* (New Haven: Yale University Press, 1972), p. 547.

Selected Bibliography

A. BOOKS AND ARTICLES

Aharoni, Yohanan. *The Land of the Bible: A Historical Geography*. London: Burns and Oates, 1966.

————, and Avi-Yonah, Michael. *The Macmillan Bible Atlas*. New York: Macmillan, 1968.

Allardt, Erik, and Rokkam, Stein, eds. *Mass Politics*. New York: The Free Press, 1970.

Allon, Yigal. *Masach shel chol: Yisrael Vearov ben Milchama Veshalom* [A curtain of sand: Israel and the Arabs between war and peace]. Tel Aviv: Kibbutz Hameuchad, 1959.

————. "Chinuch Lehumaniyut Beitot Milchama" [Education for humanism in time of war]. *Mibbifnim*, vol. 32, no. 1–2, April 1970.

————. "Istrategia Shel Shalom" [Strategy for peace]. *Mibbifnim*, vol. 35, no. 4, December 1973.

AlRoy, Gil Carl, ed. *Attitudes Toward Jewish Statehood in the Arab World*. New York: American Association for Peace in the Middle East, 1971.

AlRoy, Gil Carl. *Behind the Middle East Conflict: The Real Impasse between Arab and Jew*. New York: G. P. Putnam's Sons, 1975.

————. *The Kissinger Experience: American Policy in the Middle East*. New York: Horizon Press, 1975.

Amital, Yehuda. *Hamaalot Mimaamakim* [The stairs from the deep]. Jerusalem: Agudat Yeshivat Har Ezion, 1974.

The Anatomy of Peace in the Middle East: Proceedings of the Annual Conference. New York: American Academic Association for Peace in the Middle East, 1969.

Apter, David, ed. *Ideology and Discontent*. New York: The Free Press, 1964.

Arad, Yitzhak. "Chinuch Lochamim Leshalom Uleachvah" [The education of fighters for peace and brotherhood]. *Bamachane*, November 2, 1969.

Arian, Alan. *Ideological Change in Israel*. Cleveland: The Press of Case Western Reserve University, 1968.

Aron, Raymond. *The Opium of the Intellectuals*. New York: Doubleday, & Co., 1957.

Assaf, M. *History of the Arabs in Palestine* [in Hebrew]. Tel Aviv: Davar, 1951.

Atlas of Israel. Jerusalem: Department of Surveys, the Ministry of Labor & the Bialik Institute, 1956.

Avineri, Shlomo. "The Palestinians and Israel." *Commentary*, vol. 49, no. 6, June 1970.

Avi-Yonah, Michael. *Biymey Roma Uvizantion* [In the days of Rome and Byzantium]. Jerusalem: Bialik Institute, 1962.

————. *Geografiya Historit Shel Eretz Yisrael: Lemin Shivat Zion Vead*

Reshit Hakibush Haaravi [Historical geography of Palestine: from the end of the Babylonian exile to the Arab conquest]. 3rd ed. Jerusalem, Bialik Institute, 1962.

————, and Safrai, R. S. *Carta's Atlas of the Second Temple, the Mishnah and the Talmud* [in Hebrew]. Jerusalem: Carta, 1966.

————. *Sefer Yerushalayim* [The book of Jerusalem]. Jerusalem and Tel Aviv: Bialik Institute and Dvir, 1956.

Avnery, Uri. *Milchemet Hayom Hashvii* [War of the seventh day]. Tel Aviv: New Page, 1969. Published in English as *Israel Without Zionists: A Plea for Peace in the Middle East*. New York: Macmillan, 1966.

Banai, Ya'acov. *Chayalim Almonim* [Unknown Soldiers]. Tel Aviv: Hug Yedidim, 1958.

Bar-Deroma, H. *Wezeh Gevul Haarez* [The true boundaries of the holy land according to the sources]. Jerusalem: B. E. R. Publishing, 1958.

Bareli, Meir. *Iyunim Bimediniyut Chutz* [Studies in foreign policy]. Tel Aviv: Am Oved, 1975.

Begin, Menachem. *The Revolt*. Tel Aviv: Steimatzky's Agency, Ltd. n.d.

Bell, Daniel. *The End of Ideology*. New York: The Free Press, 1965.

Bella, Moshe, ed. *Olamo Shel Jabotinsky: Mivchar Dvarav Veikar Torato* [The world of Jabotinsky: a selection of his works and the essentials of his teaching]. Tel Aviv: Dfusim Publishers, 1972.

Ben-Ami, Aharon, ed. *Hakol!* [All of it!]. Tel Aviv: Madaf Publishers, 1967.

Ben-Arieh, Yehoshua. *Eretz Yisrael Rameah Ha-19: Giluyah Mechadash* [The rediscovery of the holy land in the nineteenth century]. Jerusalem: Carta and the Israel Exploration Society, 1970.

Ben-Ezer, Ehud, ed. *Unease in Zion*. New York: Quadrangle Press, 1974.

Ben-Gurion, David. *My Talks with Arab Leaders*. New York: The Third Press, 1973.

Ben-Porat, Y.; Carmel H.; Dan, U.; et al. *Kippur*. Tel Aviv: Special Editions Publishers, December 1973.

Ben-Shalom, Avraham. *Deep Furrows*. New York: Hashomer Hazair Organization, 1937.

Ben-Yoseph, Moshe (Hager). *Haayarah* [The townlet]. Tel Aviv: Aleph Publishers, 1968.

Ben-Zvi, Y. *Eretz Yisrael Yevishuvah Biymey Hashilton Haotomani* [Eretz Israel under Ottoman rule: four centuries of history]. Jerusalem, Bialik Institute, 1962.

Bergmann, Gustav. "Ideology." *Ethics*, vol. 61, no. 3, 1951.

Birnbaum, Norman. *The Sociological Study of Ideology 1940–60: A Trend Report and Bibliography*. Oxford: Blackwell, 1962.

Bloch, Jochanan. *Selbstbehauptung: Zionistische Aufsätze, Evangelische Zeitstimmen*, vol. 61/2. Hamburg, 1972.

————. "The Unstatesmanlike Policies of the Government of Israel." *Haumma*, no. 33.

Bodenheimer, Max I. *Prelude to Israel*. New York: Thomas Yoseloff, 1963.

Borochov, Ber. *Nationalism and the Class Struggle*. New York: Poalei Zion of America, 1937.

Brecher, Michael. *The Foreign Policy System of Israel*. New Haven: Yale University Press, 1972.

Buber, Martin. *Israel and Palestine: The History of an Idea*. London: East and West Library, 1952.

————, ed. *Towards Union in Palestine: Essays on Zionism and Jewish-Arab Cooperation.* Jerusalem: Ihud Association, 1947.

Cantril, Hadley. *The Psychology of Social Movements.* New York: John Wiley & Sons Inc., 1963.

Chambers, Clarke A. *Seedtime of Reform 1918–33.* Minneapolis, University of Minnesota Press, 1963.

Cohn, Norman. *The Pursuit of the Millenium.* London: Temple Smith, 1957.

Coser, Lewis A. *Men of Ideas: A Sociologist's View.* New York: The Free Press, 1970.

Curtis, Michael, ed. *People and Politics in the Middle East.* New Brunswick: Transaction, Inc., 1971.

Dan, Uri. *Rosh Gesher* [Sharon's bridgehead]. Tel Aviv: E. L. Special Publications, 1975.

Davies, W. D. *The Gospel and the Land: Early Christianity and Jewish Territorial Doctrine.* Berkeley, Los Angeles, London: University of California Press, 1974.

Dayan, Moshe. *Mappa Hadasha: Yechasim Acherim* [A new map: other relationships]. Tel Aviv: Maariv Books and Shikmona Publishers, 1969.

de Huszar, George B., ed. *The Intellectuals: A Controversial Portrait.* Glencoe: The Free Press, 1960.

Doriel, Joseph. *Habitachon Haleumi Shel Yisrael* [The national security of the Hebrew people]. Tel Aviv: Reshafim, 1974.

Dorman, Menachem. *Bchaf Hakela: Masot Politiyot* [Political essays]. Tel Aviv: Hakibbutz Hameuchad Publishing House, 1960.

————. "Mi 'Turim' el Ha 'Tur' Beshirat Alterman" [From 'columns' to 'the column' in the poetry of Alterman]. *Molad,* new series 3, no. 14–15, June 1970.

Edwards, Lyford P. *The Natural History of Revolution.* New York: Russell and Russell, 1965.

Eisenstadt, Samuel. "Social Institutions," *International Encyclopedia of the Social Sciences,* vol. 14, 1968.

————. *Israeli Society.* London: Weidenfeld and Nicolson, 1967.

Eitan, Eitan. 'Haderech Leshichrur Falastin" [The way to the liberation of Falastin]. *Keshet,* no. 49, fall 1970.

Eldad (Scheib), Israel. *Maaser Rishon: Pirkei Sichronot Umusar Haskel* [First tithe: memories and their lessons]. Tel Aviv: published by Lechi Veterans, 1963.

————. *The Jewish Revolution.* New York: Shengold Publishers, 1971.

Eliav, Arie Lova. *Land of the Hart: Israelis, Arabs, the Territories, and a Vision of the Future.* Philadelphia: Jewish Publication Society, 1974.

Elizur, Yuval, and Salpeter, Eliahu. *Who Rules Israel?* New York: Harper & Row, 1973.

Elon, Amos. *The Israelis: Founders and Sons.* New York: Holt, Rinehart and Winston, 1971.

————. *Herzl.* New York: Holt, Rinehart and Winston, 1975.

Evans, Laurence. *United States Policy and the Partition of Turkey, 1914–24.* Baltimore: Johns Hopkins University Press, 1965.

Fein, Leonard. *Israel: Politics and People.* Boston: Little, Brown and Company, 1967.

Fitzsimons, M. A. *Empire by Treaty: Britain and the Middle East in the Twentieth Century.* Indiana: University of Notre Dame Press, 1964.

Frankel, Joseph. *National Interest.* New York: Praeger Publishers, 1970.

Freilich, I. "Dinam Shel Hashtachim Hameshuchrarim Bemilchemet Sheshet Hayamim" [The status of the liberated territories in religious law]. *Or Hamizrach,* vol. 18, no. 4, June 1969.

Friedland, Edward; Seabury, Paul; and Wildavsky, Aaron. *The Great Détente Disaster: Oil and the Decline of American Foreign Policy.* New York: Basic Books, 1975.

Friedlander, Yehuda. *Uri Zvi Greenberg: Mivchar Maamarim al Yezirato* [Uri Zvi Greenberg: a selection of critical essays of his writing]. Tel Aviv: Am Oved, 1974.

Friedlander, Y., and Rahaman, G. "Shlmut Hazehut Hayehudit Aruva Lishlemut Haaretz" [The wholeness of Jewish identity as guarantee of the wholeness of the country]. *Mitzion Tetze Torah: Journal for Jewish Thought,* no. 7, May 1970.

Frischwasser-Ra'anan, H. F. *The Frontiers of a Nation: A Reexamination of the Forces Which Created the Palestine Mandate and Determined its Territorial Shape.* London: Batchworth Press, 1955.

Gerlach, Luther and Hine, Virginia. *People, Power, Change.* Indianapolis: Bobbs-Merrill Co., 1970.

Getter, Miriam. *Haideologia Shel Lechi* [The Ideology of Lechi]. Master's thesis, Tel Aviv University, 1967.

Gichon, Mordechai. *Atlas Carta Letoldot Eretz Yisrael Mibetar Vead Tel-Chai* [Carta's atlas of Palestine from Beththter to Tel Hai]. Jerusalem: Carta, 1969.

Goblet, Y. M. *The Twilight of Treaties.* Port Washington: Kennikat Press, 1970.

Goldman, Guido G. *Zionism Under Soviet Rule 1917–28.* New York: Herzl Press, 1960.

Goldmann, Nahum. "The Future of Israel." *Foreign Affairs,* vol. 48, no. 3, April 1970.

Gorni, Joseph. "Haideologia Shel 'Kibush Haavodah' " [The ideology of the 'conquest of labor']. *Keshet,* no. 38, winter 1968.

Greenberg, Uri Zvi. *Sefer Hakitrug Vehaemunah* [Book of Chastisement and Faith]. Jerusalem: Sdan Publishers, 1938.

Grintz, Yehoshua M. *Perakim Betoldot Bayit Sheni* [Chapters in the history of the second temple times]. Jerusalem: Y. Marcus Publishers, 1969.

Gusfield, Joseph. *Symbolic Crusade: Status Politics and the Temperance Movement.* Urbana: University of Illinois Press, 1963.

———, ed. *Protest, Reform and Revolt: A Reader in Social Movements.* New York: John Wiley & Sons, 1970.

Halevi, Judah. *The Kuzari.* New York: Shocken Books, 1968.

Haller, Paul. *National-Revolutionärer Zionismus: Untersuchung und Proklamation.* Vienna: Dr. Heinrich Glanz Verlag, 1938.

Halpern, Ben. *The Idea of the Jewish State.* Cambridge: Harvard University Press, 1961.

Hamenachem, Ezra, ed. *Hayisraeli Kiyehudi* [The Israeli as Jew]. Givataim, Yishai Ron Memorial Foundation, 1974.

Harkabi, Yehoshafat. *Arab Attitudes to Israel.* Jerusalem: Israel Universities Press, 1972.

———. *Ben Yisrael Learov* [Between Israel and the Arabs]. Tel Aviv: Maarachot Publications, 1968.

————. *Fatah Baistrategia Haaravit* [Fedayeen action and Arab strategy]. Tel Aviv: Maarachot Publications, 1969.

————. *Keitzad Husberah Haemda Haaravit Neged Yisrael Bazava Hamizri* [The indoctrination against Israel in UAR armed forces]. Tel Aviv: Maarachot Publications, 1967.

————. *Palestinians and Israel.* New York: John Wiley and Sons; Jerusalem: Israel Universities Press, 1974.

Hayoresh [The heir to the throne]. Tel Aviv: Peleg Publishers, 1975.

Hentov, J. *Communism and Zionism in Palestine: The Comintern and the Political Unrest in the 1920s.* Cambridge: Schenkman Publishers, 1974.

Hertzberg, Arthur, ed. *The Zionist Idea: An Historical Analysis and Reader.* New York: Meridian Books, 1960.

Herzl, Theodor. *A Jewish State: An Attempt at a Modern Solution to the Jewish Question.* London: David Nutt, 1896.

Herzog, Chaim, *The War of Atonement.* London: Weidenfeld and Nicolson, 1975.

Hess, Moses. *Rome and Jerusalem.* New York: Philosophical Library, 1958.

Hoffer, Eric. *The True Believer.* New York: Harper & Row, 1951.

Holzman, Haim. *Techikat Habitachon Bashtachim Hamuchsakim* [Security legislation in the occupied areas]. Givat Haviva: Center for Arabic and Afro-Asian Studies, 1968.

Hoskins, Halford. *British Routes to India.* London: Longmans, Green, 1928.

Hunter, Floyd. *Community Power Structure.* Chapel Hill: University of North Carolina Press, 1953.

Hurewitz, J. C. *Middle East Politics: The Military Dimension.* New York: Praeger, 1969.

————, ed. *Diplomacy in the Near and Middle East,* vol. 2, *A Documentary Record 1914–56.* Princeton: Princeton University Press, 1956.

Hyman, Herbert H., and Singer, Eleanor, ed. *Readings in Reference Group Theory and Research.* New York: The Free Press, 1968.

Ibn Shmuel, Yehuda. *Midreshei Geulah* [Midrashim of redemption]. Tel Aviv: Mossad Bialik, 1944.

Ichilov, Orit. "Yisrael Vehasmol Hechadash" [Israel and the new left]. *Keshet,* no. 49, fall 1970.

Isaac, Erich and Rael Jean. "Israel's Dissenting Intellectuals." *Conservative Judaism,* vol. 26, no. 3, spring 1972.

Isaacs, Samuel Hillel. *The True Boundaries of the Holy Land.* Chicago, Illinois: privately printed, 1917.

Ish Shalom, *Michael. Mas'ei Nozrim Leeretz Yisrael* [Christian travels to the holy land]. Tel Aviv: Am Oved and Dvir Co., 1965.

Jacob, Abel. "Trends in Israeli Public Opinion on Issues Related to the Arab-Israeli Conflict 1967–72." *The Jewish Journal of Sociology,* vol. 16, no. 2, December 1974.

Kallen, Horace M. *Utopians at Bay.* New York: Theodor Herzl Foundation, 1958.

Karmon, Yehuda. *Kavei Hafsakat Haesh Shel Yisrael* [Israel's cease-fire lines: a geographical survey]. Tel Aviv: Chief Educational Officer, General Staff, 1968.

————. *Israel, A Regional Geography.* London, New York, Sydney, Toronto: Wiley-Interscience, 1971.

Katz, Amnon. "Shlemut Haaretz Tluyah Bishlemut Haam" [The wholeness of the land depends on the wholeness of the people]. *M.T.T.: Mitzion Tetze Torah—Journal for Jewish Thought*, no. 7, May 1970.

Katz, Samuel. *Battleground: Fact and Fantasy in Palestine.* New York: Bantam Books, 1973.

———. *Yom Haesh* [Days of fire]. Tel Aviv: Karni Publishers, 1966. Published in English as *Days of Fire.* London: W. H. Allen, 1968.

Kaufmann, Yehezkel. *Toldot Haemunah Hayisraelit* [The history of Israelite religion], four volumes. Jerusalem: Bialik Institute, 1960.

Kedourie, Elie. *The Chatham House Version and Other Middle-Eastern Studies.* New York: Praeger, 1970.

———. *Nationalism.* London: Hutchinson University Library, 1960.

Kenan, Amos. *Israel: A Wasted Victory.* Tel Aviv: Amikam Publishers, 1970.

Killian, Lewis M. "Social Movements." *Handbook of Modern Sociology.* Skokie, Illinois: Rand McNally, 1964.

Kissinger, Henry A. *A World Restored: Metternich, Castlereagh, and the Problems of Peace 1812–22.* Boston: Houghton, Mifflin, Sentry Edition, n.d.

Klieman, Aaron S. *Foundations of British Policy in the Arab World: the Cairo Conference of 1921.* Baltimore: The Johns Hopkins University Press, 1970.

Kolet, Yisrael. "D'muto Shel Aharonson Uzmano Shel Livneh" [The personality of Aaronson and the times of Livneh]. *Molad*, New Series 3, no. 14–15, June 1970.

Kurzweil, Baruch. "The Young Hebrews." *Jewish Spectator*, September 1953.

———. *Bamaavak al Erchei Hayahadut* [In the struggle for the values of Judaism]. Jerusalem: Schocken Publishing House, 1969.

Laqueur, Walter. *A History of Zionism.* New York: Holt, Rinehart and Winston, 1972.

———. *Confrontation: The Middle East and World Politics.* New York: Bantam Books, 1974.

Lewin, Kurt. *Field Theory in Social Science: Selected Theoretical Papers.* New York: Harper & Row, 1964.

Lijphart, Arend. *The Trauma of Decolonization: The Dutch and West New Guinea.* New Haven: Yale University Press, 1966.

Lipset, Seymour M. *Agrarian Socialism.* Berkeley, California: The University of California Press, 1950.

———. *Political Man: The Social Bases of Politics.* New York: Doubleday, 1960.

Livneh, Eliezer. *Aharon Aharonson: Haish Uzmano* [Aaron Aaronson: the man and his time]. Jerusalem: Mossad Bialik, 1969.

———. *Yisrael Umashber Hatzivilisatzia Hamaaravit* [Israel and the crisis of western civilization]. Tel Aviv: Schocken Publishing House, 1972.

Lloyd George, David. *Memoirs of the Peace Conference*, two volumes. New Haven: Yale University Press, 1939.

"Ma Acharei Hashalom? Mish'al" [What after peace? a symposium]. *Keshet*, no. 31, spring 1966.

"Ma Acharei Hamilchamah? Mish'al" [What after the war? a symposium]. *Keshet*, no. 38, winter 1968.

Mannheim, Karl. *Ideology and Utopia.* New York: Harcourt, Brace and World, 1936.

Margalit, Elkana. *Hashomer Hazair: Meadat Neurim Lemarxism Mahap-chani* [Hashomer hazair: from youth community to revolutionary Marxism, 1913–36]. Tel Aviv: Hakibbutz Hameuchad Publishing House, 1971.

Marriott, Sir John A. R. *The Eastern Question—An Historical Study in European Diplomacy.* Oxford: The Clarendon Press, 1940.

Mason, Herbert, ed. *Reflections on the Middle East Crisis.* Paris and The Hague: Mouton, 1970.

McLaughlin, Barry, ed. *Studies in Social Movements.* New York: The Free Press, 1969.

Medding Peter Y. *Mapai in Israel: Political Organisation and Government in a New Society.* Cambridge: Cambridge University Press, 1972.

Merlin, Samuel. *The Search for Peace in the Middle East.* New Jersey: Thomas Yoseloff, 1968.

Middleton, K. W. B. *Britain and Russia: An Historical Essay.* Port Washington: Kennikat Press, 1947.

Mills, C. Wright. *The Power Elite.* New York: Oxford University Press, 1956.

Naamani, J. T. et al. *Israel: Its Politics and Philosophy.* New York: Behrman, 1973.

Neaman, Pinchas. *Geographical Problems in the Law of the Sabbatical Year* [in Hebrew]. Master's thesis, Tel Aviv University, 1968.

Ofry, Dan. *The Yom Kippur War.* Tel Aviv: Zohar Publishing Co., 1974.

Palestine: A Study of Jewish, Arab and British Policies, two volumes. New Haven: Published for the Esco Foundation for Palestine by Yale University Press, 1947.

Palestine Royal Commission: Minutes of Evidence Heard at Public Sessions. London: His Majesty's Stationery Office, 1937.

Parkes, James. *A History of Palestine from 135 A.D. to Modern Times.* London: Victor Gollancz, 1949.

———. *Whose Land? A History of the Peoples of Palestine.* Harmondsworth: Penguin, 1971.

Parkin, Frank. *Middle Class Radicalism.* New York: Praeger, 1968.

Patai, Raphael, ed. *Encyclopedia of Zionism and Israel,* two volumes. New York: Herzl Press and McGraw Hill, 1971.

Perlmutter, Amos. *Anatomy of Political Institutionalization: The Case of Israel and Some Comparative Analyses.* Cambridge: Harvard University Center for International Affairs, 1970.

———. *Military and Politics in Israel.* London: Frank Cass, 1969.

Pèter, D., Riftin, Y., et al. *Smol Vezionut* [Left and Zionism]. Tel Aviv: Circle for Leftist Initiative and Ideological Study, February 1974.

Pinsker, Leo. *Auto–Emancipation.* New York: ZOA Pamphlet Series, no. 3, 1916.

Prawer, Joshua. *Hayehudim Bemalkhut Yerushalayim Hatzalbanit* [The Jews in the Latin Kingdom of Jerusalem]. Jerusalem: Merkaz Press, 1946.

———. *The Crusader's Kingdom.* New York: Praeger Publishers, 1973.

Press, Y. ed. *Encylopaedia Eretz Israel,* four volumes [in Hebrew]. Jerusalem: Rubin Mass, 1948–53.

Preuss, Walter. *The Labour Movement in Israel.* Jerusalem: Rubin Mass, 1965.

Rackman, Emanuel. *Israel's Emerging Constitution.* New York: Columbia University Press, 1955.

Raphael, Yitzhak, ed. *Torah Shebeal Peh* [The Oral Torah], Lectures at the

Country-wide Conference on the Oral Torah. Jerusalem: Mossad Harav Kuk, 1969.

Roberts, Samuel J. *Survival or Hegemony? The Foundations of Israeli Foreign Policy.* Washington: Center of Foreign Policy Research of the Johns Hopkins University School of Advanced International Studies, 1973.

Rubinstein, Amnon. "And Now in Israel a Fluttering of Doves." *New York Times Magazine,* July 26, 1970.

————. "The Israelis: No More Doves." *New York Times Magazine,* October 21, 1973.

Safran, Nadav. *The United States and Israel.* Cambridge: Harvard University Press, 1963.

Samuel, Edwin. *The Structure of Society in Israel.* New York: Random House, 1969.

Schechtman, Joseph B. *Jordan: A State That Never Was.* New York: Cultural Publishing, 1968.

————. *The Vladimir Jabotinsky Story,* two volumes. New York: Thomas Yoseloff, 1956.

Schepansky, Israel. *Eretz Yisrael Besafrut Hatshuvot* [Eretz Israel in the responsa literature], two volumes. Jerusalem: Mossad Harav Kuk, 1968.

Shamir, Moshe. *Chayai in Yishmael* [My life with Ishmael]. Tel Aviv: Maariv Books, 1969. Published in English London: Vallentine, Mitchell, 1970.

Shapira, Abraham, ed. *Siach Lochamim* [Talk of fighting men]. Tel Aviv: Published by Young Members of the Kibbutz Movement, 1970. Published in English as *The Seventh Day: Soldiers Talk about the Six Day War.* New York: Scribner Publishers, 1970.

Shiloah, Zvi. *Eretz Gadola Leam Gadol: Sipuro shel Maamin* [A great country for a great people: the tale of a believer]. Tel Aviv: Ot Paz Publishers, 1970.

Shimoni, Yaakov. *Medinot Arav Beyamenu* [The Arab states in our days]. Tel Aviv: Am Oved, 1965.

Sirkin, Ronald Mark. "Coalition, Conflict, and Compromise: The Party Politics of Israel." Ph.D. dissertation, Pennsylvania State University, 1971.

Smelser, Neil J. *Theory of Collective Behavior.* New York: The Free Press, 1962.

Soloveichik, Aharon. "Yishuv Eretz Yisrael Vmilchemet Mitzvah Bazman Hazeh" [The settlement of Eretz Yisrael and the concept of 'milchemet mitzvah' in our times]. *Or Hamizrach,* vol. 19, no. 2, January 1970.

Stein, Leonard. *The Balfour Declaration.* New York: Simon and Schuster, 1961.

Stern, Samuel T. "Gevulot Eretz Yisrael" [The borders of Eretz Yisrael]. *Or Hamizrach,* vol. 18, no. 1, September 1968.

Tabenkin, Yitzhak. *Lekach Sheshet Hayamim: Yishuvah shel Eretz Bilti Mechuleket* [Lesson of the six days: the settlement of an undivided land]. Tel Aviv: Hakibbutz Hameuchad, 1970.

Teveth, Shabtai. *Moshe Dayan.* London: Weidenfeld and Nicolson, 1972.

————.*The Cursed Blessing.* New York: Random House, 1970.

Toch, Hans. *The Social Psychology of Social Movements.* Indianapolis: Bobbs-Merrill, 1965.

Tozer, H. F. *A History of Ancient Geography.* London: Hafner Publishing, 1964.

Tsur, M.; Ben Aharon, Y.; Grossman, A. *Bein Zeirim: Sichot Bezavta Batnuah Hakibutzit* [Among young people: talks in the kibbutz]. Tel Aviv: Am Oved, 1969.

Vilnay, Zev. *The New Israel Atlas, Bible to the Present Day.* New York: McGraw Hill, 1969.

Viteles, Harry. *A History of the Cooperative Movement in Israel,* two volumes. London: Vallentine Mitchell, 1967.

Weiner, Eugene, ed. *Bemilchama Veshalom* [In war and peace]. Tel Aviv: Defense Ministry, 1972.

Weisbord, Robert G. *African Zion: The Attempt to Establish a Jewish Colony in the East African Protectorate 1903–5.* Philadelphia: Jewish Publication Society, 1968.

Weiss, Hillel. *Dyokan Halochem* [The portrait of the fighter]. Ramat Gan: Bar Ilan University Press, 1975.

Weizmann, Chaim. *Trial and Error.* New York: Harper & Bros., 1949.

Wolfenson, Abraham. *David Ben-Gurion Umedinat Yisrael* [David Ben-Gurion and the state of Israel]. Tel Aviv: Am Oved, 1974.

Wolfers, Arnold. *Discord and Collaboration: Essays in International Politics.* Baltimore: Johns Hopkins University Press, 1962.

Yanai, Natan. *Kera Batzameret* [The split in the leadership]. Tel Aviv: Levin-Epstein, 1969.

Zohar, David M. *Political Parties in Israel: The Evolution of Israeli Democracy.* New York: Praeger Publishers, 1974.

Zohar, Ezra. *Bizvat Hamishtar: Madua Af Echad Lo Kam* [In the vise of the regime: why no one stood up]. Tel Aviv: Shikmona Publishers, 1974.

Zudnowski, Moshe M., and Landau, Jacob M. *Israeli Communist Party.* Stanford: Studies Series No. 9, Hoover Institute Press, 1965.

B. PAMPHLETS

Sikui [A chance]. Jerusalem: The Movement for Peace and Security, June 1970.

Sipuach oh Shalom [Annexation or peace]. Tel Aviv: Movement for a Federation of Israel-Falastin, December 1967.

Begin, Menachem. *Yehudi: Leom Vedat* [Jew: nationality and religion]. Information Department of the Herut Movement: Reprint of speech in the Knesset, February 9, 1970.

————. *Shlom Haam Veshlemut Haaretz* [The peace of the people and the wholeness of the land]. Information Department of the Herut Movement: Reprint of speech in the National Conference of the Herut Movement, April 23, 1970.

Bloch, Jochanan. *Sakanah, Ushemah Abba Even* [A menace: and its name is Abba Eban]. Beersheba: The Movement for an Undivided Land of Israel, n.d.

Borisov, J. *Palestine Underground: The Story of the Jewish Resistance.* New York: Judea Publishing, 1947.

Eldad, Israel. *Israel: The Road to Full Redemption.* New York: Kraushers Books, 1961.

Eliav, Arie Lova. *New Targets for Israel.* Tel Aviv: reprinted from three articles in *Davar,* November 1968 and February 1969.

Elman, P. *The Peninsula of Sinai.* Jerusalem: The Ministry of Justice, February 1971.

First Harvest. Tel Aviv: Minutes and Essays of the Club for Hebrew Thought, 1966.

Katz, Samuel. *Diplomatic Triumph or Geopolitical Disaster.* London: Land of Israel Movement, 1974.

Livneh, Eliezer, and Katz, Samuel. *Eretz Yisrael Ugvuloteha: Sheelot Utshuvot* [Eretz Yisrael and its boundaries: questions and answers]. Tel Aviv: Land of Israel Movement, 1968.

Palestine: A Bi-National State. New York: Ihud Association of Palestine, August 1946.

Palestine Undivided. Tel Aviv: M. Usieli, 1938.

Ratosh, Yonatan. *1967—Uma Hal'ah? Shalom Ivri* [1967—and what next? A Hebrew peace]. Tel Aviv: Hermon Publishers, 1967.

Secure and Recognized Boundaries: Israel's Right to Live in Peace Within Defensible Frontiers. Jerusalem: Carta, 1971.

Shaki, Avner. *Mihu Yehudi?* [Who is a Jew?]. Jerusalem: Gesher Foundation, n.d.

Sneh, Moshe. *The Venerated Arafat . . . And the Forgotten Lenin.* Tel Aviv: Communist Party of Israel [Maki] Information Bulletin no. 5, May 1970.

Symposium on the Problems of Peace and Security [in Hebrew]. Tel Aviv: Movement for Peace and Security, 1969.

Talmon, J. S. *Israel Among the Nations: Reflections on Jewish Statehood.* Jerusalem: World Zionist Organization, 1970.

C. NEWSPAPERS AND PERIODICALS

Aleph, Tel Aviv, irregular [Hebrew].
Al Hamishmar, Tel Aviv, daily [Hebrew].
Amudim, Tel Aviv, monthly [Hebrew].
Ba'machaneh, Tel Aviv, weekly [Hebrew].
Bead Veneged, Jerusalem, bimonthly [Hebrew].
Brit Hasmol, Tel Aviv, irregular [Hebrew].
Davar, Tel Aviv, daily [Hebrew].
Haaretz, Tel Aviv, daily [Hebrew].
Haolam Hazeh, Tel Aviv, weekly [Hebrew].
Hazofe, Tel Aviv, daily [Hebrew].
Haumma, Jerusalem, quarterly [Hebrew].
Israc, London, irregular, ceased publication.
Keshet, Tel Aviv, quarterly [Hebrew].
Kol Haam, Tel Aviv, weekly [Hebrew].
Lamerchav, Tel Aviv, daily [Hebrew]; ceased publication.
Maariv, Tel Aviv, daily [Hebrew].
Mibbifnim, Tel Aviv, quarterly [Hebrew].
New Outlook, Tel Aviv, monthly.
Ot, Tel Aviv, weekly [Hebrew].
Petachim, Jerusalem, bimonthly [Hebrew].
Siach, Tel Aviv, irregular [Hebrew].
Sulam, Jerusalem, monthly [Hebrew]; ceased publication.
The Jerusalem Post, Jerusalem, daily.
The Jerusalem Post Overseas Weekly Edition, Jerusalem, weekly.

The Jewish Week, New York and Washington, weekly.
The Macabbean, New York, monthly (December 1901–1920).
The New Judea, London, monthly (1924–48).
The Times of Israel, Tel Aviv, weekly.
Yediot Achronot, Tel Aviv, daily [Hebrew].
Zavit Acheret, Tel Aviv, irregular [Hebrew].
Zot Haaretz, Tel Aviv, biweekly [Hebrew].

Index

Library of Congress Cataloging in Publication Data
Isaac, Rael Jean.
  Israel divided.
  Bibliography: pp. 207–17
  Includes index.
  1. Israel—Politics and government.   2. Jewish-Arab
relations—1967–1973.   I. Title.
DS126.5.168   320.9'5694'05   75–36944
ISBN 0–8018–1737–4